1866-1991

125th

ANNIVERSARY

DAY OF INFAMY

WALTER LORD

Henry Holt and Company
New York

To Janet Cady

Library of Congress Catalog Card Number: 57-6189
ISBN 0-8050-1898-0

First published in hardcover by Henry Holt and Company, Inc.,
in 1957.

Printed in the United States of America
Recognizing the importance of preserving the written word,
Henry Holt and Company, Inc., by policy, prints all of its
first editions on acid-free paper. ∞

The lyrics to "Three Little Fishes," page 160,
are reprinted by permission of the copyright owner
Joy Music Inc., New York, N.Y.

CONTENTS

Foreword

It happened on December 7, 1941.

One part of America learned while listening to the broadcast of the Dodger-Giant football game at the Polo Grounds in New York. Ward Cuff had just returned a Brooklyn kickoff to this 27-yard line when at 2:26 P.M. WOR interrupted with the first flash: the Japanese had attacked Pearl Harbor.

Another part of America learned half an hour later, while tuning in the New York Philharmonic concert at Carnegie Hall. Artur Rodzinski's musicians were just about to start Shostakovich's Symphony Number 1 when CBS repeated an earlier bulletin announcing the attack.

The concertgoers themselves learned still later when announcer Warren Sweeney told them at the end of the performance. Then he called for "The Star-Spangled Banner." The anthem had already been played at the start of the concert, but the audience had merely hummed along. Now they sang the words.

Others learned in other ways, but no matter how they learned, it was a day they would never forget. Nearly every American alive at the time can describe how he first heard the news. He marked the moment carefully, carving out a sort of mental souvenir, for instinctively he knew how much his life would be changed by what was happening in Hawaii.

This is the story of that day.

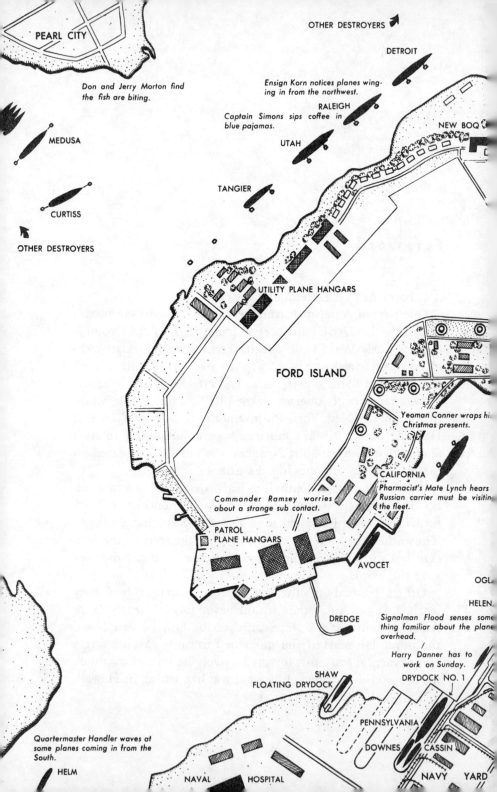

PEARL CITY

Don and Jerry Morton find
the fish are biting.

OTHER DESTROYERS

DETROIT

Ensign Korn notices planes winging in from the northwest.

RALEIGH

Captain Simons sips coffee in
blue pajamas.

NEW BOQ

UTAH

MEDUSA

TANGIER

CURTISS

OTHER DESTROYERS

UTILITY PLANE HANGARS

FORD ISLAND

Yeoman Conner wraps hi.
Christmas presents.

CALIFORNIA

Pharmacist's Mate Lynch hears
Russian carrier must be visitin
the fleet.

Commander Ramsey worries
about a strange sub contact.

PATROL
PLANE HANGARS

AVOCET

OGL

HELEN.

DREDGE

Signalman Flood senses some
thing familiar about the plane
overhead.

Harry Danner has to
work on Sunday.

DRYDOCK NO. 1

SHAW
FLOATING DRYDOCK

PENNSYLVANIA

DOWNES   CASSIN

Quartermaster Handler waves at
some planes coming in from the
South.

HELM

NAVAL   HOSPITAL

NAVY   YARD

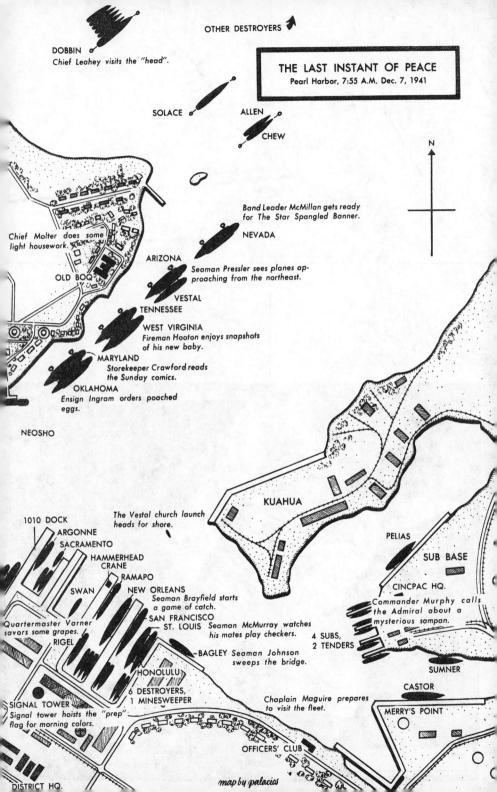

THE LAST INSTANT OF PEACE
Pearl Harbor, 7:55 A.M. Dec. 7, 1941

OTHER DESTROYERS

DOBBIN
Chief Leahey visits the "head".

SOLACE

ALLEN

CHEW

Chief Molter does some light housework.

Band Leader McMillan gets ready for The Star Spangled Banner.

NEVADA

OLD BOQ

ARIZONA
Seaman Pressler sees planes approaching from the northeast.

VESTAL

TENNESSEE

WEST VIRGINIA
Fireman Hooton enjoys snapshots of his new baby.

MARYLAND
Storekeeper Crawford reads the Sunday comics.

OKLAHOMA
Ensign Ingram orders poached eggs.

NEOSHO

KUAHUA

1010 DOCK

ARGONNE

SACRAMENTO

HAMMERHEAD
CRANE

RAMAPO

SWAN

NEW ORLEANS
Seaman Brayfield starts a game of catch.

SAN FRANCISCO

ST. LOUIS Seaman McMurray watches his mates play checkers.

Quartermaster Varner savors some grapes.

RIGEL

The Vestal church launch heads for shore.

BAGLEY Seaman Johnson sweeps the bridge.

HONOLULU

6 DESTROYERS, 1 MINESWEEPER

SIGNAL TOWER
Signal tower hoists the "prep" flag for morning colors.

PELIAS

SUB BASE

CINCPAC HQ.

Commander Murphy calls the Admiral about a mysterious sampan.

4 SUBS, 2 TENDERS

SUMNER

CASTOR

Chaplain Maguire prepares to visit the fleet.

MERRY'S POINT

OFFICERS' CLUB

DISTRICT HQ.

map by palacios

N

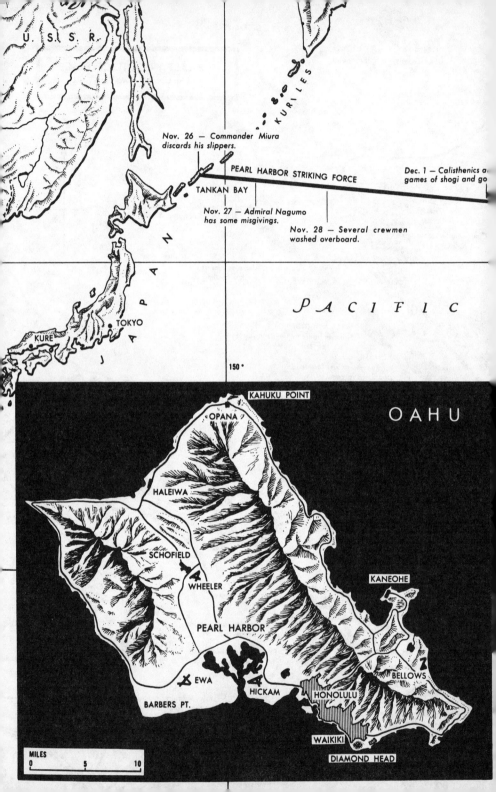

U. S. S. R.

KURILES

Nov. 26 — Commander Miura discards his slippers.

PEARL HARBOR STRIKING FORCE

Dec. 1 — Calisthenics a games of shogi and go

TANKAN BAY

Nov. 27 — Admiral Nagumo has some misgivings.

Nov. 28 — Several crewmen washed overboard.

J A P A N

PACIFIC

KURE

TOKYO

150°

OAHU

KAHUKU POINT

OPANA

HALEIWA

SCHOFIELD

WHEELER

KANEOHE

PEARL HARBOR

EWA

HICKAM

BELLOWS

HONOLULU

BARBERS PT.

WAIKIKI

DIAMOND HEAD

MILES
0   5   10

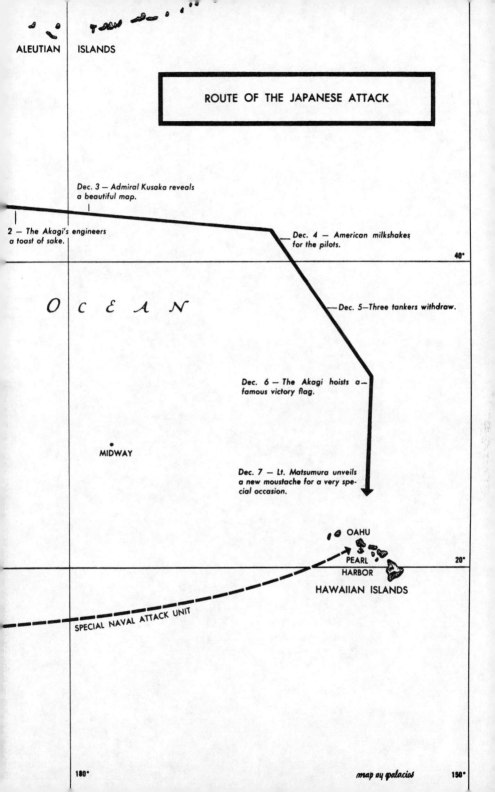

ALEUTIAN   ISLANDS

ROUTE OF THE JAPANESE ATTACK

Dec. 3 — Admiral Kusaka reveals
a beautiful map.

2 — The Akagi's engineers
a toast of sake.

Dec. 4 — American milkshakes
for the pilots.

40°

O C E A N

—Dec. 5—Three tankers withdraw.

Dec. 6 — The Akagi hoists a—
famous victory flag.

MIDWAY

Dec. 7 — Lt. Matsumura unveils
a new moustache for a very special occasion.

OAHU

PEARL
HARBOR   20°

HAWAIIAN ISLANDS

SPECIAL NAVAL ATTACK UNIT

180°   map by palacios   150°

DAY OF INFAMY

Chapter I

"Isn't That a Beautiful Sight?"

MONICA CONTER, a young Army nurse, and Second Lieutenant Barney Benning of the Coast Artillery strolled out of the Pearl Harbor Officers' Club, down the path near the ironwood trees, and stood by the club landing, watching the launches take men back to the warships riding at anchor.

They were engaged, and the setting was perfect. The workshops, the big hammerhead crane, all the paraphernalia of the Navy's great Hawaiian base were hidden by the night; the daytime clatter was gone; only the pretty things were left— the moonlight . . . the dance music that drifted from the club . . . the lights of the Pacific Fleet that shimmered across the harbor.

And there were more lights than ever before. For the first week end since July 4 all the battleships were in port at once. Normally they took turns—six might be out with Admiral Pye's battleship task force, or three would be off with Admiral Halsey's carrier task force. This was Pye's turn in, but Halsey was out on a special assignment that meant leaving his battleships behind. A secret "war warning" had been received from Washington—Japan was expected to hit "the Philippines, Thai, or Kra Peninsula or possibly Borneo"—and the carrier *Enterprise* was ferrying a squadron of Marine fighters to reinforce Wake Island. Battleships would slow the task

3

force's speed from 30 to 17 knots. Yet they were too vulnerable to maneuver alone without carrier protection. The only other carrier, the *Lexington*, was off ferrying planes to Midway, so the battleships stayed at Pearl Harbor, where it was safe.

With the big ships in port, the officers' club seemed even gayer and more crowded than usual, as Monica Conter and Lieutenant Benning walked back and rejoined the group at the table. Somebody suggested calling Lieutenant Bill Silvester, a friend of them all who this particular evening was dining eight miles away in downtown Honolulu. Monica called him, playfully scolded him for deserting his buddies— the kind of call that has been placed thousands of times by young people late in the evening, and memorable this time only because it was the last night Bill Silvester would be alive.

Then back to the dance, which was really a conglomeration of Dutch treats and small private parties given by various officers for their friends: "Captain Montgomery E. Higgins and Mrs. Higgins entertained at the Pearl Harbor Officers' Club . . . Lieutenant Commander and Mrs. Harold Pullen gave a dinner at the Pearl Harbor Officers' Club . . ."—the Honolulu Sunday *Advertiser* rattled them off in its society column the following morning.

Gay but hardly giddy. The bar always closed at midnight. The band seemed in a bit of a rut—its favorite "Sweet Leilani" was now over four years old. The place itself was the standard blend of chrome, plywood, and synthetic leather, typical of all officers' clubs everywhere. But it was cheap— dinner for a dollar—and it was friendly. In the Navy everybody still seemed to know everybody else on December 6, 1941.

Twelve miles away, Brigadier General Durward S. Wilson, commanding the 24th Infantry Division, was enjoying the same kind of evening at the Schofield Barracks Officers' Club. Here, too, the weekly Saturday night dance seemed even gayer than usual—partly because many of the troops in the 24th and 25th Divisions had just come off a long, tough week in the field; partly because it was the night of Ann Etzler's Cabaret, a benefit show worked up annually by "one of the very talented young ladies on the post," as General Wilson gallantly puts it. The show featured amateur singing and dancing—a little corny perhaps, but it was all in the name of charity and enjoyed the support of everybody who counted, including Lieut. General Walter C. Short, commanding general of the Hawaiian Department.

Actually, General Short was late. He had been trapped by a phone call, just as he and his intelligence officer, Lieutenant Colonel Kendall Fielder, were leaving for the party from their quarters at Fort Shafter, the Army's administrative headquarters just outside Honolulu. Lieutenant Colonel George Bicknell, Short's counterintelligence officer, was on the wire. He asked them to wait; he had something interesting to show them. The general said all right, but hurry.

At 6:30 Bicknell puffed up. Then, while Mrs. Short and Mrs. Fielder fretted and fumed in the car, the three men sat down together on the commanding general's *lanai*. Colonel Bicknell produced the transcript of a phone conversation monitored the day before by the local FBI. It was a call placed by someone on the Tokyo newspaper *Yomiuri Shinbun* to Dr. Motokazu Mori, a local Japanese dentist and husband of the paper's Honolulu correspondent.

Tokyo asked about conditions in general: about planes, searchlights, the weather, the number of sailors around . . . and about flowers. "Presently," offered Dr. Mori, "the flowers in bloom are fewest out of the whole year. However, the hibiscus and the poinsettia are in bloom now."

The three officers hashed it over. Why would anyone spend the cost of a transpacific phone call discussing flowers? But if this was code, why talk in the clear about things like planes and searchlights? And would a spy use the telephone? On the

other hand, what else could be going on? Was there any connection with the cable recently received from Washington
warning "hostile action possible at any moment"?

Fifteen minutes . . . half an hour . . . nearly an hour
skipped by, and they couldn't make up their minds. Finally
General Short gently suggested that Colonel Bicknell was "too
intelligence-conscious"; in any case they couldn't do anything
about it tonight; they would think it over some more and talk
about it in the morning.

It was almost 7:30 when the general and Colonel Fielder
rejoined their now seething wives and drove the fifteen
miles to Schofield. As they entered the dance floor, they
scarcely noticed the big lava-rock columns banked with ferns
for a gala evening—they were still brooding over the Mori
call.

General Short had a couple of cocktails—he never drank
after dinner—and worried his way through the next two hours.
Perhaps it was the Mori call. Perhaps it was his troubles with
training and equipment (there was never enough of anything). Perhaps it was his fear of sabotage. To General Short,
Washington's warning had posed one overwhelming danger—
an uprising by Hawaii's 157,905 civilians of Japanese blood,
which would coincide with any Tokyo move in the Far East.
He immediately alerted his command against sabotage; lined
up all his planes neatly on the ramps, where they could be
more easily guarded; and notified the War Department.
Washington seemed satisfied, but the fear of a Japanese Fifth
Column lingered—that was the way the Axis always struck.

By 9:30 he had had enough. The Shorts and the Fielders
left the officers' club, started back to Shafter. As they rolled
along the road that sloped down toward town again, Pearl
Harbor spread out below them in the distance. The Pacific
Fleet blazed with lights, and searchlight beams occasionally
probed the sky. It was a moment for forgetting the cares of
the day and enjoying the breathless night. "Isn't that a beau-

tiful sight?" sighed General Short, adding thoughtfully, "and what a target they would make."

General Short's opposite number, Admiral Husband E. Kimmel, Commander in Chief of the Pacific Fleet—known as CINCPAC in the Navy's jargon of endless initials—had an even less eventful evening back in Honolulu. He was dining quietly at the Halekulani Hotel, a Waikiki landmark that maintained a precarious balance between charm and stuffiness. Several of the Navy's top brass lived there with their wives, and tonight Admiral and Mrs. Fairfax Leary were giving a small dinner, attended by the commander in chief. It was anything but a wild party—so slow, in fact, that at least two of the wives retreated to a bedroom upstairs for some refreshment with a little more authority.

But Admiral Kimmel was no party admiral anyhow. Hard, sharp, and utterly frank, he worked himself to the bone. When he relaxed, it was usually a brisk walk with a few brother officers, not cocktails and social banter. Proudly self-contained, he looked and acted uncomfortable in easygoing surroundings—he even disapproved of the Navy's new khakis as "lessening the dignity and military point of view of the wearer."

He was a difficult man to know, and his position made him more so. He had been jumped over 32 admirals to his present job. Relations were utterly correct, but inevitably there was a mild awkwardness—a lack of informal give-and-take—between himself and some of the men who had always been his seniors. Finally, there was his responsibility as CINCPAC—enough to kill the social inclinations in any man: refitting the fleet with the new weapons that were emerging, training the swarm of new recruits that were arriving, planning operations against Japan if hostilities should explode.

Admiral Kimmel had spent the early afternoon discussing the situation with his staff. The Japanese were now burning their codes . . . their fleet had changed call letters twice in a month . . . their carriers had disappeared. On the other hand, the Japanese would naturally take precautions at a time like this; and the lost carriers might not mean anything—Navy intelligence had already lost them 12 times the past six months. Whatever happened, it would be in southeast Asia—Washington, the official estimates, the local press, everybody said so. As for Hawaii, nobody gave it much thought. To free Kimmel's hands, defense of the base was left to the Army and to the Fourteenth Naval District, technically under Kimmel but run by Admiral Claude C. Bloch pretty much as his own show. Local defense seemed fairly academic anyhow. Only a week before, when Admiral Kimmel asked his operations officer, Captain Charles McMorris, what the chances were of a surprise attack on Honolulu, the captain firmly replied, "None."

The staff meeting broke up about three o'clock. Admiral Kimmel retired to his quarters for the afternoon, went on to the Learys' party around 5:45. While they dined under the big hau tree on the Halekulani terrace, the admiral's driver waited in the car outside, slapping away at mosquitoes. At one point, Richard Kimball, the hotel manager, passed by and said he was sorry about the bugs. The driver replied he didn't mind the mosquitoes—it was the boredom that got him. If only the car had a radio. But it turned out he didn't need one tonight. The admiral left at 9:30, drove straight home, and was in bed by ten. It had been a long, tiring week, and tomorrow morning he had an early golf date with General Short.

Most of the officers stayed up later, but their evenings were hardly more spectacular. Rear Admiral Robert A. Theobald, commanding Destroyer Flotilla One, danced at the staid Pacific Club until midnight. Lieutenant Commander S. S. Isquith, engineering officer of the target ship *Utah*, played cards at the Hawaiian Bridge Center. Young Ensign Victor Delano—reared in the Navy and just out of Annapolis himself—spent a properly respectful evening at the home of

Vice Admiral Walter Anderson, commander of Battleship Division Four.

The enlisted men were less circumscribed. Radioman Fred Glaeser from Pearl Harbor . . . Sergeant George Geiger from the Army's bomber base at Hickam Field . . . two thirds of Company M, 19th Infantry, from Schofield Barracks . . . thousands of others from posts scattered throughout the island of Oahu converged on Honolulu in a fleet of buses, jalopies, and ancient taxis.

Most were dropped at the YMCA, a convenient starting point. Then, after perhaps a quick one at the Black Cat Café across the street, they fanned out on the town. Some, like Chief M. G. Montessoro, patroled the taverns of Waikiki Beach. Others watched "Tantalizing Tootsies," the variety show at the Princess. Most swarmed down Hotel Street—a hodgepodge of tattoo joints, shooting galleries, pinball machines, barber shops, massage parlors, photo booths, trinket counters—everything an enterprising citizenry could devise for a serviceman's leisure.

Juke boxes blared from Bill Lederer's bar, the Two Jacks, the Mint, the New Emma Café. Thin shafts of light escaped around the drawn shades of hotels named Rex . . . Ritz . . . the Anchor. Occasional brawls erupted as the men overflowed the narrow sidewalks.

The Shore Patrol broke up a fight between two sailors from the cruiser *Honolulu;* caught a seaman from the *California* using somebody else's liberty card; arrested a man from the Kaneohe Naval Air Station for "malicious conversation." But the night was surprisingly calm—only five serious offenses as against 43 for the whole month so far.

The MPs had a quiet time too. They found perhaps 25 soldiers passed out—out of 42,952 in the islands—and these were sent to the Fort Shafter guardhouse to sober up. Otherwise, nothing special.

A surprisingly large number stuck to their ships, bases, and military posts. As the Army and Navy swelled with reservists, an ever-growing number of men seemed to prefer the simpler pleasures. At the Hickam post theater Private Ed Arison watched Clark Gable outwit oriental chicanery in *Honky Tonk*. In the big new barracks nearby, Staff Sergeant Charles W. Maybeck played Benny Goodmans and Bob Crosbys on his new phonograph. Up at Schofield, Private Aloysius Manuszewski had some beer at the PX, spent most of the evening writing home to Buffalo.

At Pearl Harbor, Boatswain's Mate Robert E. Jones joined the crowd at the Navy's new Bloch Recreation Center. It was a place designed to give the enlisted man every kind of relaxation the Navy felt proper—music, boxing, bowling, billiards, 3.2 beer. Tonight's attraction was "The Battle of Music," the finals of a contest to decide the best band in the fleet. As the men stamped and cheered, bands from the *Pennsylvania, Tennessee, Argonne,* and *Detroit* battled it out. The *Pennsylvania* band won; everybody sang "God Bless America"; and the evening wound up with dancing. When the crowd filed out at midnight, many still argued that the battleship *Arizona's* band—which had already been eliminated—was really the best of all.

Slowly the men drifted back to their ships; the Hotel Street bars closed down; the dances broke up—Honolulu's strict blue laws took care of that. Here and there a few couples lingered. Second Lieutenant Fred Gregg of Schofield proposed to Evolin Dwyer and was accepted; Ensign William Hasler of the *West Virginia* was not so lucky, but he happily learned later that a woman can change her mind. Lieutenant Benning drove Monica Conter back to Hickam, where she was stationed. There they laid plans for the following day—lunch, swimming, a movie, some barbecued spareribs. Another engaged couple, Ensign Everett Malcolm and Marian Shaffer, drove to the Shaffer home high in the hills behind Honolulu. He arranged to meet her for golf at one.

About 2:00 A.M. Ensign Malcolm started back for Pearl Harbor but discovered he would never make the last launch to his ship, the *Arizona.* So he headed instead for the home of Captain D. C. Emerson. The old captain had been senior dentist on the *Arizona,* and his congenial bachelor establishment was a sort of shoreside bunkroom for the ship's junior officers.

On arriving, Ensign Malcolm was quickly hailed in by the captain, who sat on the floor with three other officers, arguing about (of all things) Woodrow Wilson's Fourteen Points. Mildly bewildered, Malcolm joined in and they were all still at it when the clock touched three.

Only the people who had to be up were now abroad. Radioman Fred Glaeser couldn't find a bed at the Y, resigned himself to a cramped night in his car. Lieutenant Kermit Tyler, a young pilot at Wheeler Field, was up too—but he was already starting for work. He had drawn the 4:00-8:00 A.M. shift in the Army's new interceptor center at Fort Shafter. Now as he rolled along the road to town, he flicked on his car radio and listened to KGMB playing Hawaiian records.

About 320 miles to the north, on the Japanese aircraft carrier *Akagi,* Commander Kanjiro Ono listened intently to the same program. He was a staff communications officer for Vice Admiral Chuichi Nagumo, commanding a huge Japanese task force of six carriers, two battleships, three cruisers, and nine destroyers that raced southward through the night. Admiral Nagumo was about to launch an all-out assault on the U. S. fleet at Pearl Harbor, and everything depended on surprise. He felt that if the Americans had even an inkling, the radio would somehow show it.

But there was nothing—nothing whatsoever, except the soft melodies of the islands. Admiral Nagumo settled back, relieved. There seemed a good chance that a great deal of hard work would not be wasted.

Chapter II

"A Dream Come True!"

TEN MONTHS HAD NOW PASSED since Admiral Isoroku Yamamoto, Commander of the Japanese Combined Fleet, remarked almost casually to Rear Admiral Takajiro Onishi, Chief of Staff of the Eleventh Air Fleet, "If we are to have war with America, we will have no hope of winning unless the U. S. fleet in Hawaiian waters can be destroyed."

Then he ordered Admiral Onishi to start studying the possibility of launching a surprise attack on Pearl Harbor. Onishi called in Commander Minoru Genda, a crack young airman, and ten days later Genda came up with his appraisal: risky but not impossible.

Yamamoto needed no further encouragement. A few trusted subordinates went quietly to work, and by May Rear Admiral Shigeru Fukudome of the Naval General Staff was able to toss a fat notebook at Rear Admiral Ryunosuke Kusaka.

"Go ahead, read it," invited Fukudome. Kusaka plunged into a mass of statistics on Pearl Harbor, but missed any operational plans. "That," said Fukudome, "is what I want you to do."

The job seemed overwhelming. The U. S. strength looked enormous. Hawaii was thousands of miles from Japan. There were airfields scattered all around Oahu—Hickam, Wheeler,

12

Ewa, Kaneohe, probably others. Pearl Harbor itself was narrow and shallow, making it extremely difficult to get at the ships. On top of everything else, Vice Admiral Nagumo, commander of the First Air Fleet, and slated to lead any attack, was dragging his feet. As his chief of staff, no wonder Kusaka was discouraged.

"Don't keep saying, 'It's too much of a gamble,' just because I happen to be fond of playing bridge and *shogi*," Admiral Yamamoto cheerfully admonished. "Mr. Kusaka, I am fully aware of your arguments. But Pearl Harbor is my idea and I need your support." He added that it would certainly help if Kusaka could win over Admiral Nagumo.

Kusaka worked on, and somehow the project began to make sense. Commander Genda did wonders with the torpedo problem. All summer he experimented on the Inland Sea, setting up short shallow torpedo runs. By August he was trying out shallow-draft torpedoes at Saeki. As for the short length of run—well, there was Southeast Loch, a narrow arm of water that led like a bowling alley straight to the battleship moorings in the center of Pearl Harbor.

Everything was done in the darkest secrecy. One afternoon late in August, Lieutenant (j.g.) Toshio Hashimoto, a young naval pilot, took some papers to his wing commander's office and found a group of high-ranking officers poring over charts and maps of Pearl Harbor. They were stamped *"Top Secret,"* and Lieutenant Hashimoto was appalled at his intrusion. Nobody rebuked him, but he went away petrified by the mere knowledge of such an enormous secret.

By the end of August, Admiral Yamamoto was ready to unveil the scheme to a select few. Admiral Osami Nagano, Chief of the Naval General Staff, and 13 other key officers were called to Tokyo and given the word. Then, from September 2 to 13, they all tested the idea on the game board at the Naval War College.

The attacking team "lost" two carriers; Admiral Nagano began complaining that December was too stormy; Admiral

Nagumo, commander of the all-important First Air Fleet, still had cold feet. Other officers argued that Japan could take southeast Asia without U. S. interference; that if America came in, the place to catch the fleet was nearer Japanese waters.

But Yamamoto stuck to his guns—if war came, America was bound to be in it . . . her fleet was Japan's biggest obstacle . . . the best time to crush it was right away. By the time it recovered, Japan would have everything she needed and could sit back and hold out forever.

This logic won the day, and on September 13 the Naval Command issued the rough draft of a plan that combined Pearl Harbor, Malaya, the Philippines, and the Dutch East Indies in one huge assault.

Next, the training stage. One by one, men were tapped for the key jobs. Brilliant young Commander Mitsuo Fuchida was mildly surprised to be transferred suddenly to the carrier *Akagi,* having just left her the year before. He was far more amazed to be named commander of all air groups of the First Air Fleet. Commander Genda sidled up with the explanation: "Now don't be alarmed, Fuchida, but we want you to lead our air force in the event that we attack Pearl Harbor."

Lieutenant Yoshio Shiga and about a hundred other pilots got the word on October 5 from Admiral Yamamoto himself. He swore them to secrecy, told them the plan, urged them to their greatest effort.

The men practiced harder than ever—mostly the low, short torpedo runs that had to be mastered. The torpedoes themselves continued to misbehave in shallow water, diving to the bottom and sticking in the mud. Commander Fuchida wondered whether they would ever work. But Genda only grew more excited—once perfected, they would be the supreme weapon. And by early November he had succeeded. Simple wooden stabilizers were fitted on the fins, which would keep the torpedoes from hitting even the shallow 45-foot bottom of Pearl Harbor.

Meanwhile, other pilots practiced bombing techniques, for nobody except Genda was completely sold on torpedoes. Besides, the meticulous intelligence now pouring in from Consul General Nagao Kita in Honolulu showed that the battleships were often moored in pairs; torpedoes couldn't possibly reach the inboard ship. To penetrate tough armor-plated decks, ordnance men fitted fins on 15-inch and 16-inch armor-piercing shells. These converted missiles would go through anything.

While the pilots practiced and the inventors worked their miracles, Admiral Kusaka battled the red tape that snarls anybody's navy. Some time during October he flew to Tokyo to argue headquarters into giving him eight tankers for the task force that was now taking shape. It meant the difference between using four or six carriers, and at a time like this it seemed incredible that there should be any question about it. But headquarters hemmed and hawed, and it took several weeks to wangle the extra ships.

Thirty-three-year-old Suguru Suzuki, youngest lieutenant commander in the service, had a more stimulating job. Around the end of October he boarded the Japanese liner *Taiyo Maru* for an interesting journey to Honolulu. Instead of following her usual course, the ship sailed far to the north, crossed over between Midway and the Aleutians, and then cut south to Hawaii—exactly the course the task force planned to follow to avoid detection.

Lieutenant Commander Suzuki whiled away the trip taking reams of notes. He checked the winds, the atmospheric pressure, the roll of the vessel. Could a scouting seaplane be launched in these seas? It could. Would any special refueling problems arise? They would. He observed that during the entire voyage the *Taiyo Maru* didn't sight a single ship.

In Honolulu, Lieutenant Commander Suzuki spent a busy

week. From occasional visitors to his ship he learned that the fleet wasn't now assembling at Lahaina Anchorage as it used to. He confirmed that the week end was a universally observed American institution. He picked up some choice titbits —structural data on the Hickam Field hangars, interesting aerial shots of Pearl Harbor taken October 21. These were made from a private plane that took up sight-seers at nearby John Rogers Airport. Anybody could do it.

Then back to Tokyo again, guardedly comparing notes with Lieutenant Commander Toshihide Maejima, who was also on board. Commander Maejima seems to have had much the same interests, but directed rather more toward submarines.

By now things were moving fast in Tokyo. November 3, Admiral Nagano's final blessing . . . November 5, Combined Fleet Top Secret Order Number 1, spelling out the plan . . . November 7, Admiral Nagumo officially named commander of the Pearl Harbor Striking Force. The same day Yamamoto tentatively set the date—December 8, or Sunday, December 7, Hawaii time. Good for a number of reasons: favorable moonlight . . . perfect coordination with the Malay strike . . . the best chance to catch the ships in port and the men off duty.

A few more people were let in on the secret. Admiral Kusaka confided in Commander Shin-Ichi Shimizu, a middle-aged supply officer. The problem: how to draw winter gear without attracting attention, when everybody else was getting ready for the tropics. Commander Shimizu's solution: requisition both summer and winter gear. He glibly told the startled depot that if war came, you never knew where you might go. Then he piled everything on the freighter *Hoko Maru* and chugged off to sea about November 15. Once out of sight, he swung north and made for Hitokappu Bay in the bleak, cold Kuriles—the secret rendezvous point for the Pearl Harbor Striking Force.

Admiral Nagumo himself was not far behind. His flagship,

the carrier *Akagi*, left Saeki in the late evening of the 17th. His chief of staff, Admiral Kusaka, tingled with optimism. Only the day before, he had received a letter from his old housekeeper, telling of a pleasant dream—the Japanese submarine fleet had achieved a splendid surprise victory at Pearl Harbor. A strange dream for a housekeeper, but Admiral Kusaka thought it was a good omen.

On November 19 Lieutenant Commander Suzuki arrived back from his junket to Honolulu and took a fast launch to the battleship *Hiei*, anchored off Yokohama. Suzuki climbed aboard with his bulging brief case, and the *Hiei*, too, steamed off for Hitokappu.

One by one they slipped away. Always separately, never any apparent connection. Once out of sight, the sea simply swallowed them up. At the great Kure naval base a lively radio traffic crackled from the rest of the ships, designed to give the impression that the fleet was still at home. The regular carrier operators stayed behind to give these signals their usual "swing." (A wireless operator's touch is as distinctive as his handwriting.) The camouflage was so good it even fooled Admiral Kusaka, who bawled out his communications man for breaking radio silence, only to find the "message" was a fake concocted back home.

One by one they glided into Hitokappu Bay—the lumbering carriers *Akagi* and *Kaga;* the huge new flattop *Zuikaku;* the light carriers *Hiryu* and *Soryu;* the old battleships *Hiei* and *Kirishima;* the crack new cruisers *Tone* and *Chikuma;* nine destroyers led by the light cruiser *Abukuma;* three screening submarines; the eight tankers finally wangled from headquarters. Last to arrive in the twilight of November 21 was the great carrier *Shokaku*, which had put on such an effective masquerade of turbine trouble that she was almost late.

Now they were all there—32 ships incongruously packed in a desolate harbor. Snow crowned the mountains that ringed the cold, gray bay. Three lonely radio masts stood against the sky. Three small fishermen's huts and one bare concrete pier were the only other traces of civilization. Even so, Nagumo took no chances—no shore leaves, no rubbish overboard. When Seaman Shigeki Yokota got the *Kaga's* garbage detail, he had to burn it right beside the pier.

Commander Shimizu and the other supply ship skippers gradually transferred food, clothes, and thousands of drums of fuel oil to the task force. Five-gallon tins of oil were crammed into every empty space. When all was loaded, Shimizu told his crew to stay put until December 10: "Go fishing. Do anything you want, but you can't leave the area." Then he transferred to the *Akagi*—he couldn't resist going along for the ride.

Admiral Nagumo held a last conference on the *Akagi* on the night of the 23rd. Lieutenant Commander Suzuki told about his interesting trip to Honolulu. Commander Fuchida, who would lead the air strike, scribbled away at his notes. The meeting ended with a toast of *sake* and three *banzais* for the emperor.

On the 25th Yamamoto ordered the fleet to get going the following day, and inevitably Admiral Nagumo spent a restless last night. At 2:00 A.M. he finally called in Lieutenant Commander Suzuki, apologized for waking him, and said he just had to check one point again: "You're absolutely certain about not spotting the U. S. Pacific Fleet in Lahaina?"

"Yes, Admiral."

"Nor is there any possibility that it might assemble at Lahaina?"

Suzuki reassured him and went back to bed, deeply moved by the sight of the old admiral, all alone with his worries, pacing away the night in his kimono.

At dawn Suzuki left the *Akagi* and stood on the shore waving good-by as the anchor chains rattled upward and the ships got under way. On the bridge of the *Akagi* Admiral Kusaka tugged at his coat collar to escape the bitter wind that swept the cheerless morning.

An unexpected hitch arose when a piece of cable snarled in the *Akagi's* propeller, but a diver got it free in half an hour, and by 8:00 A.M. the whole task force was clear of the harbor. As the *Akagi* glided by, a patrol boat's blinkers flashed through the gloom, "Good luck on your mission."

Commander Gishiro Miura, the *Akagi's* navigation officer, certainly needed it. He had no easy job in weather like this —pounding seas, steady gales, the thickest kind of fog. Miura was famous throughout the fleet for his sloppy, easy-going amiability; but it was all gone now. He stood stern and tense on the bridge. He wore a pair of shoes instead of his usual carpet slippers.

Most of the time the ships managed to keep in formation: the carriers in two parallel columns of three . . . the eight tankers trailing behind . . . the battleships and cruisers guarding the flanks . . . the destroyers screening the whole force . . . the subs scouting far ahead. But at night the tankers, not used to this sort of work, would stray far and wide. Every morning the destroyers herded them back to the fleet.

The second day out, Admirals Nagumo and Kusaka clung to the plunging bridge of the *Akagi,* trying as usual to round up the tankers. Suddenly Nagumo blurted, "Mr. Chief of Staff, what do you think? I feel that I've undertaken a heavy responsibility. If I had only been more firm and refused. Now we've left home waters and I'm beginning to wonder if the operation will work."

Admiral Kusaka came up with the right answer: "Sir, there's no need to worry. We'll make out all right."

Nagumo smiled. "I envy you, Mr. Kusaka. You're such an optimist."

Admiral Nagumo must have felt even more discouraged when they first tried refueling on the 28th. This turned out to be dangerous, back-breaking work. As the ships bucked and plunged, the big hoses running from the tankers would snap loose and whiplash across the deck. Several crewmen were swept overboard, but nothing could be done about it.

By the 30th they were getting better at refueling, but now they had another problem. As the weather grew worse, oil drums stored on the deck of the light carrier *Hiryu* spilled, turning her into a skating rink. Commander Takahisa Amagai, the flight deck officer, wrapped straw rope around his boots to keep from falling, but barked his shins anyhow.

On they plowed, through nerve-wracked days and sleepless nights. Admiral Kusaka cat-napped in a canvas chair on the *Akagi's* bridge. Her chief engineer, Commander Yoshibumi Tanbo, did the same far below. He and his 350 men rarely left the engine room, lived in a life of oil and sweat beside their beloved machines. Mess attendants carried down all their meals—usually rice balls with pickled plums and radishes, wrapped in bamboo bark.

Everyone grew more and more restless. From the bridge of the *Akagi* Admiral Kusaka watched the pilots endlessly check their planes, warm up the engines, run through daily calisthenics. On the *Shokaku*, Commander Hoichiro Tsukamoto never knew that time could pass so slowly—his mind was always wandering to his watch or clock. Captain Tadataka Endo, the ship's doctor, whiled away the hours playing *shogi* and *go*. On the *Hiryu*, everyone speculated about the gauze mask that Group Leader Lieutenant Haita Matsumura wore over his mouth. He mumbled something about the unhealthy climate, and they marked him off as a hopeless hypochondriac.

But they speculated most of all on where they were going. Fighter pilot Yoshio Shiga on the *Kaga* was sure it would be in the north—all the planes had been changed to winter oil. Lieutenant (j.g.) Sukao Ebina, the *Shokaku's* junior medical officer, guessed Dutch Harbor. Commander Tanbo down in the *Akagi's* engine room enjoyed a special advantage: he knew how far she could go on the fuel she carried. It all added up to the Philippines.

Hardly anybody yet knew the truth. Last-ditch negotiations were being conducted by Japanese envoys in Washington, trying to win for Japan a free hand in Asia. If these talks unexpectedly succeeded, orders would be sent to Nagumo to turn around and come home. And if this were done, the world must never know what almost happened. So at this point Nagumo couldn't risk telling anybody.

But it was far more likely that the attack would come off; so the main job was to keep the fleet from being discovered. No waste could be thrown overboard—it might leave a tell-tale track. The ships used the highest grade fuel to keep smoke at a minimum. The empty oil drums were carefully stowed away. Complete blackout and strict radio silence. On the *Hiei*, Commander Kazuyoshi Kochi, chief communications officer for the whole task force, disconnected an essential part of his transmitter, put it in a wooden box, and used it as a pillow whenever he managed to get in some sleep.

They had several bad scares. Once Tokyo radioed that an unknown submarine had been detected. The fleet hastily changed course, only to discover that it was all a mistake. Another night Admiral Kusaka suddenly spotted a light in the sky, thought it might be an unknown aircraft. It turned out to be a spark from the *Kaga's* funnel. She got a stiff warning to be more careful.

One morning the report spread that a Soviet ship was cruising nearby, en route from San Francisco to Russia. Every ship went on alert, but nothing came of it. Nor was there any way of checking such reports—Nagumo would not allow any planes in the air for fear of disclosing the fleet's presence.

Arguments rambled over what to do if they were spotted by a neutral ship. At least one member of Nagumo's staff cheerfully advised, "Sink it and forget it."

On December 2 this sort of bull session ended abruptly. The day before, the imperial council had decided on war, and now Admiral Yamamoto radioed the task force: "Climb

Mount Niitaka." It was code for "Proceed with the attack."

Another message later that day confirmed the date: "X-Day will be 8 December"—which was, of course, Sunday, December 7, in Hawaii.

At last the men were mustered and told. On the *Kaga*, Seaman Shigeki Yokota, a 23-year-old farm boy, was frightened but philosophical. Down in the heat and noise of the *Akagi's* engine room Commander Tanbo's men drank a quiet toast of *sake* . . . somehow no one felt like more than one cup. But most of the crew howled *banzais* and shared Seaman Iki Kuramoti's ecstasy: "An air attack on Hawaii! A dream come true!"

Next morning everyone seemed to take a new lease on life. The pilots were briefed on their specific assignments—the Army airfields at Hickam and Wheeler . . . Schofield Barracks . . . the naval air stations at Kaneohe and Ford Island . . . the Marine base at Ewa . . . the U. S. fleet. On the *Akagi*, Admiral Kusaka produced a beautiful plaster-of-Paris relief map of Pearl Harbor. Previously, he had kept it under lock and key in his stateroom, accessible only to a few top officers; now he had it installed on the hangar deck, where everybody could use it. On the *Kaga* the pilots played identification games. An air officer would hide silhouettes of the American ships behind his back. Then he would flash them one at a time for the fliers to name. Lieutenant Yoshio Shiga just never could get the *Utah*.

The fliers were now pampered by everybody—daily baths, special rations of fresh milk and eggs. Despite all the Shinto cult could do, these were promptly converted into American milkshakes.

On the flagship, Admiral Nagumo worried more than ever about being discovered. He was indeed in a ticklish spot. If sighted by the enemy at any time before December 6, he was to turn around and go home. If sighted on the 6th, he was to use his own judgment. Only on the 7th was he committed, no matter what happened.

In the radio room of the *Hiei,* Commander Kochi listened intently to detect any sign that the Americans were onto the game. The intercepts were very reassuring.

Soon a flow of messages began to arrive from home, so important that Kochi let his staff do the monitoring, and devoted his own attention entirely to Tokyo. Yamamoto was relaying the latest Honolulu intelligence on the U. S. fleet. On December 3 he radioed:

> "November 28—0800 (Local Time) Pearl Harbor: 2 Battleships (*Oklahoma, Nevada*); 1 Aircraft carrier (*Enterprise*); 2 Class-A Cruisers; 12 Destroyers Depart. 5 Battleships; 3 Class-A Cruisers; 3 Class-B Cruisers; 12 Destroyers; 1 Seaplane Carrier Enter . . ."

The following day Nagumo refueled and crossed the international date line. This made no difference to the Japanese, who always kept their watches on Tokyo time, but to an American it explains why it is December 3 again.

By evening the fleet was 900 miles north of Midway . . . 1300 miles northwest of Oahu. Admiral Nagumo began veering southeast. On the *Hiei,* Commander Kochi caught another useful message relayed by Tokyo from Honolulu:

> "November 29 P.M. (Local Time) Vessels Anchored in Pearl Harbor: A-Zone (Between Navy Arsenal and Ford Island) KT (NW dock Navy Arsenal) Battleships, *Pennsylvania, Arizona;* FV (Mooring buoy) Battleships, *California, Tennessee, Maryland, West Virginia.* KS (Navy Arsenal Repair Dock) Class-A Cruiser *Portland* . . ."

More refueling on the 4th, and another morsel from Honolulu: "Unable to ascertain whether air alert has been issued. There are no indications of sea alert . . ."

On the 5th, part of the fleet refueled most of the day and night. Admiral Kusaka then ordered three of the tankers to withdraw and wait for him to return. It was one of those

sentimental moments the Japanese love so well, and the crew
kept waving their caps as the tankers slowly disappeared.
Down below Commander Shimizu—the supply officer who
was just along for the ride—wistfully listened to a Japanese
program, Mrs. Hanako Muraoka's "Children's Hours." It was
now so faint that he finally gave up and twirled the dial
until he caught some American music. It came in bright and
lively.

At dawn on the 6th Kusaka refueled the rest of the task
force, then once again the ships that had been refueled the
day before. His idea was to have the tanks as full as possible
for the day of the attack. By late morning the job was done,
and the five remaining tankers also withdrew. More fond
farewells.

Meanwhile Yamamoto had radioed a final, stirring call to
arms: "The moment has arrived. The rise or fall of our
empire is at stake . . ."

Everyone who could be spared assembled on deck, and on
each ship the message was read to all hands. Speeches followed, and cheers split the air. Then up the *Akagi's* mast ran
the same "Z" flag flown by Admiral Heihachiro Togo at his
great victory over the Russians in 1905. Down in the *Akagi's*
engine room Chief Engineer Tanbo couldn't see it happen,
but as he listened over the voice tube, his heart pounded and
tears came to his eyes. He still regards it as his most dramatic
single moment during the entire war.

It was hardly the moment for an earache. But as Group
Leader Lieutenant Rokuro Kijuchi resumed briefing a group
of pilots on the flight deck of the *Hiryu,* he felt a throbbing
pain. He went to the ship's doctor and got the bad news—
he couldn't go; he had mastoids.

The fleet was now some 640 miles due north of Oahu.
With the slow tankers gone, it could make its final thrust
southward. Shortly before noon Admiral Kusaka turned his
ships and gave the order: "Twenty-four knots, full speed
ahead!"

By 3:00 P.M. they had closed the gap to 500 miles. And in the radio room of the *Hiei*, Commander Kochi had a new message from Honolulu: as of 6:00 P.M., December 5, Pearl Harbor contained "8 battleships; 3 Class-B Cruisers; 16 Destroyers. Entering Harbor, 4 Class-B Cruisers (*Honolulu* Type); 5 Destroyers."

At 4:55 P.M. the submarine *I-72*, already on the scene, sent some up-to-the-minute information: "American fleet is not in Lahaina waters."

So they were either still at Pearl or had just left for sea. Nagumo's staff hashed it over. Lieutenant Commander Ono, the admiral's intelligence officer, pointed out that five of the battleships had been in port eight days; he was afraid they would be gone now. But Chief of Staff Kusaka, who was a bug on statistics, didn't think they would leave on a week end.

Commander Genda, the enterprising torpedo specialist, bemoaned the absence of carriers, but Ono comforted him that a couple of them might return at the last minute. Genda cheered up: "If that happened, I don't care if all eight battleships are away."

Late that evening another reassuring message from Honolulu: "No barrage balloons sighted. Battleships are without crinolines. No indications of an air or sea alert wired to nearby islands . . ."

The deceptive measures obviously were working. And Tokyo must have felt quite self-satisfied, for everything possible had been done. The authorities had even brought busloads of sailors from the Yokosuka Naval Barracks and paraded them conspicuously all over town on sight-seeing tours.

At 1:20 A.M. a last message was relayed by Tokyo from Honolulu:

"December 6 (Local Time) Vessels moored in Harbor: 9 Battleships; 3 Class-B Cruisers; 3 Seaplane Tenders; 17

Destroyers. Entering Harbor are 4 Class-B Cruisers; 3
Destroyers. All Aircraft Carriers and Heavy Cruisers
have departed Harbor . . . No indication of any
changes in U. S. Fleet or anything else unusual."

More regrets that the carriers were gone. Some even wondered whether the raid should be called off. But Admiral
Nagumo felt there was no turning back now. Eight battleships were bound to be in port, and it was time to stop
worrying "about carriers that are not there."

A last restless night of peace settled over the darkened
ships as they pounded on toward Oahu, now less than 400
miles away. On the *Kaga,* Fighter Pilot Shiga took a tub
bath, prepared a complete new change in clothing before
retiring. Pilot Ippei Goto, who had just been promoted, laid
out his new ensign's uniform for the first time. On the *Hiryu,*
Bomber Pilot Hashimoto put his things in order and tried to
get some sleep. But he kept tossing in his bunk. Finally he
got up, went to the ship's doctor, and talked him out of some
sleeping pills.

They must have worked, for when Commander Amagai,
the *Hiryu's* flight deck officer, dropped by a little later to
see how his boys were getting on, they were all sound asleep.

He then went up to the hangar deck and carefully checked
the wireless in each plane. To make doubly sure that nobody
accidentally touched a set and gave away the show, he slipped
small pieces of paper between each transmitter key and its
point of contact.

On the *Akagi,* Lieutenant Commander Ono hunched over
his radio and continued his all-night vigil, monitoring the
Honolulu radio stations. Two . . . 2:30 . . . 3:00 A.M.
passed; still there was just KGMB playing Hawaiian songs.

Some 360 miles to the south, Lieutenant Commander
Mochitsura Hashimoto, special torpedo officer of the Japanese
submarine *I-24,* sat listening to the same radio program. The

I-24 was one of 28 large cruising subs that had been stationed off Oahu. They were to catch any U. S. warships lucky enough to escape to sea.

Also listening to the program in the *I-24* was Ensign Kazuo Sakamaki, who had just turned 23 the day they left Japan. Sakamaki lived dreams of naval glory, but so far he was just a passenger. He was skipper of a two-man midget sub, which the *I-24* carried papoose-style on her afterdeck.

There were five of these midgets altogether, each carried by a mother sub. The plan was to launch them shortly before the air attack. With luck they might sneak inside the harbor and bag a ship or two themselves.

The whole idea had an implausible touch that didn't appeal to the superpractical Admiral Yamamoto. But it also had that touch of military suicide dear to the Japanese heart, and finally Commander Naoji Iwasa persuaded the high command to incorporate the midgets—by now called the "Special Naval Attack Unit"—into the over-all plan. Then, since Iwasa had thought it up, he was put in charge.

At first Yamamoto set an important condition—the midgets couldn't enter Pearl Harbor itself . . . they might give away the show before it began. But Commander Iwasa insisted that they could sneak in undetected, and finally Yamamoto relented on this point too.

Commander Iwasa quickly whipped his project into shape. Five long-range cruising subs were stripped of their aircraft and catapults and fitted instead with the new secret midgets. Four big clamps and one auxiliary clamp held them in place. Each of the midgets was about 45 feet long, carried two torpedoes, ran on storage batteries, and required a two-man crew.

The crews—hand-picked and trained for more than a year —gathered in the Naval Command's private room at Kure Naval Base on the morning of November 16. There they learned that the great day was at hand, that they would sail on the 18th for Hawaii.

The following night Ensign Sakamaki took a last stroll through Kure with his classmate and fellow skipper, Ensign Akira Hirowo. At a novelty shop they each bought a small bottle of perfume. In the best tradition of the old Japanese warriors, they planned to put it on before going to battle. Then they could die gloriously—as Sakamaki explained, "like cherry blossoms falling to the ground."

Next morning they were off. Straight across the Pacific they sailed, cruising about 20 miles apart. Usually they ran submerged by day, on the surface at night. During these evening runs Sakamaki and his crewman, Seaman Kyoji Inagaki, would climb all over the midget, making sure that everything was all right. In his enthusiasm, Sakamaki was twice washed overboard. Fortunately he had remembered to tie himself to the big sub with a rope; so each time he was hauled in, dripping but full of pep, ready to go back to work.

On December 6 they sighted Oahu. After nightfall they surfaced and eased closer to shore. Finally they lay to in the moonlight, about ten miles off Pearl Harbor. From the conning tower Commander Hashimoto studied with interest the red and green lights off the port . . . the glow of Honolulu itself . . . the illuminated twin towers of the Royal Hawaiian Hotel . . . and all the way to his right the Elks Club that glittered and twinkled at the foot of Diamond Head.

So at last they were there. Sakamaki and Inagaki ran through the million details that needed last minute checking. Suddenly they discovered the gyrocompass wasn't working. This was important—without it they couldn't navigate under water. Sakamaki corralled the *I-24*'s gyrocompass man, ordered Inagaki to help him on the repair job, and went below for a last nap.

About 12:30 A.M. he left his bunk and wandered up to the conning tower for a little fresh air. Oahu was darker now and seemed wrapped in haze. The stars were out, and the moon beat on a choppy, restless sea.

He went below and checked on the gyrocompass. Inagaki

and the specialist were getting nowhere. Sakamaki's heart sank and he wondered whether this was just bad luck or if he had somehow failed. In any case, he was determined to go on.

He packed his personal belongings and wrote a farewell note to his family. In it he thoughtfully included a lock of hair and one of his fingernail parings. He cleaned up and changed to his midget submarine uniform—a leather jacket and *fundoshi*, which was a sort of Japanese G-string. He sprinkled himself with the perfume he bought at Kure and put on a white *hashamaki*, the Japanese warrior's traditional headband. Then he made the rounds of the sub, embracing the crew. By now it was well after 3:30 A.M., the time the midgets were meant to start for Pearl Harbor.

Chapter III

"Gate Open—White Lights"

At 3:42 a.m. the small mine sweeper *Condor* was plying her trade just outside Pearl Harbor, when watch officer Ensign R. C. McCloy suddenly sighted a strange white wave to port. It was less than 100 yards away, gradually converging on the *Condor* and moving toward the harbor entrance. He pointed it out to Quartermaster B. C. Uttrick, and they took turns looking at it with McCloy's binoculars. They decided it was the periscope of a submerged submarine, trailing a wake as it moved through the water.

Soon it was only 50 yards away—about 1000 yards from the entrance buoys. Then it apparently saw the *Condor,* for it quickly veered off in the opposite direction. At 3:58 the *Condor's* signal light blinked the news to the destroyer *Ward,* on patrol duty nearby: "Sighted submerged submarine on westerly course, speed nine knots."

The message came to Lieutenant (j.g.) Oscar Goepner, a young reserve officer from Northwestern University, who had just taken over the watch. He had been on the *Ward* doing this sort of inshore patrol work for more than a year, but to-night was the first time anything like this had ever happened. He woke up the skipper, Lieutenant William W. Outer-bridge.

For Outerbridge it was more than his first sub alert—it was his first night on his first patrol on his first command. Until now his naval career had been very uneventful, considering a rather colorful background. He had been born in Hong Kong —the son of a British merchant captain and an Ohio girl. After his father's death, the widow moved back home, and Outerbridge entered Annapolis, Class of 1927. He managed to scrape through, and spent the next 14 years inching up from one stripe to two—it was always a slow climb in the prewar Navy.

Until a few days before, he had been executive officer on the destroyer *Cummings,* where all the officers were Academy men except one reservist. Now he was the only Academy man on a ship full of reservists. He recalled how sorry he had felt for the *Cummings'* lonely reserve officer. Now the tables were turned—Goepner still recalls how sorry everybody on the *Ward* felt for Outerbridge, alone among the heathens.

On reading the *Condor's* message, Outerbridge sounded general quarters, and the men tumbled to their battle stations. For the next half-hour the *Ward* prowled about—her lookouts and sonar men straining for any sign of the sub. No luck. At 4:43 A.M. the crew were released, and most of them went back to bed. The regular watch continued to search the night.

Four minutes later the gate in the antitorpedo net across the harbor entrance began to swing open. This always took eight to ten minutes; and it wasn't until 4:58 A.M. that a crewman noted in the gate vessel log, "Gate open—white lights."

At 5:08 the mine sweeper *Crossbill,* which had been working with the *Condor,* passed in. Normally the gate would now be closed again—this was always supposed to be done at night—but the *Condor* was due in so soon, it just didn't seem worth the trouble.

By 5:32 the *Condor* was safely in, but still the gate stayed

open. The tug *Keosanqua* was due to pass out around 6:15
A.M. Once more it didn't seem worth the trouble to close the
gate, only to open it again in a little while.

As the *Condor* closed up shop, the *Ward* radioed for a few
final words of advice that might help her carry on the search:
"What was the approximate distance and course of the sub
you sighted?"

"The course was about what we were steering at the time,
020 magnetic, and about 1000 yards from the entrance."

This was far to the east of the area first indicated, and
Outerbridge felt he must have been looking in the wrong
place. Actually, the *Condor* was talking about two different
things. Her first message gave the sub's course when last
seen; this new message gave it when first seen. She never
explained that in between times the sub had completely
changed course.

So the *Ward* moved east, combing an area where the sub
could never be. And as she scurried about, she remembered
at 5:34 to acknowledge the *Condor's* help: "Thank you for
your information . . . We will continue search."

The radio station at nearby Bishops Point listened in on
this exchange, but didn't report it to anybody—after all, a
ship-to-ship conversation between the *Ward* and the *Condor*
was none of their business. The *Ward* didn't report anything
either—after all, the *Condor* didn't, and she was the one who
said she saw something. She must have decided it wasn't a
sub after all.

In any event, it wasn't the sub piloted by Ensign Kazuo
Sakamaki. He wasn't even ready to leave until 5:30, a good
two hours behind schedule. Meanwhile there had been more
futile last-minute efforts to fix the broken gyroscope. Then
another round of ceremonial good-bys.

When the *I-24's* skipper, Lieutenant Commander Hiroshi
Hanabusa, asked if the broken gyrocompass had altered his
plans, Sakamaki proudly replied, "Captain, I am going

ahead." And then, carried away by it all, they both shouted, "On to Pearl Harbor!"

Dawn was just breaking when Sakamaki and Inagaki left the bridge of the *I-24* and scrambled aft along the catwalk to their midget. Each man held a bottle of wine and some lunch in his left hand, and shook a few more hands with his right. As Sakamaki's friend, Ensign Hirowo observed when climbing into his midget on the *I-20*, "We must look like high school boys happily going on a picnic."

Sakamaki was far beyond such mundane thoughts. He and Inagaki said nothing as they climbed up the side of the small sub, squirmed through the hatch in the conning tower, and slammed it shut behind them.

The *I-24* slowly submerged, and the crew took their stations to release the four big clamps that held the midget. Quietly they waited for the signal.

Sakamaki and Inagaki were waiting too. Their electric motor was now purring, and they could feel the mother sub picking up speed to give them a better start.

Suddenly there was the terrific bang of the releasing gear, and they were off on their own. Immediately everything went wrong. Instead of thrusting ahead on an even keel, the midget tilted down, nearly standing on end. Sakamaki switched off the engines and began trying to correct the boat's trim.

Chapter IV

"You'd Be Surprised What Goes on Around Here"

LIEUTENANT HARAUO TAKEDA, 30-year-old flight officer on the cruiser *Tone*, was a disappointed, worried man as the Japanese striking force hurtled southward, now less than 250 miles from Oahu.

He was disappointed because last-minute orders kept him from piloting the *Tone's* seaplane, which was to take off at 5:30 A.M., joining the *Chikuma's* plane in a final reconnaissance of the U. S. fleet. And he was worried because—as the man in charge of launching these planes—he feared that they would somehow collide while taking off. True, the two ships were some eight miles apart, but it was still pitch black. Besides, when the stakes are so high, a man almost looks for things to worry about.

Nothing went wrong. The planes shot safely from their catapults and winged off into the dark—two small harbingers of the great armada that would follow. Admiral Nagumo planned to hit Pearl Harbor with 353 planes in two mighty waves. The first was to go at 6:00 A.M.—40 torpedo planes . . . 51 dive bombers . . . 49 horizontal bombers . . . 43 fighters to provide cover. The second at 7:15 A.M.—80 dive bombers . . . 54 high-level bombers . . . 36 more fighters. This would still leave 39 planes to guard the task force in case the Americans struck back.

34

By now the men on the carriers were making their final preparations. The deck crews—up an hour before the pilots—checked the planes in their hangars, then brought them up to the flight decks. Motors sputtered and roared as the mechanics tuned up the engines. On the *Hiryu*, Commander Amagai carefully removed the pieces of paper he had slipped into each plane's wireless transmitter to keep it from being set off by accident.

Down below, the pilots were pulling on their clean underwear and freshly pressed uniforms. Several wore the traditional *hashamaki* headbands. Little groups gathered around the portable Shinto shrines that were standard equipment on every Japanese warship. There they drank jiggers of *sake* and prayed for their success.

Assembling for breakfast, they found a special treat. Instead of the usual salted pike-mackerel and rice mixed with barley, today they ate *sekihan*. This Japanese dish of rice boiled with tiny red beans was reserved for only the most ceremonial occasions. Next, they picked up some simple rations for the trip—a sort of box lunch that included the usual rice balls and pickled plums, emergency rations of chocolate, hardtack, and special pills to keep them alert.

Now to the flight operations rooms for final briefing. On the *Akagi* Commander Mitsuo Fuchida, leader of the attacking planes, sought out Admiral Nagumo: "I am ready for the mission."

"I have every confidence in you," the admiral answered, grasping Fuchida's hand.

On every carrier the scene was the same: the dimly lit briefing room; the pilots crowding in and spilling out into the corridor; the blackboard revised to show ship positions at Pearl Harbor as of 10:30 A.M., December 6. Time for one last look at the enemy line-up; one last run-down on the charts and maps. Then the latest data on wind direction and velocity, some up-to-the-minute calculations on distance and flying time to Hawaii and back. Next a stern edict: no one except

Commander Fuchida was to touch his radio until the attack began. Finally, brief pep talks by the flight officers, the skippers, and, on the *Akagi*, by Admiral Nagumo himself.

A bright dawn swept the sky as the men emerged, some wearing small briefing boards slung around their necks. One by one they climbed to the cockpits, waving good-by—27-year-old Ippei Goto of the *Kaga*, in his brand-new ensign's uniform . . . quiet Fusata Iida of the *Soryu*, who was so crazy about baseball . . . artistic Mimori Suzuki of the *Akagi*, whose Caucasian looks invited rough teasing about his "mixed blood." When it was Lieutenant Haita Matsumura's turn, he suddenly whipped off the gauze mask which had marked him as such a hypochondriac. All along, he had been secretly growing a beautiful mustache.

Commander Fuchida headed for the flight leader's plane, designated by a red and yellow stripe around the tail. As he swung aboard, the crew chief handed him a special *hashamaki* headband: "This is a present from the maintenance crews. May I ask that you take it along to Pearl Harbor?"

In the *Agaki's* engine room, Commander Tanbo got permission and rushed topside for the great moment—the only time he left his post during the entire voyage. Along the flight decks the men gathered, shouting good luck and waving good-by. Lieutenant Ebina, the *Shokaku's* junior surgeon, trembled with excitement as he watched the motors race faster and the blue exhaust smoke pour out.

All eyes turned to the *Akagi*, which would give the signal. She flew a set of flags at half-mast, which meant to get ready. When they were hoisted to the top and swiftly lowered, the planes would go.

Slowly the six carriers swung into the wind. It was from the east, and perfect for take-off. But the southern seas were running high, and the carriers dipped 15 degrees, sending high waves crashing against the bow. Too rough for really safe launching, Admiral Kusaka thought, but there was no other choice now. The Pearl Harbor Striking Force was poised

230 miles north and slightly east of Oahu. The time was 6:00 A.M.

Up fluttered the signal flags, then down again. One by one the fighters roared down the flight decks, drowning the cheers and yells that erupted everywhere. Commander Hoichiro Tsukamoto forgot his worries as navigation officer of the *Shokaku,* decided this was the greatest moment of his life. The ship's doctors, Captain Endo and Lieutenant Ebina, abandoned their professional dignity and wildly waved the fliers on. Engineer Tanbo shouted like a schoolboy, then rushed back to the *Akagi's* engine room to tell everybody else.

Now the torpedo planes and dive bombers thundered off, while the fighters circled above, giving protection. Plane after plane rose, flashing in the early-morning sun that peeked over the horizon. Soon all 183 were in the air, circling and wheeling into formation. Seaman Iki Kuramoti watched, on the verge of tears. Quietly he put his hands together and prayed.

For Admiral Kusaka it had been a terrible strain, getting the planes off in these high seas. Now they were on their way, and the sudden relief was simply too much. He trembled like a leaf—just couldn't control himself. And he was embarrassed, too, because he prided himself on his grasp of Buddhism, *bushido,* and *kendo* (a form of Japanese fencing) —all of which were meant to fortify a man against exactly this sort of thing. Finally he sat on the deck—or he thinks possibly in a chair—and meditated Buddha-fashion. Slowly he pulled himself together again as the planes winged off to the south.

At the main target of this onslaught, the only sign of life was a middle-aged housewife driving her husband to work. Mrs. William Blackmore headed through the main Pearl Harbor gate . . . past the Marine sentry, who checked her windshield sticker . . . and headed down to the harbor craft pier. Mr. Blackmore—16 years in the Navy and presently chief engineer of the tug *Keosanqua*—was to get under way at 6:00 A.M. to meet the supply ship *Antares* and take over a steel barge she was towing up from Palmyra.

As Mrs. Blackmore dropped her husband, the first gray light of morning gave the rows of silent warships an eerie, ghostly look. "This," she observed, "is the quietest place I've ever seen."

"You'd be surprised what goes on around here," Blackmore replied cheerfully, and he jumped aboard the tug for another day's work.

The *Keosanqua* moved down the harbor, through the long narrow entrance channel, and past the open torpedo net, which was kept open still longer for whenever the tug should return. It was now 6:30 A.M. and the *Antares* was already in sight, towing the barge about a hundred yards behind her. The *Ward* hovered about a mile away, and a Navy PBY circled above, apparently looking at something.

Seaman H. E. Raenbig, the *Ward's* helmsman, was looking at something too. As the *Antares* came up from the southwest and crossed the *Ward's* bow to port, he suddenly noticed a curious black object that seemed to be fastened to the towline between the *Antares* and her barge. They were about a mile away, and so he asked Quartermaster H. F. Gearin to use his glasses for a closer look.

Gearin immediately saw that the black object was not hanging on the hawser but was merely in line with it. Actually, the object was in the water on the far side of the *Antares.* He showed it to Lieutenant Goepner, who said it looked like a buoy to him, but to keep an eye on it.

Gearin did, and about a minute later said he thought it was a small conning tower. It seemed to be converging on the *Antares'* course, as though planning to fall in behind the barge. At this point the Navy patrol bomber began circling overhead. Goepner needed no further convincing.

"Captain, come on the bridge!" he shouted. Outerbridge jumped from his cot in the chartroom, pulled on a Japanese kimono, and joined the others. He took one look and sounded general quarters. It was just 6:40 A.M.

Seaman Sidney Noble stumbled out of his bunk in the forecastle for the second time in three hours—so sleepy he could hardly wipe the sand from his eyes. He pulled on dungarees, shoes but no socks, and a blue shirt, which he didn't bother to button. Then he joined the other men racing up the ladder to their battle stations.

Gunner's Mate Louis Gerner stayed below long enough to slam and dog the hatch leading to the anchor engine room, then dashed after the rest. As he ran aft toward his station in the after well deck, Outerbridge leaned over the bridge railing and frantically waved him away from Number 1 gun, which was now swinging out, trained on the conning tower ahead.

Along the afterdeck Ensign D. B. Haynie ran past Number 2, 3, and 4 guns, shouting to the men to break out the ammunition. He might have spared himself the trouble at Number 3. Seaman Ambrose Domagall, the first loader, had been on duty as bridge messenger. As soon as general quarters sounded, he went directly to the gun, yanked open the ready rack, and was waiting with a three-inch shell in his arms when the rest of the crew rushed up.

Outerbridge had signaled "All engines ahead full," and the old *Ward* was now surging forward—bounding from five to ten to 25 knots in five minutes.

"Come left," he called to Helmsman Raenbig, and the 1918 hull wheezed with the strain as she heeled hard to port. Outerbridge headed her straight for the gap between the barge and the conning tower, now some 400 yards off the *Ward's* starboard bow.

At this point the *Antares* caught on—her blinker flashed the news that she thought she was being followed. Up above, the PBY dropped two smoke pots to mark the sub's position.

To Ensign William Tanner, pilot of the PBY, this was simply the act of a good Samaritan. He had been on the regular morning patrol when he first spotted the submarine. It was well out of the designated area for friendly subs. His immediate reaction—"My God, a sub in distress!"

Then he saw the *Ward* steaming in that direction. Quickly he swooped down and dropped his two smoke bombs. They would help the *Ward* come to the rescue. From his position this was the best he could do for the sub.

The *Ward* didn't need any markers—the submarine was just to starboard, pointing straight at the ship. It was running awash, with the conning tower about two feet out of water. In the choppy sea the men caught brief glimpses of a small cigar-shaped hull. They were utterly fascinated. Chief Commissary Steward H. A. Minter noticed that it was painted a dingy green. Quartermaster Gearin saw a layer of small barnacles . . . Helmsman Raenbig noticed moss on the conning tower . . . most of the men thought it looked rather rusty. Everyone agreed there were no markings on the squat, oval conning tower.

Curiously enough, the sub didn't seem to see the *Ward* at all. It just kept moving ahead, trailing the *Antares* at about eight or nine knots.

"Commence firing," Outerbridge ordered. They were now only 100 yards away and Boatswain's Mate A. Art, captain of Number 1 gun knew they were much too close to use his sights. So he aimed the gun like a squirrel rifle and let her go. It was exactly 6:45 A.M. when this first shot whistled over the conning tower and plunged into the sea beyond.

They were better squirrel hunters at Number 3 gun on the galley house roof. Gun Captain Russell Knapp gave his order to fire about 30 seconds later, with the target less than 50 yards away. The shell hit the base of the conning tower, just where it touched the water. The sub staggered but came on.

Now it was right alongside, sucked almost against the ship. For an instant it seemed to hang there—long enough to give Gunner's Mate Louis Gerner an indelible picture of the glass

in its stubby periscope—and then it was behind them, writh-
ing and spinning in the *Ward's* wake.

Four quick whistle blasts told Chief Torpedoman W. C.
Maskzawilz to release his depth charges. One . . . two . . .
three . . . four rolled off the stern. Huge geysers erupted and
the sub was instantly swallowed in a mountain of foam. Maskzawilz, who set the pistols at 100 feet, noted with satisfaction
that the sub "seemed to wade right into the first one."

Up in the PBY Ensign Tanner was doing some soul-
searching. Helping the sub might be the decent thing to do,
but his orders were very strict—"Depth bomb and sink any
submarines found in the defensive sea area without authority." Now he looked down, the *Ward* was doing just that. A
pang of hesitation, and Tanner made another run. This time
he dropped some depth bombs of his own.

All these fireworks were watched with mild interest by the
men on the tug *Keosanqua*. She loafed about two miles away,
just off the harbor mouth, still waiting to pick up the *Antares'* barge. Like everybody else on board, Engineer Blackmore thought it was merely some early-morning practice.

On the *Ward*, Lieutenant Goepner had a far more harrowing thought. He had the awful feeling that it might be an
American sub. Of course, it shouldn't have been there and,
of course, it didn't look like anything he had ever seen before;
but could there have been a mistake?

In the PBY, Ensign Tanner had the same feeling. He and
his copilot, Ensign Clark Greevey, assured each other that
orders were orders. But if Tanner's judgment was wrong, a
lot of good that would do. He could see the court-martial
now. And he could see himself labeled for the rest of his life
as the man who sank the American sub. In a wave of youth-
ful self-pity he began picturing himself trying to get any job
anywhere. As the plane resumed its patrol, he grimly reported the sinking to the Kaneohe Naval Air Station and settled back to await the inevitable end of his career.

Only Outerbridge seemed absolutely confident. In fact, he decided that the report radioed at 6:51 A.M. wasn't strong enough. It ran: "Depth-bombed sub operating in defensive sea area." This might imply just a periscope sighting or a sonar contact. Throughout the years there had been too many spars and whales bombed for headquarters to get overly excited about a message like that. But the *Ward* had seen the sub itself, and that was the all-important point to put over. It was the one hope of stirring up some action, instead of the standard "verify and repeat."

So Outerbridge quickly drafted another message. At 6:53 he again radioed the Fourteenth Naval District Headquarters. This time the report ran: "Attacked, fired on, depth-bombed, and sunk, submarine operating in defensive sea area." He felt that "fired on" was the key phrase. Now they would know he used his guns. Now they would know that he at least saw something.

Even Outerbridge didn't go all the way. He might have reported this extraordinary encounter in the clear instead of in code, and thus saved a few minutes. He might have used his blinker to signal the harbor control tower. He might have sent the more jolting message that was drafted but ended up crumpled in his file—it began with the words: "Sighted conning tower of strange sub, fired two rounds at point-blank range . . ." But at least he did something. At least he was willing, when other men were hypnotized by peace, to announce that he had blasted the daylights out of someone.

Whoever it was, it wasn't Ensign Sakamaki. At 6:30 he and Inagaki were still trying to correct their boat's trim. It was no easy job. Only one man at a time could wriggle on his stomach along the cramped tunnel that led fore and aft from the control room. They took turns slithering back and forth . . . shifting lead ballast, twisting the dials that released the air and filled the tanks with water. It took an hour to get the sub back on an even keel.

At last they started off again and even found time for a spot of lunch. They sat facing each other in the tiny control room, munching rice balls and exchanging cups of grape wine. As they finished, they grasped each other's hands and again pledged success.

Ten minutes later Sakamaki, peeking through the periscope, was appalled to see that they were approximately 90 degrees off course. With the gyrocompass out of order, he was depending on an auxiliary compass, which he thought would at least show the right directions. Apparently it was out of order too.

He tried to reset his course with his periscope, but it wasn't much help. Blindly the sub moved this way and that, always seeming to end up in the wrong direction. His hands grew wet with sweat. It was now about 7:00 A.M., and Ensign Kazuo Sakamaki was still a long way from the mouth of Pearl Harbor.

Chapter V

"Well, Don't Worry About It"

IT WAS AN UNEVENTFUL MORNING at the Army's Opana radar station near Kahuku Point on the northern tip of Oahu. Normally Privates Joseph Lockard and George Elliott made 25 plane contacts during the regular 4:00 to 7:00 A.M. watch, but this Sunday there was hardly anything.

The Opana station was one of five mobile units set up at strategic points around the perimeter of Oahu. They were all linked to an information center at Fort Shafter, which kept track of the plots picked up by the stations. The system could pick up any plane within 150 miles—when it worked. But it had just started operating around Thanksgiving and was still full of bugs. Lockard, Elliott, and the others spent most of their time training and making repairs.

At first they practiced from 7:00 A.M. to 4:00 P.M. But after Washington's warning of November 27, they went on duty every morning from four to seven—General Short felt these were the critical hours. Then they trained until 11:00 and knocked off for the day. On Sundays they worked only the four-to-seven shift. To the men this was simply a change in hours, not a change in routine or approach.

It was all very casual at Opana. This was the most remote of the five stations, and the six men who ran it were left pretty much to themselves. They had a small camp at Ka-

44

waiola, nine miles down the coast, and commuted to work
by pickup truck. They were meant to work in three-man
shifts, but this Sunday they decided that a two-man shift
would do. Lockard served as operator, Elliott as both plotter
and motorman. The regular motorman stayed in the sack.

They went on duty at noon December 6. They had the
double job of guarding the set with a .45 pistol and seven
rounds of ammunition, and running it during the four-to-
seven watch the following morning. That night they set the
alarm for 3:45 A.M., tuned in the set on schedule at 4:00, and
spent the next three hours waiting for something to happen.
There was a flicker or so around 6:45—apparently a couple
of planes were coming in from the northeast about 130 miles
away—but nothing more than that. They weren't surprised
when the Shafter Information Center phoned at 6:54 and
told them they could start closing up.

At the information center, Lieutenant Kermit Tyler, the
only officer on duty, was having an equally quiet time. Usually the place was quite busy as the five stations phoned in
their contacts and the spotters moved little arrows around
the big wooden plotting table. It was all make-believe, for the
other services hadn't yet assigned liaison officers to help
screen out friendly planes, but still it made for lively practice. The control officer would plan the interception of the
"enemy." His assistant, the pursuit officer, would relay his
orders to mythical squadrons of Army fighters. Sometimes
they even practiced with real planes.

But this Sunday there was little action. Few contacts; nobody to evaluate the planes that were spotted; no control officer to direct any interception. Except for the enlisted men
at the plotting table, only the pursuit officer, Lieutenant Tyler, was on hand. But with nobody to give him orders and no
planes to relay orders to, he had nothing to do. Nor did he
really know what he was meant to do—he had only drawn
this duty once before.

Actually, he was there purely for training. Major Kenneth

Bergquist—in charge of the radar network—wanted the
young pilots to learn as much about the systems as possible,
so they could use it more effectively in interception work.
Since the center had to operate from four to seven anyhow,
this was a good chance to brush up. Today was Tyler's turn,
and it was enough if he kept his eyes peeled.

For the first two hours nothing happened. Around 6:10
one of the stations finally phoned in a contact, and the spotters began shoving their arrows around the board. At 6:45
some plots began to show up 130 miles north of Oahu—not
much, but enough to make Lieutenant Tyler wander over
and see how the clerk would mark them on the daily record.
They showed up as little hen scratches pointing toward Oahu.
Then suddenly it was 7:00 A.M., and everyone went off to
breakfast.

Tyler was left alone in the room. For one of those reasons
known only to the Army, his orders ran from 4:00 to 8:00—
an hour beyond everybody else's. He settled back alone—no
one to obey . . . no one to command . . . and now no one
even to talk to.

The 7:00 A.M. closing time made little difference to Privates Lockard and Elliott at Opana. They were at the mercy
of the breakfast truck. It usually came about seven, but a
man couldn't set his watch by it. With this in mind, they decided to keep the set running until the truck came. Elliott
wanted to practice operating the set. After two weeks in the
outfit, he could do the plotting pretty well, but still was no
operator. Lockard was willing to teach him.

At 7:02 Elliott sat down and began fiddling with the controls. Lockard leaned over his shoulder and started explaining
the various echoes or blips. Suddenly a blip flashed on the
screen far bigger than anything Lockard had ever seen before. It was almost as big as the main pulse the unit always
sent out. So big he thought the set was broken . . . that
somehow the main pulse and mileage scale had gotten out of
kilter. It was a pinball machine gone haywire.

He shoved Elliott aside and took over the controls himself. Quickly he saw there was nothing wrong with the set—it
was just a huge flight of planes. By now Elliott was at the
plotting table, and in a few seconds they nailed down the position: 137 miles to the north, three degrees east.

At 7:06 Elliott tried the headphones that connected directly with one of the spotters in the information center.
The line was dead. Then he tried the regular Army circuit.
After the clicks and hums and wheezes that are the overture
to any phone call in Hawaii, he finally got through to the information center switchboard operator, Private Joseph
McDonald. McDonald worked in a small cubicle just outside
the plotting room and remained on duty even though the
center was now closed.

Breathlessly Elliott broke the news: "There's a large number of planes coming in from the north, three degrees east."

McDonald thought there was nobody left at the information center, so he wrote down the message and turned around
to time it by the big clock on the plotting room wall.
Through the open door he suddenly noticed Lieutenant Tyler, sitting alone at the plotting table—there was someone in
the building after all.

McDonald took the message to the lieutenant. Helpfully
he explained that it was the first time he had ever received
anything like this—"Do you think we ought to do something
about it?" He suggested they call the plotters back from
breakfast. They didn't get too much practice, and this certainly seemed "an awful big flight."

Tyler was unimpressed. McDonald returned to the switchboard and called back Opana. This time he got Lockard, who
was excited too. The blips looked bigger than ever; the distance was shrinking fast—7:08 A.M., 113 miles . . . 7:15
A.M., 92 miles. At least 50 planes must be soaring toward
Oahu at almost 180 mph.

"Hey, Mac!" he protested when McDonald told him the
lieutenant said everything was all right. Then Lockard asked

to speak directly to Tyler, explaining he had never seen so many planes, so many flashes, on his screen.

McDonald traipsed back to Tyler: "Sir, I would appreciate it very much if you would answer the phone."

Tyler took over, listened patiently, and thought a minute. He remembered the carriers were out—these might be Navy planes. He recalled hearing the radio on his way to work; remembered that it stayed on all night whenever B-17s came in from the coast—these might be Flying Fortresses. In either case, the planes were friendly. Cutting short any further discussion, he told Lockard, "Well, don't worry about it."

Lockard was now in no mood to keep on; he thought they might as well shut down the set. But Elliott wanted to practice some more, so they followed the flight on in—7:25 A.M., 62 miles . . . 7:30 A.M., 47 miles . . . 7:39 A.M., 22 miles. At this point they lost it in the "dead zone" caused by the hills around them.

Conveniently, the pickup truck arrived just then to take them back to Kawaiola for breakfast. They slammed shut the doors of the mobile unit, turned the lock, hopped in the truck, and bounced off down the road at 7:45.

At the Shafter Information Center Private McDonald was still uneasy. He asked Lieutenant Tyler what he really thought of the blips, and was glad to hear the lieutenant say, "It's nothing." Shortly after 7:30 another operator took over the switchboard, and as McDonald left the building he suddenly stuck the original Opana message in his pocket. He had never done anything like this before, but he wanted to show it to the fellows.

Alone again in the plotting room, Lieutenant Tyler settled back to wait out the last dragging minutes of his own tour of duty. He had no qualms about the Opana message, and although he didn't know it, on one count at least he was absolutely right—the all-night radio did mean some B-17s were coming in from the mainland. At this very moment 12 of the big bombers were approaching from the northeast.

But the planes that showed upon the Opana screen were a little less to the east, far more numerous, and at this moment infinitely closer.

Commander Mitsuo Fuchida knew they must be nearly there—they had been in the air now almost an hour and a half. But a carpet of thick white clouds stretched endlessly below, and he couldn't even see the ocean to check the wind drift. He flicked on the radio direction finder and picked up an early-morning program from Honolulu. By twisting his antenna he got a good bearing on the station and discovered he was five degrees off course. He made the correction, and the other planes followed suit.

They were all around him. Behind were the other 48 horizontal bombers. To the left and slightly above were Lieutenant Commander Kakwichi Takahashi's 51 dive bombers. To the right and a little below were Lieutenant Commander Shigeharu Murata's 40 torpedo planes. Far above, Lieutenant Commander Shigeru Itaya's 43 fighters provided cover. The bombers flew at 9000 feet, the fighters as high as 15,000. All of them basked in the bright morning sun that now blazed off to the left.

But below, the clouds were still everywhere. Fuchida began to worry—would it be as bad over Pearl Harbor? If so, what would that do to the bombing? He wished the reconnaissance planes would report—they should be there by now. And then through the radio music he suddenly heard a weather broadcast. He tuned closer and caught it clearly: ". . . partly cloudly . . . mostly over the mountains . . . ceiling 3500 feet . . . visibility good."

Now he knew he could count on the clouds to break once he reached Oahu. Also that it would be better to come in from the west and southwest—those clouds over the mountains made an eastern approach too dangerous. Then, as if to cap this run of good luck, the clouds below him parted, and almost directly ahead he saw a white line of surf breaking against a rugged green shore. It was Kahuku Point, Oahu.

Lieutenant Toshio Hashimoto, piloting one of Fuchida's bombers, was simply charmed. The lush green island, the clear blue water, the colored roofs of the little houses seemed in another world. It was the kind of scene one likes to preserve. He pulled out his camera and snapped some pictures.

For fighter pilot Yoshio Shiga, this warm, sunlit land had a deeper meaning. Back in 1934 he had been to Honolulu on a naval training cruise . . . a visit full of good times and pleasant memories. To see Oahu again, still so green and lovely, gave him a strange, nostalgic feeling. He thought about it for a moment, then turned to the business at hand.

The time had come to deploy for the attack, and Commander Fuchida had a difficult decision to make. The plan provided for either "Surprise" or "Surprise Lost" conditions. If "Surprise," the torpedo planes were to go in first, then the horizontal bombers, finally the dive bombers, while the fighters remained above for protection. (The idea was to drop as many torpedoes as possible before the smoke from the dive bombing ruined the targets.) On the other hand, if the raiders had been detected and it was "Surprise Lost," the dive bombers and fighters would hit the airfields and antiaircraft defenses first; then the torpedo planes would come in when resistance was crushed. To tell the planes which deployment to take, Commander Fuchida was to fire his signal gun once for "Surprise," twice for "Surprise Lost."

Trouble was, Commander Fuchida didn't know whether the Americans had caught on or not. The reconnaissance planes were meant to tell him, but they hadn't reported yet. It was now 7:40 A.M., and he couldn't wait any longer. They were already well down the west coast and about opposite Haleiwa. Playing a hunch, he decided he could carry off the surprise.

He held out his signal pistol and fired one "black dragon." The dive bombers began circling upward to 12,000 feet; the horizontal bombers spiraled down to 3500; the torpedo planes dropped until they barely skimmed the sea, ready for the honor of leading the assault.

As the planes orbited into position, Fuchida noticed that the fighters weren't responding at all. He decided that they must have missed his signal, so he reached out and fired another "black dragon." The fighters saw it this time, but so did the dive bombers. They decided it was the second "black dragon" of the "Surprise Lost" signal. Hence, they would be the ones to go in first. In a welter of confusion, the High Command's plan for carefully integrated phases vanished; dive bombers and torpedo planes eagerly prepared to slam into Pearl Harbor at the same time.

They could already see it on their left. Lieutenant Shiga was attracted by the unusual color gray of the warships. Commander Itaya was struck by the way the battleships were "strung out and anchored two ships side by side in an orderly manner." Commander Fuchida was more interested in counting them—two, four, eight. No doubt about it, they were all there.

Chapter VI

"Joe, This Is One for the Tourist!"

THIRTEEN-YEAR-OLD JAMES B. MANN, JR., stood with his father, squinting at the planes that circled high above their beach house at Haleiwa on the northwest coast of Oahu. The Manns liked to come to Haleiwa for a restful week end, but this morning there was no rest at all. First the planes set off their two pug dogs; then the barking woke the family up. Mrs. Mann thought it might be that Lieutenant Underwood from Wheeler Field—he was always buzzing the beach—but Mr. Mann and Junior quickly discovered that it was a much bigger show.

More than 100 planes were orbiting about, gradually breaking up into smaller groups of three, five, and seven. Soon, several fighters dropped down low enough for Junior to observe, "They've changed the color of our planes." Then the fighters sped off to the east, down the road toward Schofield and Wheeler Field. Now the other groups were flying away too, and by 7:45 A.M. they had all disappeared.

Twelve miles further south, another 13-year-old, Tommy Young, was surf-casting with his father off Maile Beach. Suddenly Tommy's attention was attracted by the drone of airplane motors. Looking up, he saw a big formation of silvery planes flying southeast. His father counted 72 of them.

Fourteen miles to the southeast, two other young fisher-

52

Japanese crewmen cheer the attacking planes on their way, as they take off in the early-morning light of December 7. Commander Tsukamoto, navigation officer of the carrier *Shokaku,* decided this was the greatest moment of his life.

The American commanders who received the attack: at top, Admiral Husband E. Kimmel, commanding the U.S. Pacific Fleet, and, below, Lieut. General Walter C. Short, commanding U.S. Army ground and air forces in Hawaii.

The Japanese commander who delivered the attack: Vice Admiral Chuichi Nagumo.

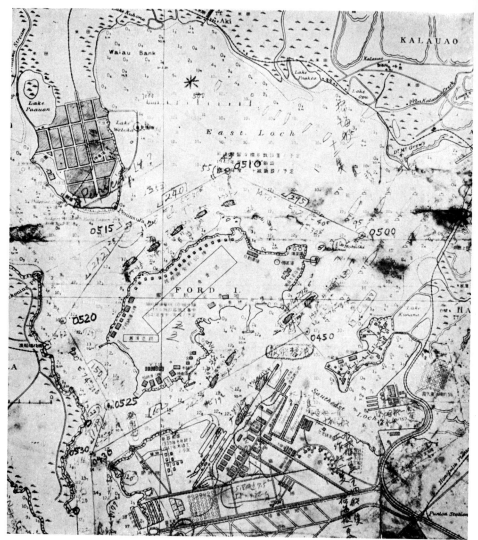

This Japanese chart marks the supposed position of various ships in Pearl Harbor. Although quite inaccurate, it was relied on faithfully—the old target ship *Utah*, mislabeled the carrier *Saratoga*, took two torpedoes right away. The proposed course of a Japanese midget sub is plotted around Ford Island, leading to later reports that the map was recovered from one of these subs. But Japanese comments scribbled on the chart—for instance, that the tanks circled at the bottom can be seen "at about five nautical miles"—indicate that it really came from a plane shot down. This is in line with the recollection of General Kendall Fielder, who helped recover the chart.

Official U.S. Navy Photo

The raid begins. Japanese torpedo plane peels off after direct hit on the *Oklahoma* . . . the torpedoed *Utah* lists to port off the near side of Ford Island . . . smoke boils up from dive-bombed hangars at extreme right. This and the next two pictures were later captured from the Japanese.

Battleship Row through Japanese eyes. Telltale torpedo tracks lead straight to the listing *West Virginia* and *Oklahoma*. Gray smoke across the channel is from the torpedoed *Helena*; white smoke in the background, from dive-bombing at Hickam Field.

Top, looking straight down on Battleship Row from a Japanese bomber. Oil gushes from the torpedoed *Oklahoma* and *West Virginia.* Astern, the *Arizona* has just been hit by a bomb. The same scene, below, viewed three days later from a U.S. Navy plane. The *Oklahoma* has turned turtle, the *West Virginia* is awash, the *Arizona* blown apart. Fifteen years later oil still seeped from *Arizona's* hulk.

Height of the attack. The *West Virginia* lies sunk but still upright, thanks to Lieutenant Ricketts' impromptu counterflooding. Inboard is the *Tennessee,* less seriously damaged but threatened at the moment by burning oil.

Rescue launch edges in to pick up swimmers from the *West Virginia.* One survivor needed no such help: Ensign Fowler, the ship's disbursing officer, pushed off on a raft, using his cash ledger as a paddle.

No one ever finished raising the American flag, as the torpedoed *Utah* rolls over at her berth on the northwest side of Ford Island.

cru[...]
cruise[...]
greater [...]
Navy ha[...]
order, most [...]
by 1944. Each [...]
of approximate[...]
to man its fifteen [...]
four to eight planes [...]
gray hull it carries four [...]
turbines which turn up [...]
100,000 horsepower, the pow[...]
than 1,000 average automobiles [...]

Right—A bow on view of the
U. S. S. Arizona as she plows into a
huge swell. It is significant that despite the claims of air enthusiasts no
battleship has yet been sunk by bombs.

180

Courtesy of Walker Lewis

From the Army-Navy game program, November 29, 1941: "despite
the claims of air enthusiasts no battleship has yet been sunk by
bombs."

Newsreel Pool

Eight days later—the *Arizona* exploding from direct bomb hit.

The *Arizona* burning after the great explosion.

After the attack the shattered *Arizona* lies, a tomb for 1102 men.

Japanese fighters cruise by one of the unarmed B-17s that arrived from California during the raid. Most of the bombers were attacked, but this one led a charmed life—the enemy pilots apparently thought Staff Sergeant Lee Embree's camera was a gun and veered away whenever he pointed it at them.

Lieutenant Robert Richards' B-17 couldn't make Hickam, ground-looped into tiny Bellows Field across the island.

Captain Ray Swenson's B-17 was the only one from the Coast destroyed. Japanese bullets set off some flares, which burned the ship in half as it crash-landed at Hickam.

Wheeler Field, viewed from a Japanese plane. The Army fighters are parked in neat rows on the runway to prevent sabotage.

At Ewa Field, Marine ground crews fire back at the raiders with rifles.

Courtesy of Milton Holst

While men grimly fought back at the bases, the average civilian awakened to noise and smoke, gradually shook off his Sunday morning torpor, and tried to grasp what was happening. This local resident investigates the smoke at Kaneohe Naval Air Station.

men were trying their luck in Pearl Harbor. Thirteen-year-old Jerry Morton and his kid brother Don, 11, sat on the enlisted men's landing at Pearl City, a peninsula that juts southward into the middle of the anchorage. Like most service children, Jerry and Don regarded Pearl Harbor not as a naval base but as a huge, fascinating play pool. Almost every morning when they weren't at school, they ran down to the landing—only 200 yards from the house—and let out a ball of string. Occasionally a gullible perch took a chance; rarely anything worthy of the dinner table. But there were always the ships, the planes, the sailors—a wonderful kaleidoscope that never grew dull.

This morning they set out as usual—barefoot, khaki pants rolled up, T-shirts stuffed in their pockets as soon as their mother wasn't looking. Little gusts of wind stirred the harbor waters, but the sun poked through the clouds often enough to make the day hot and lazy. It was a typical Sunday morning, except for one thing: incredibly, the fish were biting. By 7:45 the boys had used up all their bait, and Don was dispatched to the house for more. Jerry, the senior partner, lolled in the morning sun.

Around him, the ships of the Pacific Fleet lay in every direction. To the north and east, little nests of destroyers clustered about their tenders at anchor. To the southeast, most of the cruisers pointed into the Navy Yard piers. Still further to the south, the cruiser *Helena* lay at 1010 dock . . . then the battleship *Pennsylvania,* sharing Drydock No. 1 with two destroyers. To their west was another destroyer, high in the floating drydock . . . and finally, completing the circle, more destroyers, the repair ship *Medusa,* and the aircraft tender *Curtiss* lay moored offshore.

Dominating the whole scene—and squarely in the middle of the harbor—was Ford Island, where Don and Jerry's stepfather, Aviation Ordnanceman Thomas Croft, had duty this Sunday at the seaplane hangars. The Navy PBY patrol planes were based here; also the carrier planes when they were in port. The carriers themselves moored along the northwest side of the island, while the battleships used the southeast side.

This Sunday, of course, the carriers were all at sea, and the moorings opposite Pearl City offered little in the way of excitement—only the old cruisers *Detroit* and *Raleigh* . . . the ex-battleship *Utah*, now demoted to target ship . . . the seaplane tender *Tangier*. But on the far side of the island a thrilling line of masts and funnels sprouted from "Battleship Row"—*Nevada, Arizona, Tennessee, West Virginia, Maryland, Oklahoma*, and *California* were all there.

Other less glamorous craft elbowed their way into the picture. The "honey barge" *YG-17* crawled from ship to ship, collecting garbage. The tanker *Neosho* squatted toward the southern end of Battleship Row. The cruiser *Baltimore*—a veteran of Teddy Roosevelt's Great White Fleet—lingered in rusty retirement, anchored among the sleek destroyers in East Loch. The poky little seaplane tender *Swan* perched on a marine railway near the cruisers (Radio Operator Charles Michaels estimates she could do 12.6 knots with a clean bottom and all laundry aloft). The old gunboat *Sacramento* hovered nearby—her tall, thin smokestack looked like something designed by Robert Fulton. The ancient mine layer *Oglala* lay next to the cruiser *Helena* at 1010 dock. She had the romantic past of a Fall River liner, but it was all over now. These days she was almost always tied up; once so long that a family of birds built a nest in her funnel.

The large and the small, the mighty and the meek, they all added up to 96 warships in Pearl Harbor this Sunday morning.

Assembled together, the U. S. Pacific Fleet was a big family—yet it was a small family too. Most of the men knew everybody else in their line of work, regardless of ship. Walter Simmons, who served a long hitch as mess attendant on the *Curtiss*, recalls that it was almost impossible for him to board any other ship in the fleet without meeting someone he knew.

In these prewar days everybody stayed put. Chief Boatswain's Mate Joseph Nickson had been on the *San Francisco* nine years; Chief Jack Haley on the *Nevada* 12 years. Ensign Joseph Taussig, brand-new to the ship, thought that several of the chief petty officers on the *Nevada* had been there before he was born. These old chiefs played an important part in keeping the family spirit. They were almost like fathers to the young ensigns—taught them beer baseball in the long, dull hours when nothing was happening; called them "Sonny" when no one else was listening. But they were also the first to accept an officer's authority, and believed implicitly in the Navy chain of command.

For the officers it was a small world too. Year after year they had come from the same school, taken the same courses, followed the same careers, step by step. They too knew one another's service records and "signal numbers" by heart. They all shared the same hard work, wardroom Cokes, starched white uniforms, Annapolis traditions. Like all true professionals, they were a proud, sensitive, tightly knit group.

But signs were beginning to appear that this small, little world might be in for a change. Reservists were now pouring in from the various training programs. They were enthusiastic enough, but they lacked the background of Navy tradition. Where they were involved, sometimes the old way of doing things just wouldn't work.

Doris Miller, a huge mess attendant on the *West Virginia,* was one of the regulars faced with this problem of reconciling the old with the new. Every morning he had the colossal job of waking up Ensign Edmond Jacoby, a young reservist from the University of Wichita. At first Miller used to yank at Jacoby, much like a Pullman porter arousing a passenger. This was fine with Jacoby, but an Annapolis man reminded Miller that an enlisted man must never touch an officer.

Faced with the problem of upholding an ensign's dignity and still getting Jacoby up, Miller appeared the following morning with a brilliant solution. Standing three inches from Jacoby's ear, he yelled, "Hey, Jake!" and fled the room.

This Sunday morning Doris Miller had no problems. Ensign Jacoby was off duty and free to sleep. Miller was working as mess attendant in the junior officers' wardroom, but there were only two officers on hand and there wasn't much to do.

It was just about as easy for the other men on duty. At 1010 dock Coxswain Ralph Haines was touching up the bright work on Admiral William Calhoun's gig. The admiral, who gloried in the title "COMTRAINRON 8" (Commander, Training Squadron Eight), ran a group of supply ships. He had been scheduled to arrive this morning on the *Antares*, but for some reason was late.

On the *Nevada*, Ensign Taussig was officer of the deck. He whiled away the time trying to think of something useful to do. It occurred to him that one boiler had been carrying the burden all four days the ship had been in port. He ordered another lit off.

On the *Arizona*, Coxswain James Forbis had a working party on the fantail, rigging the ship for church services. The awning flapped and snapped in the breeze, and standing on the shore waiting to go out, Fleet Chaplain William A. Maguire made a mental note to have an extra windbreak rigged to keep his altar things in place. But the sun was warm, the clouds were high, and all things considered, the day was perfect. Turning to his assistant, Seaman Joseph Workman, Maguire burst out, "Joe, this is one for the tourist!"

The men off duty seemed to agree. On ship after ship they were getting ready to go ashore. Some, like Seaman Donald Marman of the cruiser *Honolulu*, were preparing for Catholic mass at the base arena. Others, like Signalman John Blanken on the *San Francisco*, were headed for swimming at Waikiki. Ensign Thomas Taylor on the *Nevada* hoped to get in some tennis. The *Helena* marine detachment was warming up for softball. Ensign William Brown had a very special project in mind as he stood on the deck of his PT boat, which was loaded on the tanker *Ramapo* for shipment to the Philippines. His wife was coming over in two weeks, and he had just rented a little house in town. This would be the perfect day to fix the place up.

The less ambitious loafed about the decks. On the *St. Louis*, Seaman Robert McMurray watched his mates playing checkers. Pharmacist's Mate William Lynch on the *California* remembered this was his sister's birthday, and began planning a letter to her. Machinist's Mate R. L. Hooton sat on a bucket in front of his locker on the *West Virginia*, enjoying some snapshots just received from his wife. They were of his eight-month-old son whom he had never seen.

Storekeeper Felder Crawford sat on his desk in the *Maryland's* supply room, absorbed in that great American institution, the Sunday comics: Dagwood was having his usual troubles with Mr. Dithers . . . Daddy Warbucks' private plane made a forced landing, leading the Asp to observe, "I have never trusted the air" . . . Navy Bob Steele successfully deflected a surprise air attack on his destroyer by an unidentified navy.

A number of the men turned their thoughts to Christmas —there were only 15 more shopping days left. Yeoman Durrell Conner sat in the flag communications office of the *California* wrapping presents. Seaman Leslie Short climbed up to one of the *Maryland's* machine-gun stations, where he wasn't likely to be disturbed, and addressed his Christmas cards.

On every ship there were men still at breakfast. Captain Bentham Simons of the *Raleigh* lounged in a pair of blue pajamas, sipping coffee in his cabin. On the *Oklahoma*, Ensign Bill Ingram, son of Navy's great football coach, ordered poached eggs. Quartermaster Jim Varner took a large bunch

of grapes from the serving line on the repair ship *Rigel,* then
retired below to enjoy them properly. He hung them from
the springs of an empty upper bunk and climbed into the
lower, lay there happily plucking the grapes and wondering
what to do the rest of the day.

The shoreside breakfasts offered more variety, fewer re-
strictions. At the target repair base, Seaman Marlin Ayotte's
meal showed real faith in his cooking—four eggs, bacon, two
bowls of cereal, fruit, toast, three cups of coffee. At the
civilian workers' cantonment—affectionately known to the
residents as "Boystown"—Ben Rottach entertained a couple
of friends from the *Raleigh* at a breakfast of ham and eggs
with whisky chasers.

In the repair shops and at Drydock No. 1, a few luckless
souls had duty. Civilian yard worker Harry Danner struggled
to align the boring bars on the *Pennsylvania's* starboard propeller shafts. But there was a Sunday spirit even about the
men at work. At the main Pearl Harbor gate, for instance,
the Marine guard was getting ready to have its picture taken
by Tai Sing Loe, who seemed to be the whole Navy's un-
official photographer. He was a wonderfully colorful Chinese,
who stalked his prey wearing a huge elephant hunter's hat.

Just down the road from the Pearl Harbor gate—a few hundred yards closer to Honolulu—lay the main entrance to
Hickam Field, where the Army bombers were based. Normally there was a good deal of practice flying here, including
some friendly buzzing of the Navy next door. The carrier
planes, in turn, would occasionally stage mock raids on
Hickam. But this morning all was quiet. The carriers were at
sea, and the bombers were lined up in neat rows beside the
main concrete runway.

General Short's sabotage alert was in full force, and obviously the best way to guard the planes was to group them
together, out in the open. So there they all were—or at least
all that mattered, for only six of the B-17s could fly . . .

only six of the 12 A-20s . . . and only 17 of the 33 out-moded B-18s.

Their hangars stood silent and empty along the Pearl Harbor side of the field (there were only boondocks on the Honolulu side); but the control tower, near the left end of the hangar line, hummed with excitement. Captain Gordon Blake, the tall, young base operations officer, had been in his office since seven. Next, his friend, Major Roger Ramey, arrived. Then Colonel Cheney Bertholf, adjutant general of the Hawaiian Air Force. Finally, even the base commandant, Colonel William Farthing, steamed up. Everybody who was in the know wanted to see the B-17s arrive from the mainland. They were new, fabulous planes; to have 12 of them come at once was a big event indeed. Down on the field, Captain Andre d'Alfonso, medical officer of the day, prepared his own special welcome. As soon as they arrived, his job was to spray them with Flit guns.

Elsewhere hardly anything was going on. Sergeant Robert Hey began dressing for a rifle match with Captain J. W. Chappelman. Captain Levi Erdmann mulled over the base tennis tournament. Nurse Monica Conter—in between dates with Lieutenant Benning—took pulses and temperatures at the new base hospital. Private Mark Layton squeezed under the 7:45 breakfast deadline, but most of the men didn't even try. At the big new consolidated barracks, Staff Sergeant Charles Judd lay in bed, reading an article debunking Japanese air power in the September issue of *Aviation* magazine.

It was the same story at Wheeler Field—the Army fighter base in the center of the island. Here, too, the planes were lined up in neat rows—62 of the Army's brand-new P-40s. Here, too, most people were still in bed. Two exceptions—Lieutenants George Welch and Ken Taylor, a couple of pilots stationed at the small Haleiwa air strip on the west coast of the island. Welch and Taylor had come over for the weekly Saturday dance. Then they got involved in an all-night poker game.

Now Welch was arguing that they should forget all about bed and drive back to Haleiwa for an early-morning swim. This debate was perhaps the liveliest thing happening at Wheeler.

Just to the north, the five big quadrangles of Schofield Barracks were equally quiet. Many of the men in the 24th and 25th Divisions were on week-end pass to Honolulu; others had straggled home in the early hours and were dead to the world. A few, like Sergeant Valentine Lemanski, were in the washroom fumbling with toothpaste, towels, and shaving kits. There never seemed enough space on the washbowl shelves. But in the nearby officers' housing area, Colonel Virgil Miller's little girl Julia was up, fed, and dressed in her Sunday best. Now she was about to enter the family car on her way to church with her mother and brother.

It was also time for church at Fort Shafter, the Army's administrative center near Honolulu. Pfc. William McCarthy joined a group approaching the Catholic chapel. But many of the men stayed in bed or lolled in the morning sunshine. Colonel Fielder, feeling fresh and rested after his early evening with General Short, had pulled on blue slacks and a blue sport shirt. He was about to drive over to the windward side of the island for a picnic at Bellows Field.

Bellows was a small Army fighter base near the eastern end of Oahu. It had only two small squadrons, and only 12 of the planes were modern P-40s, but all of them were lined up just as neatly as the planes at Hickam and Wheeler. The men were all taking it easy or planning the usual Sunday projects.

Five miles farther up the coast lay the Kaneohe Naval Air Station, the only other post on the windward side of Oahu. Thirty-three of the Navy's new PBYs operated out of here. This morning three of them were out on patrol. The others were in the hangars or riding at anchor in the choppy blue water of Kaneohe Bay.

At 7:45 this lazy Sunday morning Kaneohe looked as serene as any of the Army airfields. Mess Attendant Walter

Simmons was setting the table in the officers' wardroom, but nobody had turned up to eat. Lieutenant Commander H.P. McCrimmon, the post medical officer, was sitting in his office with his feet on his desk, wondering why the Sunday paper was late.

That was what the people in Honolulu were wondering, too. Normally they counted on the *Advertiser* as an indispensable part of Sunday breakfast, but this morning the presses had broken down after running off only 2000 copies. The papers already printed had gone to Pearl Harbor for distribution among the ships. Everyone else was simply out of luck. Getting something repaired on Sunday in Honolulu was a tall order, although Editor Ray Coll worked hard at the problem.

Across town, Editor Riley Allen of the *Star-Bulletin* had no press troubles and his afternoon paper didn't come out on Sunday, but he was miles behind on his correspondence. This morning he hoped to catch up, and now sat in his office dictating to his secretary, Winifred McCombs. It was her first day on the job, and at 7:45 A.M. she perhaps wondered whether she had been wise in leaving her last position.

Most of the people in Honolulu were enjoying more civilized hours, many of them sleeping off the island's big football week end. Saturday afternoon the University of Hawaii beat Willamette 20-6 in the annual Shrine game, and the victory had been celebrated in standard mainland fashion. Now the fans bravely faced the morning after. Webley Edwards, manager of radio station KGMB and a popular broadcaster himself, tackled a grape and soda. It looked like a constructive way to start the new day.

In sharp contrast to Oahu's Sunday morning torpor, the destroyer *Ward* scurried about off the entrance to Pearl Harbor. A lot had happened since she polished off the midget sub. At 6:48 A.M. she sighted a white sampan well inside the restricted area. She scooted over to investigate, and the sampan took off. Quickly overhauled, the sampan's skipper, a

Japanese, shut off his engines and waved a white flag. This struck Outerbridge as rather odd—these sampans often sneaked into the restricted area for better fishing, but when caught the surrender was rarely so formal. On the other hand, the skipper had already heard plenty of firing and might be just emphasizing his own peaceful inclinations. In any case, the *Ward* started escorting the offender toward Honolulu to turn him over to the Coast Guard.

At 7:03 A.M. the *Ward* picked up another sub on her sound apparatus. Outerbridge raced over to the spot indicated, unloaded five depth charges, and watched a huge black oil bubble erupt 300 yards astern. Then back to the sampan. Everyone remained at general quarters, and Outerbridge alerted Fourteenth Naval District Headquarters to stand by for further messages.

At headquarters, all of this fell into the lap of Lieutenant Commander Harold Kaminsky, an old reservist who had been in the Navy off and on ever since he was an enlisted man in World War I. Regularly in charge of net and boom defenses, he took his Sunday turn as duty officer like everyone else. This morning he held down the fort with the aid of one enlisted man, a Hawaiian who understood little English and nothing about the teletype.

Due to various delays in decoding, paraphrasing, and typing, it was 7:12 by the time Commander Kaminsky received the *Ward's* 6:53 message about sinking the submarine. First he tried to phone Admiral Bloch's aide but couldn't reach him. Then he put in a call to the admiral's chief of staff, Captain John B. Earle. The phone woke up Mrs. Earle, and she immediately put her husband on the wire. To Kaminsky, the captain sounded astonished and incredulous. Captain Earle later recalled that he first felt it was just one more of the sub "sightings" that had been turning up in recent months. On the other hand, this did seem too serious to be brushed off—it was the first time he heard of a Navy ship firing depth charges or anything else at one of these contacts.

So he told Kaminsky to get the dispatch verified, also to notify the CINCPAC duty officer and Commander Charles Momsen, the Fourteenth Naval District operations officer. Earle said he would take care of telling Admiral Bloch.

The admiral was on the phone by 7:15. Captain Earle relayed the news, and the two men spent the next five or ten minutes trying to decide whether it was reliable or not. In the course of passing from mouth to mouth, the message had lost the point Outerbridge tried to make by saying he "fired on" the sub, hence must have seen it. Now neither Bloch nor Earle could tell whether this was just a sound contact or whether the *Ward* had actually seen something. Finally they made up their minds. Since they had asked the *Ward* to verify, since Commander Momsen was investigating, and since they had referred the matter to CINCPAC, they decided (using Captain Earle's phrase) "to await further developments."

Meanwhile Kaminsky had notified CINCPAC Headquarters over at the sub base. The assistant duty officer, Lieutenant Commander Francis Black, estimated that he got the call around 7:20. He relayed the report to the duty officer, Commander Vincent Murphy, who was dressing in his quarters on the spot. Murphy asked, "Did he say what he was doing about it? Did he say whether Admiral Bloch knew about it or not?"

Nothing had been said on these points, so Murphy told Black to call back and find out. He dialed and dialed, but the line was always busy. By now Murphy was dressed and told Black, "All right, you go to the office and start breaking out the charts and positions of the various ships. I'll dial one more time, and then I'll be over."

The line was still busy, so Murphy told the operator to break in and have Kaminsky call the CINCPAC office. Then he ran on down to get there in time for the call.

Small wonder Kaminsky's line was busy. After talking to Black, he had to phone Commander Momsen, the district

operations officer. Then Momsen said to call Ensign Joseph
Logan. Then a call to the Coast Guard about that sampan
the *Ward* caught. Then Momsen on the line again at 7:25—
have the ready-duty destroyer *Monaghan* contact the *Ward*.
Then a call to Lieutenant Ottley to get the Honolulu harbor gate closed. Phone call by phone call, the minutes slipped
away.

Commander Murphy dashed into his office a little after
7:30 to find the phone ringing. But it wasn't the call that he
expected from Kaminsky; it was a call from Commander Logan Ramsey, the operations officer at Patrol Wing (Patwing)
2, the Ford Island headquarters for all Navy patrol plane
work. Ramsey was bursting with news—a PBY reported it
had just sunk a sub about a mile off the Pearl Harbor entrance. Murphy told him he already had a similar report, and
for the next minute or so the two men compared notes.

The PBY message had been sent by Ensign Tanner. It
was logged in at seven o'clock, but there had been the usual
delays in decoding, then the usual incredulity. Commander
Knefler McGinnis, who was Tanner's commanding officer
and in charge of Patwing 1 at Kaneohe, felt it must be a case
of mistaken identity. He checked to make sure that all information on U. S. subs was in the hands of the patrol planes.
Ramsey himself received the message around 7:30 from the
Patwing 2 duty officer, and his first reaction was that some
kind of drill message must have gotten out by mistake. He
ordered the duty officer to request "authentication" of the
message immediately. But to be on the safe side he decided to
draw up a search plan and notify CINCPAC—that was what
he was doing now.

As Murphy hung up, the phone began ringing again. This
time it was Kaminsky, finally on the wire. He assured Murphy that Bloch had been told . . . that the ready-duty destroyer was on its way to help . . . that the stand-by destroyer had been ordered to get up steam. Murphy asked,

"Have you any previous details or any more details about this attack?"

"The message came out of a clear sky," Kaminsky replied.

Murphy decided he'd better call Admiral Kimmel, and by 7:40 CINCPAC himself was on the telephone. The admiral, who had left Mrs. Kimmel on the mainland as a defensive measure against any diverting influences, lived alone in a bare new house at Makalapa, about five minutes' drive away. As soon as he heard the news, he told Murphy, "I'll be right down."

Next, Ramsey phoned again, asking if there was anything new. Murphy said there wasn't, but warned him to keep search planes available, in case the admiral wanted them.

Now Kaminsky was back on the wire, reporting the *Ward's* run-in with the sampan. He had already told Earle, and the captain regarded it as evidence that nothing was really the matter—if there was a submarine around, what was the *Ward* doing escorting a mere sampan to Honolulu? He apparently didn't realize that the submarine incident was at 6:45, and the *Ward* had considered it definitely sunk.

Commander Murphy thought the sampan report was sufficiently interesting to relay to Admiral Kimmel, and he put in another call about 7:50.

Out in the harbor, Lieutenant Commander Bill Burford made the best of things as skipper of the ready-duty destroyer *Monaghan*. She was due to be relieved at eight o'clock, and Burford had planned to go ashore. In fact, the gig was already alongside. Then at 7:51 a message suddenly came in from Fourteenth Naval District Headquarters to "get under way immediately and contact *Ward* in defensive sea area." The message didn't even say what he should prepare for, but obviously it might be a couple of hours before he would be free again to go ashore.

Whatever was in store for the *Monaghan,* the other ships

in Pearl Harbor had only morning colors to worry about. This ceremoney was always the same. At 7:55 the signal tower on top of the Navy Yard water tank hoisted the blue "prep" flag, and every ship in the harbor followed suit. On each ship a man took his place at the bow with the "jack," another at the stern with the American flag. Then, promptly at 8:00, the prep flag came down, and the other two went up. On the smaller ships a boatswain piped his whistle; on the larger a bugler sounded colors; on the largest a band might even play the National Anthem.

As the clock ticked toward 7:55, all over the harbor men went to their stations. On the bridge of the old repair ship *Vestal,* Signalman Adolph Zlabis got ready to hoist the prep flag. On the fantail of the sleek cruiser *Helena* at 1010 dock, Ensign W. W. Jones marched to the flagstaff with a four-man Marine honor guard. On the big battleship *Nevada,* the ship's band assembled for a ceremony that would have all the trimmings. The only trouble was, the officer of the deck, Ensign Taussig had never stood watch for morning colors before and didn't know what size American flag to fly. He quietly sent an enlisted man forward to ask the *Arizona* people what they were going to do. While everybody waited around, some of the bandsmen noticed specks in the sky far to the southwest.

Planes were approaching, and from more than one direction. Ensign Donald L. Korn, officer of the deck on the *Raleigh,* noticed a thin line winging in from the northwest. Seaman "Red" Pressler of the *Arizona* saw a string approaching from the mountains to the east. On the destroyer *Helm,* Quartermaster Frank Handler noticed another group coming in low from the south. The *Helm*—the only ship under way in all of Pearl Harbor—was in the main channel, about to turn up West Loch. The planes passed only 100 yards away, flying directly up the channel from the harbor entrance. One of the pilots gave a casual wave, and Quartermaster Handler cheerfully waved back. He noticed that, unlike most American planes, these had fixed landing gear.

As the planes roared nearer, Pharmacist's Mate William Lynch heard a *California* shipmate call out, "The Russians must have a carrier visiting us. Here come some planes with the red ball showing clearly."

Signalman Charles Flood on the *Helena* picked up a pair of binoculars and gave the planes a hard look. They were approaching in a highly unusual manner, but all the same there was something familiar about them. Then he recalled the time he was in Shanghai in 1932, when the Japanese Army and Navy invaded the city. He remembered their bombing technique—a form of glide bombing. The planes over Ford Island were diving in the same way.

In they hurtled—Lieutenant Commander Takahashi's 27 dive bombers plunging toward Ford Island and Hickam . . . Lieutenant Commander Murata's 40 torpedo planes swinging into position for their run at the big ships. Commander Fuchida marked time off Barbers Point with the horizontal bombers, watching his men go in. They were all attacking together instead of in stages as originally planned, but it would apparently make no difference—the ships were sitting ducks.

A few minutes earlier, at 7:49 A.M., Fuchida had radioed the signal to attack: "To . . . to . . . to . . . to . . ." Now he was so sure of victory that at 7:53—even before the first bomb fell—he signaled the carriers that the surprise attack was successful: "Tora . . . tora . . . tora . . ."

Back on the *Akagi,* Admiral Kusaka turned to Admiral Nagumo. Not a word passed between them. Just a long, firm handshake.

Chapter VII

"I Didn't Even Know They Were Sore at Us"

COMMANDER LOGAN RAMSEY jumped from his desk at the Patwing 2 Command Center on Ford Island. He had been working out a search plan for the sub reported by the PBY when a single dive bomber screamed down on the seaplane ramp at the southern tip of the island. It looked like a young aviator "flathatting," and both he and the duty officer tried to get the offender's number. But they were too late, and Ramsey remarked that it was going to be hard to find out who it was. Then a blast . . . a column of dirt and smoke erupted from the foot of the ramp.

"Never mind," said Ramsey, "it's a Jap."

The plane pulled out of its dive and veered up the channel between Ford Island and 1010 dock. It passed less than 600 feet from Rear Admiral William Furlong as he paced the deck of his flagship, the antique mine layer *Oglala*. The admiral took one glance at the flaming orange-red circle on the fuselage and understood too. He shouted for general quarters, and as SOPA (Senior Officer Present Afloat), he hoisted the signal, "All ships in harbor sortie." The time was 7:55 A.M.

Now two more planes screeched down. This time the aim was perfect. Parts of the big PBY hangar at the head of the ramp flew in all directions. Radioman Harry Mead, member of a utility plane squadron based on the island, couldn't un-

68

derstand why American planes were bombing the place. Seaman Robert Oborne of the same outfit had a plausible explanation: it was an Army snafu. "Boy," he thought, "is somebody going to catch it for putting live bombs on those planes."

All this passed unnoticed by Ensign Donald Korn of the cruiser *Raleigh,* moored on the northwest side of Ford Island at one of the berths normally used by the carriers. He was turning over his deck watch to Ensign William Game and couldn't see much of anything happening down by the seaplane ramp. But he did have a fine view of the valley leading up the center of Oahu. At 7:56 he noticed some planes flying in low from that direction.

Now they were gliding past the algarroba trees at Pearl City. Splitting up, two headed for the *Utah* just astern, one for the *Detroit* just ahead, and one for the *Raleigh* herself. Ensign Korn, thinking the planes were Marines on maneuvers, called out his antiaircraft crews to practice with them. The men were just taking their stations when the torpedo struck home about opposite the second funnel. A shattering roar, a sickening lurch. Through a blinding mixture of smoke and dirt and muddy water, men caught a brief glimpse of the *Raleigh's* splintered church launch; it had been easing alongside where the torpedo hit. The *Detroit* got off scot-free, but the *Utah* shuddered under two solid blows. Watching from the destroyer *Monaghan* several hundred yards to the north, Boatswain's Mate Thomas Donahue thought that this time the U.S. Army really had a hole in its head.

A fifth plane in this group saved its torpedo, skimmed across Ford Island, and let fly at the *Oglala* and *Helena,* moored side by side at 1010 dock—the berth normally used by the battleship *Pennsylvania,* flagship of the whole Pacific Fleet. The torpedo passed completely under the *Oglala,* moored outboard, and barreled into the *Helena* midships—her engine-room clock stopped at 7:57. The concussion burst the seams of the old *Oglala* alongside, hurling Musician Don

Rodenberger from his upper bunk. He could only think that the ancient boilers had finally exploded.

Ensign Roman Leo Brooks, officer of the deck on the *West Virginia* across the channel, was thinking along these same lines. He, too, was in no position to see the plane diving on the seaplane hangars or on the ships moored across Ford Island. All he saw was the sudden eruption of flames and smoke at 1010 dock. He lost no time—in seconds the ship's bugler and PA system were blaring, "Away the fire and rescue party!"

Even the men who saw the planes couldn't understand. One of them was Fireman Frank Stock of the repair ship *Vestal,* moored beside the *Arizona* along Battleship Row. Stock and six of his mates had taken the church launch for services ashore. They moved across the channel and into Southeast Loch, that long, narrow strip of water pointing directly at the battleships. On their right they passed the cruisers, nosed into the Navy Yard piers; on the left some subs tucked into their berths. As they reached the Merry's Point landing at the end of the loch, six or eight torpedo planes flew in low from the east, about 50 feet above the water and heading down the loch toward the battleships.

The men were mildly surprised—they had never seen U. S. planes come in from that direction. They were even more surprised when the rear-seat gunners sprayed them with machine-gun bullets. Then Stock recalled the stories he had read about "battle-condition" maneuvers in the Southern states. This must be the same idea—for extra realism they had even painted red circles on the planes. The truth finally dawned when one of his friends caught a slug in the stomach from the fifth plane that passed.

On the *Nevada* at the northern end of Battleship Row, Leader Oden McMillan waited with his band to play morning colors at eight o'clock. His 23 men had been in position since 7:55, when the blue prep signal went up. As they moved into formation, some of the musicians noticed planes diving at the other end of Ford Island. McMillan saw a lot of dirt and sand go up, but thought it was another drill. Now it was 7:58—two minutes to go—and planes started coming in low from Southeast Loch. Heavy, muffled explosions began booming down the line . . . enough to worry anyone. And then it was eight o'clock.

The band crashed into "The Star-Spangled Banner." A Japanese plane skimmed across the harbor . . . dropped a torpedo at the *Arizona* . . . and peeled off right over the *Nevada's* fantail. The rear gunner sprayed the men standing at attention, but he must have been a poor shot. He missed the entire band and Marine guard, lined up in two neat rows. He did succeed in shredding the flag, which was just being raised.

McMillan knew now but kept on conducting. The years of training had taken over—it never occurred to him that once he had begun playing the National Anthem, he could possibly stop. Another strafer flashed by. This time McMillan unconsciously paused as the deck splintered around him, but he quickly picked up the beat again. The entire band stopped and started again with him, as though they had rehearsed it for weeks. Not a man broke formation until the final note died. Then everyone ran wildly for cover.

Ensign Joe Taussig, officer of the deck, pulled the alarm bell. The ship's bugler got ready to blow general quarters, but Taussig took the bugle and tossed it overboard. Somehow it seemed too much like make-believe at a time like this. Instead he shouted over the PA system again and again, "All hands, general quarters. Air raid! This is no drill!"

Ship after ship began to catch on. The executive officer of the supply ship *Castor* shouted, "The Japs are bombing us! The Japs are bombing us!" For an instant Seaman Bill Deas drew a blank and wondered whether the man was speaking to him. On the submarine *Tautog*, the topside anchor watch shouted down the forward torpedo hatch, "The war is on, no fooling!"

Everybody was racing for the alarm signals now. On the little gunboat *Sacramento* in the Navy Yard, Seaman Charles Bohnstadt dashed over to pull the switch, lost the race to a mess attendant. On the cruiser *Phoenix*, out where the destroyers were moored, the loud-speaker had just announced, "Lay up to the quarter deck the Catholic church party"— then the general alarm bell drowned out anything else. On Battleship Row the *Maryland's* bugler blew general quarters over the PA system, while the ship's klaxon lent added authority.

The *Oklahoma's* call to arms needed no extra punch. First came an air raid alert; then general quarters a minute later. This time the voice on the PA system added a few well-chosen words, which one crew member recalls as follows: "Real planes, real bombs; this is no drill!" Other witnesses have a less delicate version of the last part. The language alone, they say, convinced them that this was it.

But on most ships the men down below still needed convincing. Even as the torpedo hit, Fireman Joseph Messier of the *Helena* was sure the alarm bell was just another of the executive officer's bright ideas to get the crew to go to church.

"This is a hell of a time to hold general drills," echoed through the firemen's quarters of the *California*, the signalmen's compartment on the *San Francisco*, the after "head" on the *Nevada*. On the destroyer *Phelps* Machinist's Mate William Taylor engaged in a sort of one-man slowdown. He deliberately took plenty of time getting dressed. Then he ambled topside, yawned, and strolled toward the stern to get a drink of water before going below to his station in the boiler room. As he started down the after gangway, a chief gunner's mate came charging down behind him, shouting, "Get to hell out of the way—don't you know we're at war?" Taylor thought to himself, "You mumbling jackass, isn't this drill enough without added harassment from you?"

Commander Herald Stout, skipper of the destroyer-minecraft *Breese*, was even more annoyed. He had left standing orders never to test general quarters before eight on Sunday. When the alarm sounded, he left his breakfast to chew out the watch.

Captain Harold C. Train, Admiral Pye's chief of staff on the *California*, was sure the alarm had been set off by mistake. And on the destroyer *Henley* it really was a mistake. Her crew was normally mustered on Sundays at 7:55 by sounding the gas-attack alarm; this morning someone pressed the wrong button—general quarters.

Chaplain Howell Forgy of the cruiser *New Orleans* also thought someone had blundered. He drifted to his station in sick bay completely unconcerned. A moment later the ship's doctor arrived and hesitantly remarked, "Padre, there's planes out there and they look like Japs."

The word spread faster. A boatswain dashed into the CPO wardroom on the *Maryland*, sat down white as a sheet: "The Japs are here . . ." As Ensign Charles Merdinger of the *Nevada* pulled on his clothes, someone outside his stateroom yelled, "It's the real thing; it's the Japs!" With that, Merdinger stepped completely through his sock. Watertender Samuel Cucuk looked into the "head" on the destroyer tender *Dobbin*, called to Fireman Charles Leahey, "You better cut that short, Charlie, the Japs are here."

A few skeptics still held out. In the *Honolulu's* hoist room Private Roy Henry bet another Marine a dollar that it was the Army, pulling a surprise on the Navy with dummy torpedoes. The men in the repair ship *Rigel's* pipe and copper shop remained unperturbed when a seaman wearing only underwear burst in with the news—they figured the fellow was pretending he was crazy so he could get back to the Coast. When a sailor on the *Pennsylvania* said the Japs were attacking, Machinist's Mate William Felsing had a snappy comeback: "So are the Germans."

The last doubts vanished in an avalanche of shattering evidence. Pharmacist's Mate William Lynch took a skeptical metalsmith to his porthole on the *California*, pointed to the chaos erupting outside. The man sagged away, sighing, "Jesus Christ . . . Jesus Christ." On the *West Virginia* a sailor spattered with fuel oil ran by Ensign Maurice Featherman shouting, "Look what the bastards did to me!"

One and all, they accepted it now—some with a worldly grasp of affairs, some with almost ingenuous innocence. Captain Mervyn Bennion, skipper of the *West Virginia*, calmly remarked to his Marine orderly, "This is certainly in keeping with their history of surprise attacks." A seaman on the destroyer *Monaghan* told Boatswain's Mate Thomas Donahue, "Hell, I didn't even know they were sore at us."

Down the corridors . . . up the ladders . . . through the hatches the men ran, climbed, milled, and shoved toward their battle stations. And it was high time. The alarm was no sooner given when the *Oklahoma* took the first of five torpedoes . . . the *West Virginia* the first of six. These were the golden targets—directly across from Southeast Loch. Next the *Arizona* took two, even though a little to the north and partly blocked by the *Vestal*. Then the *California* got two, even though far to the south and a relatively poor target. Only the inboard battleships seemed safe—*Maryland* alongside *Oklahoma* and *Tennessee* beside *West Virginia*.

As the torpedoes whacked home, the men struggled to keep going, sometimes fell in jumbled heaps. On the *West Virginia* Ensign Ed Jacoby went out like a light when one of the first explosions toppled a steel locker over on his head. Seaman James Jensen kept his feet through the first two blasts, but the next two hurled him into another compartment, and a fifth knocked him out. Quartermaster Ed Vecera, trying to get from the quarterdeck aft to his post on the bridge, ran a regular obstacle course: torpedoes . . . Japanese strafing . . . watertight doors slammed in his face . . . a tide of men who always seemed headed the other way. Finally he fell in behind Captain Bennion, and for a while everything opened up to let the skipper pass. But soon they were separated, and Vecera was shunted off in another direction. Somehow he got to the main deck and was stopped again. He never made it to the bridge.

On the *Helena*, the mess hall crashed around Machinist's Mate Paul Weisenberger, as he struggled toward his post in the forward engine room. A table, unhooked from the overhead, bounced off his shoulder. By the time he picked himself up, the next door forward was dogged shut. He had to settle for the after engine room instead.

The mess hall on the *Oglala*—racked up by the same torpedo—was a shambles too. Broken glass and china littered the deck, as Musician Frank Forgione dashed through barefoot on his way to his station in the sick bay. He cut his feet terribly—never even noticed it until hours later.

Worst of all was the *Oklahoma*. The second torpedo put out her lights; the next three ripped open what was left of her port side. The sea swirled in, driving Seaman George Murphy from his post in the print shop on third deck as soon as he got there. His group retreated midships, slamming a watertight door behind them. The list grew steeper, and within seconds the water was squirting around the seams, filling that compartment too. As the ship heeled further, Chief Yeoman George Smith shifted over to a starboard ladder to reach his battle station. Everybody else had the same idea. In the flicker of a few emergency lamps men pushed and shoved, trying to climb over and around each other on the few usable ladders. It was a dark, sweat-smeared nightmare.

No matter how bad things were, men remembered to take care of absurd details. Radioman Robert Gamble of the *Tennessee* ignored the old shoes beside his bunk, went to his locker, and carefully put on a brand-new pair to start the war right. The *Nevada* musicians put their instruments away before going to their stations. (Exception—one man took along his cornet and excitedly threw it into a shell hoist along with some shells for the antiaircraft guns above.)

On the other hand, there was always the danger of forgetting something important. As Radioman James Lagerman raced for his battle station in the Ford Island Administration Building, he kept saying again and again to himself, "Just gotta try to remember this date . . ."

In the confusion many of the ships—unlike the *Nevada*—never carried out morning colors. Others did, but in somewhat unorthodox fashion. On the sub alongside the oil barge *YO-44*, a young sailor popped out of the conning tower and ran to the flagstaff at the stern. Just then a torpedo plane roared by, the rear-seat man swiveling his guns. The sailor scurried back to the conning tower, hugging the flag. Next try, he clipped it on; then another plane sent him diving back to shelter. Third time he got it up—just before another plane sent him ducking for cover again. The men on *YO-44* laughed and clapped and cheered.

But at the sub base headquarters a few yards away, Chief Torpedoman's Mate Peter Chang, in charge of the Navy's Submarine Torpedo School, could only watch with sickened admiration as the Japanese planes grooved one strike after another down the narrow alley of Southeast Loch. It was a real demonstration for the reluctant students who had to watch it, and Chang didn't hesitate to draw on it for material to be used in future lectures.

At CINCPAC Headquarters in the sub base administration building, Commander Vincent Murphy was still phoning Admiral Kimmel about the *Ward's* sampan report when a yeoman burst into the room: "There a message from the signal tower saying the Japanese are attacking Pearl Harbor, and this is no drill." Murphy relayed the message to his boss, then told the communications officer to radio the Chief of Naval Operations, the C-in-C Atlantic Fleet, the C-in-C Asiatic Fleet, and all forces at sea: AIR RAID ON PEARL HARBOR. THIS IS NO DRILL. The message went out at 8:00 A.M., but Admiral Bellinger had radioed a similar message to all ships in the harbor at 7:58; so Washington already knew.

Murphy now phoned Commander Ramsey over at Patwing 2 and optimistically asked how many planes were available. The commander showed a keen grasp of the situation: "I don't think I have any, but I'm scraping together what I can for search."

In the Navy housing areas around Pearl Harbor, people couldn't imagine what was wrecking Sunday morning. Captain Reynolds Hayden, enjoying breakfast at his home on Hospital Point, thought it was construction blasting—then his young son Billy rushed in shouting, "They're Jap planes!" Lieutenant C. E. Boudreau, drying down after a shower, thought an oil tank had blown up near his quarters behind Bloch Arena until a Japanese plane almost grazed the bathroom window. Chief Petty Officer Albert Molter, puttering around his Ford Island flat, thought a drill was going on until his wife Esther called, "Al, there's a battleship tipping over."

As 11-year-old Don Morton scuffed back to his house in Pearl City for more fishing bait, an explosion almost pitched him on his face. Then another, and still another. He scrambled home and asked his mother what was happening. She just told him to go fetch his brother Jerry. He ran out to find several planes now gliding by at house-top level. One was strafing the dirt road, kicking up little puffs of dust. Don was scared to go any further. As he ran back to the house, he saw his next-door neighbor, a Navy lieutenant, standing in his pajamas on the grass, crying like a child.

Up on the hill at Makalapa, where the senior officers lived, Admiral Kimmel ran out to his yard right after Commander Murphy reported the attack. He stood there for a minute or two, watching the planes make their first torpedo runs. Near him stood Mrs. John Earle, wife of Admiral Bloch's chief of staff. At one point she remarked quietly, "Looks like they've got the *Oklahoma*."

"Yes, I can see they have," the admiral answered.

In a house directly across the street—and just a little down the hill—Mrs. Hall Mayfield, wife of Admiral Bloch's intelligence officer, buried her head in the pillow and tried to forget the noise. Makalapa was just being developed, and since it was on the side of an old volcano, they had to do a lot of dynamiting through the lava. It occurred to Mrs. Mayfield that they must now be blasting the hole for her mailbox post.

But the pillow was useless. Mrs. Mayfield surrendered and opened her eyes. Her Japanese maid Fumiyo was standing in the doorway . . . each hand clutching the frame, the long sleeves of her kimono making her look curiously like a butterfly. Fumiyo was trying to say something, but the noise drowned it out. Mrs. Mayfield jumped out of bed and went to her. "Oh, Mrs. Mayfield," Fumiyo was saying, "Pearl Harbor is on fire!"

Glancing through a window, she saw her husband in pajamas, standing on the back lawn. He was leveling binoculars on the harbor, which lay below the house. Seconds later the two women joined him. Mrs. Mayfield's first words were a bit of wifely advice: "Hall, go right back inside and put in your teeth."

The captain's dentures were quickly forgotten as she watched the smoke billow up in the harbor. His wishful suggestion that it might be a drill failed to convince her. When two planes flashed by with the rising-sun insignia, all three of them turned and dashed back to the house.

Captain Mayfield was now pawing about his closet, hurling clothes and hangers in every direction. Mrs. Mayfield chose this moment to make a fatal mistake. "Why," she asked, "don't the Navy planes do something?"

The captain's glare showed that her question was treason. "Why," he yelled back, "doesn't the *Army* do something?"

In the control tower of Hickam Field just east of Pearl Harbor, Colonel William Farthing was still waiting for the B-17s from the mainland when he saw a long, thin line of aircraft approaching from the northwest. They looked like Marine planes from Ewa Field. As they began diving, Farthing remarked to Colonel Bertholf, "Very realistic maneuvers.

I wonder what the Marines are doing to the Navy so early Sunday."

Watching the same show from the parade ground nearby, Sergeant Robert Halliday saw a big splash go up near Ford Island; he decided the Navy was practicing with water bombs. Then one of the bombs hit an oil tank, which exploded in a cloud of smoke and flames. A man said some poor Navy pilot would get into trouble for that. At this point a plane suddenly swooped down on Hickam—a rising sun gleamed on its fuselage. Somebody remarked, "Look, there goes one of the red team."

Next instant, the group was scattering for cover. The plane dropped a bomb and followed it into the huge maintenance hangar of the Hawaiian Air Depot. It was the first in a long line of bombers diving on Hickam from the south. No one is completely sure whether these planes, or those pulling out of their dives on Ford Island, reached Hickam first. Within seconds, both groups were everywhere at once—strafing the men and the neat rows of planes . . . dive-bombing the hangars and buildings.

In the mess hall at the center of Hickam's big, new consolidated barracks, Pfc. Frank Rom yelled a frantic warning to the early risers eating breakfast. It was too late. Trays, dishes, food splattered in all directions as a bomb crashed through the roof. Thirty-five men were wiped out instantly; the injured crawled to safety through the rubble—including one man wounded by a gallon jar of mayonnaise.

In the barracks, where most of the men were still asleep, the first explosions at Pearl Harbor woke up Corporal John Sherwood. Cursing the Navy, he got up and looked for something to read. As he padded about, he glanced out the window just in time to see the Hawaiian Air Depot get pasted. He took off in his shorts for a safer place, shouting, "Air raid! It's the real thing!"

Someone dashing through the barracks woke up Sergeant

H. E. Swinney. Only then did he notice the bomb bursts and low-flying aircraft. Even so, he was more curious than alarmed. But he half sensed something was wrong—the barracks were never that empty on Sunday. He got up and slipped downstairs to investigate. In the hallway a group of men were chattering in excited whispers. He could get nothing out of them and looked around for a better clue. Near a doorway he saw a man with a Springfield rifle; then another man came in with blood running down his face. Swinney peeked out just in time to see a Zero fighter streak by Hangar 7. At last he caught on—he recalls it was almost the way an idea used to come to a comic-strip character, complete with light bulb above the head.

The men were desperately trying to get to their stations now. Some never made it—Private Mark Creighton, pinned down by strafers, dived into a latrine and hugged a toilet bowl for shelter. Others got there too late—Pfc. Emmett Pethoud found that the plane he had to guard was already blown to bits. More bombs were coming, so he ducked under a table—but not before he carefully replaced a phone receiver that had fallen off its hook.

A few were able to carry out their duties. Pfc. Joseph Nelles, the Catholic chaplain's assistant, was returning from early-morning mass when the planes struck. His first thoughts were to safeguard the Blessed Sacrament in the chapel. He ran back and must have just reached the altar when the chapel took a direct hit and vanished in the blast.

While Pearl and Hickam rocked with explosions, all was still quiet at Wheeler Field, the Army's fighter base in the center of the island. Staff Sergeant Francis Clossen, changing his clothes for a date at Waikiki, glanced out his third-floor window in the main barracks, saw a line of six to ten planes come through Kole Kole Pass to the west. They banked left and disappeared, blending into the background of the Waianae Mountains.

They circled back, joined others coming in from the northwest, and charged down on the field. At 8:02 A.M., Pfc. Arthur Fusco, guarding some P-40s with his rifle, froze in his tracks as the first dive bomber peeled off. He recognized those red balls and rushed into the hangar for a machine gun. He couldn't break the lock of the armament shack, but by now it made no difference.

Pfc. Carroll Andrews flattened against his barracks wall as bullets tore through the men's lockers, shattered and splintered the windows around him. Somebody yanked Pfc. Leonard Egan from his cot in one of the tents along the hangar line, and for a moment he stood dazed and naked watching the dive bombers and strafers at work. Then he grabbed his shoes and a pair of coveralls and started running.

In the housing areas families poured into their back yards in pajamas and bathrobes. A man wrapped in a bath towel raced up the post's main street. In the officers' club, Lieutenants Welch and Taylor stopped debating whether to go swimming. Welch grabbed the phone and called Haleiwa, where their P-40s were kept. Yes, the planes were all right . . . yes, they would be gassed up and loaded right away. Welch slammed down the receiver, hopped into Taylor's car, and the two careened off to Haleiwa, prodded along by a strafing Zero.

Just north of Wheeler, Major General Maxwell Murray, commanding the 25th Division, heard a plane diving over his quarters in the General's Loop at Schofield Barracks. He rushed to the window determined to report the pilot. The plane zoomed by only 75 yards away, but the general couldn't catch the number. So he ran to the front door, glancing at his watch—he would at least get the landing time. To his surprise the plane dropped a bomb.

Private Lester Buckley was unloading manure nearby at the Schofield compost heap. He took one look at flames billowing up from Wheeler, jumped in his wagon, and raced back to the barracks so fast that the pitchforks rattled out.

In the barracks, Pfc. Raymond Senecal, jolted from his

sleep, thought the engineers were blasting. He got out of bed and found the air full of strange-looking airplanes with fixed landing gear. Soon they were diving on the big Schofield quadrangles, where most of the men ate and slept. Senecal saw the bright red circles clearly, but still he couldn't quite believe it. Turning to his sergeant, he offered the advice of a true citizen-soldier: "Get someone on the telephone . . ."

Corporal Maurice Herman ran out on his barracks porch and started cranking away at the air raid siren. Down below, the Sunday morning chow lines wound through the quadrangle. It was an incongruous picture—heads raised to view the planes . . . excited discussions . . . questions being yelled to Herman on the porch . . . and every man reluctant to give up his place in the chow line. Then a plane swept by, raking the lines of men. Wild confusion, as the men scattered for their guns and stations.

Bugles began sounding. Corporal Harry Foss thought the old call to arms did more than anything else to pull the men together in the 65th Combat Engineers. Private Frank Gobeo of the 98th Coast Artillery didn't know how to blow call to arms, but he made a brilliant substitution that brought the men swarming from the barracks—he blew pay call.

Supply Sergeant Valentine Lemanski of 27th Infantry rocketed down the stairs of Quadrangle D, found the men in his company had already smashed open the supply room doors. A young private in the 19th Infantry seized a Browning Automatic Rifle (known as a BAR in the Army) and shot off a clip while still in the building. Some men in the 27th Infantry couldn't get guns at all—their sergeant refused to issue the ammunition because a sign said it couldn't be released without orders from the adjutant.

In the radar information center at Fort Shafter, Lieutenant Tyler had heard the first explosions just before his watch ended at eight. He strolled outside and for a moment or so watched what appeared to be "Navy practice at Pearl." Then he heard a few bursts of antiaircraft fire, somewhat closer. He hung around even though his watch was now over, and a few minutes after eight got a call from Sergeant Storry up at the base: "There's an air attack at Wheeler Field." Tyler knew just what to do: he instantly recalled the headset operators.

General Short listened with interest to the bedlam in his quarters nearby. He decided that the Navy must be having some kind of battle practice. The explosions increased, and he wandered out on his *lanai* for a look. There was a lot of smoke to the west, but he couldn't make much out of it. Then Colonel Philips, his chief of staff, burst in at 8:03 with the news—Hickam and Wheeler had just phoned that this was "the real thing."

Pfc. William McCarthy felt the Catholic chapel at Shafter shake and tremble with every explosion. The windows rattled all through mass and the sermon. Right after the sermon a GI ran up to the priest and told him what was happening. Quickly the padre turned to the congregation: "God bless you all, the Japanese are attacking Pearl Harbor. Return to your units at once."

Twelve miles away—across the Koolau Mountains and on the windward side of Oahu—Lieutenant Commander H. P. McCrimmon heard some low-flying planes roar past the dispensary at the Kaneohe Naval Air Station.

Someone in the room mentioned Army maneuvers, and McCrimmon got up to get a better look. Three planes were flying in close formation at about treetop height, shooting tracer bullets. They made three separate passes at the hangars two blocks away, always firing their guns as they approached. Soon black smoke began pouring from one of the buildings. McCrimmon immediately sent an ambulance to the fire in accordance with base regulations.

Another plane flew by, flashing those telltale red circles. This time McCrimmon told his yeoman to "call up Pearl Harbor and ask for some help." The call went through, but Pearl said this was one day they couldn't lend a hand. McCrimmon next called his wife and told her not to pick him up when his duty ended—the place was under attack. Her cheerful reply: "Oh, come on home; all is forgiven."

In the officers' mess a little farther away from the hangers, Attendant Walter Simmons had just finished setting up the tables when the firing began. He had a few minutes to kill and went out to watch the show. After he saw the burning hangar, he darted back in, collared an officer who had just appeared for breakfast, and the pair of them rushed off to the pilots' sleeping quarters—a two-man task force faced with the formidable job of waking up several hundred aviators Sunday morning.

Ensign George Shute burst into Ensign Hubert Reese's room, shouting, "Some damn Army pilot has gone buster—he's diving on BOQ and shooting!" He held out a warm bullet as evidence.

Reese looked out the window, saw the red circles, and joined the little group spreading the alarm. He woke up Ensign Bellinger, who reacted promptly: "Are you guys drunk? Get out and leave me alone!" Now it was Bellinger's turn to look. Then he too was running up and down the halls, banging on doors, spreading the word.

"They is attacking! They is attacking!" shouted a cook, who had joined the group, as he crashed into Ensign Charles Willis' room beating a cake pan with a spoon.

Five pilots crowded into Willis' car and started off for the hangars. Bullets ripped through the roof, the men piled out, then back in again when Willis found that the car still worked. They reached the hangar this time, but just barely. As they got out, another strafer hit the car and this time the gasoline tank went up. It was nothing compared to the blaze they found around them: 33 planes—everything at Kaneohe except the three PBYs on patrol—were burning.

The story was much the same at Ewa Field, the Marine base west of Pearl Harbor. Captain Leonard Ashwell, officer of the day, first sensed something was wrong when he saw two lines of torpedo bombers cruising eastward along the coast toward the Navy base. Unlike almost everybody else in Hawaii, he instantly recognized them. As he ran to sound the alarm, 21 Zeroes barreled in over the Waianae Mountains and began shooting up the base.

Some headed for the planes parked in neat rows; others for the hangars and roadways. One strafer caught Lieutenant Colonel Claude Larkin, base commander, just coming to work in his 1930 Plymouth jalopy. Larkin didn't even turn off the motor—he catapulted out of the car and into a roadside ditch as the plane swept past. Then he scrambled back in and raced for the base about a mile away. He arrived by 8:05, but 33 of his 49 planes were blazing wrecks.

At Waikiki Mrs. Larkin had already put in a big day. She and the colonel had finally found an apartment, and this morning she was moving everything over from the Halekulani Hotel, where they had set up temporary quarters. Other Halekulani guests were enjoying a typical, quiet Sunday morning. Captain J. W. Bunkley of the *California* slipped into his swimming trunks for a prebreakfast dip. Correspondent Joseph Harsch of *The Christian Science Monitor* awoke hearing sounds of explosions in the distance. They immediately reminded him of the air raids they used to have when he was in Berlin the winter before. He woke his wife and told her, "Darling, you often have asked me what an air raid sounds like. Listen to this—it's a good imitation."

"Oh, so that's what it sounds like," she replied. Then they both dozed off to sleep again.

Most of Honolulu was equally uninterested. Author Blake Clark heard the noise at his home on Punahou Street, wrote it off as artillery practice. When he came down to breakfast, he was disturbed only because the Sunday *Advertiser* hadn't come. He walked down to Blackshear's drugstore, picked up an early edition, and came back to enjoy it. When the Japanese cook began talking about planes outside, he strolled onto the *lanai* with Mr. and Mrs. Frear, who shared the house. There were plenty of planes, all right, and Mr. Frear observed that it was just as well in times like these.

Some civilians couldn't help learning. Jim Duncan, foreman for a private contractor at Pearl, was taking flying lessons from Tommy Tommerlin, an inter-island pilot who gave instruction on the side. This was the day for Duncan's cross-country check flight, and now they were cruising leisurely around the island in the Hui Lele Flying Club's yellow Aeronca.

They had just passed the Mormon Temple near Kahuku Point when they heard machine-gun fire and the plane gave a heavy lurch. Then it happened again. At first Duncan thought some playful Army pilot was trying to scare him, but he changed his mind as he saw the red tracers pouring toward him and heard the bullets chopping into his fuselage. Two planes had come up from below, firing and passing so close that they tossed him about in their backwash. Now they turned and were charging back down on him. As they swerved by, he saw for the first time the orange-red circles on the wings. Nothing ever looked bigger.

Duncan dived for the shoreline, hoping to find cover by hugging the steep hills that came almost down to the sea. It was a good decision—the Japanese planes circled once or twice, then flew off to rejoin the armada heading for Pearl. The crippled Aeronca limped down the coast, over the *pali*, and back to the John Rogers Airport, the civilian field just east of Hickam and Pearl Harbor.

Another amateur pilot, lawyer Roy Vitousek, had almost as much trouble right over John Rogers. He, too, had gone up in an Aeronca for an early-morning spin, taking along his son Martin. They were just getting ready to land again when they saw the first explosion on Ford Island. Some planes were circling nearby, but Vitousek didn't link them to the blast. Now more explosions ripped the harbor . . . then the hangars at Hickam . . . and if he still had any doubt, he knew for certain when he saw some planes flying below him and caught a glimpse of the rising sun.

Two of the planes came after Vitousek, and he gunned the Aeronca out to sea, hoping nobody would go to very much trouble just to get him. He was right—the two Japanese gave him a perfunctory burst and turned to John Rogers instead. At the first break Vitousek himself went into Rogers, landed, and found the place seething with indignation: "Did you see those fools? They must be drunk, practicing with live am-munition!"

For a long time the field tried its best to conduct normal business. When the dispatcher announced the 8:oo A.M. inter-island flight to Maui, the passengers filed through the gate as usual. Among them went Dr. Homer Izumi, a physi-cian from the Kula Sanitarium on Maui, who had been in Honolulu on business. His hosts, Dr. and Mrs. Harold John-son, saw him off as he boarded the plane, gingerly carrying a box of his favorite cookies. Waving good-by through the cabin window, he noticed somebody running across the field from the Andrew Flying Service hangar. The plane door opened and everyone was ordered out.

Dr. Izumi climbed down and went back to the Johnsons. There had been more strafing—civilian pilot Bob Tyce had been killed—and the Johnsons urged Dr. Izumi to drive home with them. But he guessed it was nothing . . . the plane was sure to leave soon.

Dr. Izumi guessed wrong. The place was soon in chaos— smoke, shrapnel, strafers everywhere. When a big plane droned toward him from the sea, he dived for a palm tree in the middle of the parking circle. His first thought—protect the cookies; his second—if only he had kissed his son Allen good-by the day he left Maui.

Chapter VIII

"I Can't Keep Throwing Things at Them"

UP IN THE *Maryland's* FORETOP, Seaman Leslie Vernon Short had abandoned his hopes of a quiet morning addressing Christmas cards. After a quick double take on the planes diving at Ford Island, he loaded the ready machine gun and hammered away at the first torpedo planes gliding in from Southeast Loch.

In the destroyer anchorage to the north, Gunner's Mate Walter Bowe grabbed a .50-caliber machine gun on the afterdeck of the *Tucker* and fired back too. So did Seaman Frank Johnson, who was sweeping near the bridge of the destroyer *Bagley* in the Navy Yard. Seaman George Sallet watched the slugs from Johnson's gun tear into a torpedo plane passing alongside, saw the rear gunner slump in the cockpit, and thought it was just like in the movies.

Others were firing too—the *Helena* at 1010 dock . . . the *Tautog* at the sub base . . . the *Raleigh* on the northwest side of Ford Island. Up in the *Nevada's* "bird bath," a seaman generally regarded as one of the less useful members of the crew seized a .30-caliber machine gun and winged a torpedo plane headed directly for the ship. It was to be an important reprieve.

Here and there other guns joined in, but at first they were pitifully few. A "Number 3 condition of readiness" was in

88

effect—that meant one antiaircraft battery in each sector—
and orders had been given to man additional guns on the
battleships. But whatever the official directives, the men actually on the ships recall no difference from any other peacetime Sunday.

On some ships key men were still ashore—five of the battleship captains . . . 50 per cent of the destroyer officers. On
others, men were pinned down by strafing, blocked by watertight doors, dazed by the suddenness of it all. Seaman Robert Benton, a sight-setter of a five-inch gun on the *West Virginia,* stood helplessly at his post—the rest of the gun crew
never did appear. Yeoman Alfred Horne waited alone so long
on the signal bridge of the sub tender *Pelias* that he finally
gave up. He started back down the ladder, almost into the
arms of the skipper, who thundered, "Where the hell do you
think you're going?"

There were more delays once the men reached their stations. First, the canvas awnings that stretched over the decks
and guns. On the *Sacramento* Watertender Gilbert Hawkins
found himself carefully untying each knot—he just couldn't
shake off the peacetime way of doing things. Finally a cook
ran up and slashed the lines with a butcher's knife.

Other men struggled to get guns and ammunition. At Ford
Island a supply officer took a firm stand: no .30-caliber machine guns without a BuSandA 307 Stub Requisition. On the
Helm a gunner's mate asked Commander Carroll's permission to get the keys to open the magazine locks. The skipper
said, "Damn the keys—cut the locks!"

On the *New Orleans* they used fire axes to smash open the
ammunition ready boxes. The *Pennsylvania* locks were
knocked off by a gunner's mate who walked around swinging
a big hammer—he had been bombed by the Japanese on the
gunboat *Panay* in 1937 and announced he wasn't going to
be caught again. On the *Monaghan* Boatswain's Mate Thomas
Donahue—relieved of all duties to return to the mainland—
ran back to his old job as the captain of No. 4 gun. While

the ammunition locks were being sawed off, Donahue whiled away the time slinging wrenches at low-flying planes. Then somebody called up from the magazine and asked what he needed. "Powder," he called back, "I can't keep throwing things at them."

They took him literally and sent up powder without shells. Nothing daunted, he used a drill shell for his first shot at the enemy—at least it was better than a wrench.

On the afterdeck of the *Detroit,* men banged their three-inch shells against the gun shields to get the protector caps off the fuses, and Aviation Metalsmith George Dorfmeister wondered why the whole ship didn't go up in smoke. On the *Bagley,* a five-inch gun crew trained on a low-flying strafer . . . Seaman George Sallet squeezed the trigger . . . and nothing happened. Somebody on the *Honolulu* just astern yelled and pointed to the barrel—nobody had taken out the tampion, a decorative brass plug that seals the barrel when not in use. Whereupon, the crew on one of the *Honolulu's* after guns forgot their own tampion—but here it didn't seem to matter: the first shot blew it out, and on they fought.

More and more guns were firing now, but ten priceless minutes had passed. At a time like this, they made a life-and-death difference on Battleship Row.

Another plane glided toward the *Nevada.* Again the machine guns in her foretop blazed away. Again the plane wobbled and never pulled out of its turn. The men were wild with excitement as it plowed into the water alongside the dredge pipe just astern. The pilot frantically struggled clear and floated face up past the ship. But this time they got him too late. Marine Private Payton McDaniel watched the torpedo's silver streak as it headed for the port bow. He remembered pictures of torpedoed ships and half expected the *Nevada* to break in two and sink enveloped in flames. It didn't happen that way at all. Just a slight shudder, a brief list to port.

Then she caught a bomb by the starboard antiaircraft director. Ensign Joe Taussig was at his station there, standing in the doorway, when it hit. Suddenly he found his left leg tucked under his arm. Almost absently he said to himself, "That's a hell of a place for a foot to be," and was amazed to hear Boatswain's Mate Allen Owens, standing beside him, say exactly the same words aloud.

In the plotting room five decks below, Ensign Charles Merdinger at first felt that it was all like the drills he had been through dozens of times. But it began to seem different when he learned through the phone circuit that his roommate Joe Taussig had been hit.

The men on the *Arizona,* forward of the *Nevada,* hardly had time to think. She was inboard of the *Vestal,* but the little repair ship didn't offer much protection—a torpedo struck home almost right away—and nothing could stop the steel that rained down from Fuchida's horizontal bombers now overhead. A big one shattered the boat deck between No. 4 and 6 guns—it came in like a fly ball, and Seaman Russell Lott, standing in the antiaircraft director, had the feeling he could reach out and catch it. Another hit No. 4 turret, scorched and hurled Coxswain James Forbis off a ladder two decks below.

The PA system barked, "Fire on the quarter-deck," and then went off the air for good. Radioman Glenn Lane and three of his shipmates rigged a hose and tried to fight the fire. No water pressure. They rigged phones and tried to call for water. No power. All the time explosions somewhere forward were throwing them off their feet.

Alongside, the *Vestal* seemed to be catching everything that missed the *Arizona.* One bomb went through an open hatch, tore right through the ship, exploding as it passed out the bottom. It flooded the No. 3 hold, and the ship began settling at the stern. A prisoner in the brig howled to be let out, and finally someone shot off the lock with a .45.

Forward of the *Arizona* and *Vestal,* the *Tennessee* so far was holding her own; but the *West Virginia* on the outside was taking a terrible beating. A Japanese torpedo plane headed straight for the casemate where Seaman Robert Benton waited for the rest of his gun crew. He stood there transfixed—wanted to move but couldn't. The torpedo hit directly underneath and sent Benton and his headphones flying in opposite directions. He got up . . . ran across the deck . . . slipped down the starboard side of the ship to the armor shelf, a ledge formed by the ship's 15-inch steel plates. As he walked aft along the ledge, he glanced up, saw the bombers this time. Caught in the bright morning sun, the falling bombs looked for a fleeting second like snowflakes.

The men below were spared such sights, but the compensation was questionable. Storekeeper Donald Brown tried to get the phones working in the ammunition supply room, third deck forward. The lines were dead. More torpedoes— sickening fumes—steeper list—no lights. Men began screaming in the dark. Someone shouted, "Abandon ship!" and the crowd stampeded to the compartment ladder. Brown figured he would have no chance in this clawing mob, felt his way to the next compartment forward, and found another ladder with no one near it at all. Now he was on the second deck, but not allowed any higher. Nothing left to do, no place else to go—he and a friend brushed a bunch of dirty breakfast dishes off a mess table and sat down to wait the end.

Down in the plotting room—the gunnery nerve center and well below the water line—conditions looked just as hopeless. Torpedoes were slamming into the ship somewhere above. Through an overhead hatch Ensign Victor Delano could see that the third deck was starting to flood. Heavy yellowish smoke began pouring down through the opening. The list grew steeper; tracking board, plotting board, tables, chairs, cots, everything slid across the room and jumbled against the port bulkhead. In the internal communications room next door, circuit breakers were sparking and electrical units ran wild. The men were pale but calm.

Soon oily water began pouring through the exhaust trunks of the ventilation system. Then more yellow smoke. Nothing further could be done, so Delano led his men forward to central station, the ship's damage control center. Before closing the watertight door behind him, he called back to make sure no one was left. From nowhere six oil-drenched electrician's mates showed up—they had somehow been hurled through the hatch from the deck above. Then Warrant Electrician Charles T. Duvall called to please wait for him. He sounded in trouble and Delano stepped back into the plotting room to lend a hand. But he slipped on some oil and slid across the linoleum floor, bowling over Duvall in the process. The two men ended in a tangled heap among the tables and chairs now packed against the "down" side of the room.

They couldn't get back on their feet; the oil was everywhere. Even crawling didn't work—they still got no traction. Finally they grabbed a row of knobs on the main battery switchboard, which ran all the way across the room. Painfully they pulled themselves uphill, hand over hand along the switchboard. By now it was almost like scaling a cliff.

In central station at last, they found conditions almost as bad. The lights dimmed, went out, came on again for a while as some auxiliary circuit took hold. Outside the watertight door on the lower side, the water began to rise . . . spouting through the cracks around the edges and shooting like a hose through an air-test opening. Delano could hear the pleas and cries of the men trapped on the other side, and he thought with awe of the decision Lieutenant Commander J. S. Harper, the damage control officer, had to make: let the men drown, or open the door and risk the ship as well as the people now in central station. The door stayed closed.

Delano suggested to Harper that he and his men might be more useful topside. For the moment Harper didn't even have time to answer. He was desperately trying to keep in touch with the rest of the ship and direct the counterflooding that might save it, but all the circuits were dead.

The counterflooding was done anyhow. Lieutenant Claude

V. Ricketts had once been damage control officer and liked
to discuss with other young officers what should be done in
just this kind of situation. More or less as skull practice, they
had worked out a plan among themselves. Now Ricketts began counterflooding on his own hook, helped along by Boatswain's Mate Billingsley, who knew how to work the knobs
and valves. The *West Virginia* slowly swung back to starboard and settled into the harbor mud on an even keel.

There was no time for counterflooding on the *Oklahoma*,
lying ahead of the *West Virginia* and outboard of the *Maryland*. Lying directly across from Southeast Loch, she got
three torpedoes right away, then another two as she heeled
to port.

Curiously, many of the men weren't even aware of the torpedoes. Seaman George Murphy only heard the loud-speaker
say something about "air attack" and assumed the explosions
were bombs. Along with hundreds of other men who had no
air defense stations, he now trooped down to the third deck,
where he would be protected by the armor plate that covered the deck above. Seaman Stephen Young never thought
of torpedoes either, and he was even relieved when the water
surged into the port side of No. 4 turret powder handling
room. He assumed that someone was finally counterflooding
on that side to offset bomb damage to starboard.

The water rose . . . the emergency lights went out . . .
the list increased. Now everything was breaking loose. Big
1000-pound shells rumbled across the handling rooms, sweeping men before them. Eight-foot reels of steel towing cable
rolled across the second deck, blocking the ladders topside.
The door of the drug room swung open, and Seaman Murphy watched hundreds of bottles cascade over a couple of seamen hurrying down a passageway. The boys slipped and
rolled through the broken glass, jumped up, and ran on.

On the few remaining ladders, men battled grimly to get
to the main deck. It was a regular log jam on the ladder to
S Division compartment, just a few steps from open air.

Every time something exploded outside, men would surge down the ladder, meeting head-on another crowd that surged up. Soon it was impossible to move in either direction. Seaman Murphy gave up even trying. He stood off to the side— one foot on deck, the other on the corridor wall, the only way he could now keep his footing.

Yeoman L. L. Curry had a better way out. He and some mates were still in the machine shop on third deck amidships when the list reached 60 degrees. Someone spied an exhaust ventilator leading all the way to the deck, and one by one the men crawled up. As they reached fresh air, an officer ran over and tried to shoo them back inside, where they would be safe from bomb splinters. That was the big danger, he explained: a battleship couldn't turn over.

Several hundred yards ahead of the *Oklahoma*—and moored alone at the southern end of Battleship Row—the *California* caught her first torpedo at 8:05. Yeoman Durrell Conner watched it come from his station in the flag communications office. He slammed the porthole shut as it struck the ship directly beneath him.

Another crashed home farther aft. There might as well have been more—the *California* was wide open. She was due for inspection Monday, and the covers had been taken off six of the manholes leading to her double bottom. A dozen more of these covers had been loosened. The water poured in and surged freely through the ship.

It swept into the ruptured fuel tanks, contaminating the oil, knocking out the power plant right away. It swirled into the forward air compressor station, where Machinist's Mate Robert Scott was trying to feed air to the five-inch guns. The other men cleared out, calling Scott to come with them. He yelled back, "This is my station—I'll stay here and give them air as long as the guns are going." They closed the watertight door and let him have his way.

With the power gone, men desperately tried to do by hand the tasks that were meant for machines. Yeoman Conner joined a long chain of men passing powder and shells up from an ammunition room far below. Stifling fumes from the ruptured fuel tanks made their work harder, and word spread that the ship was under gas attack. At the wounded collecting station in the crew's reception room Pharmacist's Mate William Lynch smashed open lockers in a vain search for morphine. Near the communications office a man knelt in prayer under a ladder. Numb to the chaos around him, another absently sat at a desk typing, "Now is the time for all good men . . ."

Around the harbor nobody noticed the *California's* troubles—all eyes were glued on the *Oklahoma*. From his bungalow on Ford Island, Chief Albert Molter watched her gradually roll over on her side, "slowly and stately . . . as if she were tired and wanted to rest." She kept rolling until her mast and superstructure jammed in the mud, leaving her bottom-up—a huge dead whale lying in the water. Only eight minutes had passed since the first torpedo hit.

On the *Maryland* Electrician's Mate Harold North recalled how everyone had cursed on Friday when the *Oklahoma* tied up alongside, shutting off what air there was at night.

Inside the *Oklahoma* men were giving it one more try. Storekeeper Terry Armstrong found himself alone in a small compartment on the second deck. As it slowly filled with water, he dived down, groped for the porthole, squirmed through to safety. Seaman Malcolm McCleary escaped through a washroom porthole the same way. Nearby, Lieutenant (j.g.) Aloysius Schmitt, the Catholic chaplain, started out too. But a breviary in his hip pocket caught on the coaming. As he backed into the compartment again to take it out, several men started forward. Chaplain Schmitt had no more time to spend on himself. He pushed three, possibly four, of the others through before the water closed over the compartment.

Some men weren't even close to life as they knew it, but

were still alive nevertheless. They found themselves gasping, swimming, trying to orient themselves to an upside-down world in the air pockets that formed as the ship rolled over. Seventeen-year-old Seaman Willard Beal fought back the water that poured into the steering engine room. Seaman George Murphy splashed about the operating room of the ship's dispensary . . . wondering what part of the ship had a tile ceiling . . . never dreaming he was looking up at the floor.

Topside, the men had it easier. As the ship slowly turned turtle, most of the men simply climbed over the starboard side and walked with the roll, finally ending up on the bottom. When and how they got off was pretty much a matter of personal choice. Some started swinging hand over hand along the lines that tied the ship to the *Maryland*, but as she rolled, these snapped, and the men were pitched into the water between the two ships. Seaman Tom Armstrong dived off on this side—his watch stopped at 8:10. Tom's brother Pat jumped off from the outboard side. Their third brother Terry was already in the water after squeezing through the porthole on the second deck. Marine Gunnery Sergeant Leo Wears slid down a line and almost drowned when someone used him as a stepladder to climb into a launch. His friend Sergeant Norman Currier coolly walked along the side of the ship to the bow, hailed a passing boat, and stepped into it without getting a foot wet. Ensign Bill Ingram climbed onto the high side just as the yardarm touched the water. He stripped to his shorts and slid down the bottom of the ship.

As Ingram hit the water, the *Arizona* blew up. Afterward men said a bomb went right down her stack, but later examination showed even the wire screen across the funnel top still intact. It seems more likely the bomb landed alongside the second turret, crashed through the forecastle, and set off the forward magazines.

In any case, a huge ball of fire and smoke mushroomed 500 feet into the air. There wasn't so much noise—most of the men say it was more a "whoom" than a "bang"—but the concussion was terrific. It stalled the motor of Aviation Ordnanceman Harand Quisdorf's pickup truck as he drove along Ford Island. It hurled Chief Albert Molter against the pipe banister of his basement stairs. It knocked everyone flat on Fireman Stanley H. Rabe's water barge. It blew Gunner Carey Garnett and dozens of other men off the *Nevada* . . . Commander Cassin Young off the *Vestal* . . . Ensign Vance Fowler off the *West Virginia*. Far above, Commander Fuchida's bomber trembled like a leaf. On the fleet landing at Merry's Point a Navy captain wrung his hands and sobbed that it just couldn't be true.

On the *Arizona*, hundreds of men were cut down in a single, searing flash. Inside the port antiaircraft director, one fire control man simply vanished—the only place he could have gone was through the narrow range-finder slot. On the bridge Rear Admiral Isaac C. Kidd and Captain Franklin Van Valkenburgh were instantly killed. On the second deck the entire ship's band was wiped out.

Over 1000 men were gone.

Incredibly, some still lived. Major Allen Shapley of the Marine detachment was blown out of the foremast and well clear of the ship. Though partly paralyzed, he swam to Ford Island, detouring to help two shipmates along the way. Radioman Glenn Lane was blown off the quarter-deck and found himself swimming in water thick with oil. He looked back at the *Arizona* and couldn't see a sign of life.

But men were there. On the third deck aft Coxswain James Forbis felt skinned alive, and the No. 4 turret handling room was filling with thick smoke. He and his mates finally moved over to No. 3 turret, where conditions were a little better, but soon smoke began coming in around the guns there too. The men stripped to their skivvie drawers and crammed their clothes around the guns to keep the smoke out. When somebody finally ordered them out, Forbis took off his newly shined shoes and carefully carried them in his hands as he left the turret. The deck was blazing hot and covered with oil. But there was a dry spot farther aft near No. 4 turret, and before rejoining the fight, Forbis carefully placed his shoes there. He lined them neatly with the heels against the turret—just as though he planned to wear them up Hotel Street again that night.

In the portside antiaircraft director, Russell Lott wrapped himself in a blanket and stumbled out the twisted door. The blanket kept him from getting scorched, but the deck was so hot he had to keep hopping from one foot to the other. Five shipmates staggered up through the smoke, so he stretched the blanket as a sort of shield for them all. Then he saw the *Vestal* still alongside. The explosion had left her decks a shambles, but he found someone who tossed over a line, and, one by one, all six men inched over to the little repair ship.

At that particular moment they were lucky to find anyone on the *Vestal*. The blast had blown some of the crew overboard, including skipper Cassin Young, and the executive officer told the rest to abandon ship. Seaman Thomas Garzione climbed down a line over the forecastle, came to the end of it, and found himself standing on the anchor. He just froze there—he was a nonswimmer and too scared to jump the rest of the way. Finally he worked up enough nerve, made the sign of the cross, and plunged down holding his nose. For a nonswimmer, he made remarkable time to a whale boat drifting in the debris.

Signalman Adolph Zlabis dived off the bridge and reached a launch hovering nearby. He and a few others yelled encouragement to a young sailor who had climbed out on the *Vestal's* boat boom and now dangled from a rope ladder five feet above the water. Finally the man let go, landed flat in the water with a resounding whack. The men in the launch couldn't help laughing.

Still on board the *Vestal,* Radioman John Murphy watched a long line of men pass his radio room, on their way to abandon ship. One of the other radiomen saw his brother go by. He cried, "I'm going with him," and ran out the door. For no particular reason Murphy decided to stay, but he began feeling that he would like to get back home just once more before he passed on.

At this point Commander Young climbed back on the *Vestal* from his swim in the harbor. He was by no means ready to call it a day. He stood sopping wet at the top of the gangway, shouting down to the swimmers and the men in the boats, "Come back! We're not giving up this ship yet!"

Most of the crew returned and Young gave orders to cast off. Men hacked at the hawsers tying the *Vestal* to the blazing *Arizona*. Inevitably, there was confusion. One officer on the *Arizona's* quarter-deck yelled, "Don't cut those lines." Others on the battleship pitched in and helped. Aviation Mechanic "Turkey" Graham slashed the last line with an ax, shouting, "Get away from here while you can!"

Other help came from an unexpected source. A Navy tug happened by, whose skipper and chief engineer had both put in many years on the *Vestal*. They loyally eased alongside, took a line from the bow, and towed their old ship off toward Aiea landing, where she could safely sit out the rest of the attack.

When the *Arizona* blew up, Chief Electrician's Mate Harold North on the *Maryland* thought the end of the world had come. Actually he was lucky. Moored inboard of the *Oklahoma*, the *Maryland* was safe from torpedoes and caught only two bombs. One was a 15-inch armor-piercing shell fitted with fins—it slanted down just off the port bow, smashing into her hull 17 feet below the water line. The other hit the forecastle, setting the awnings on fire. When a strafer swept by, Chief George Haitle watched the firefighters scoot for shelter. One man threw his extinguisher down a hatch, where it exploded at the feet of an old petty officer, who grabbed for a mask, shouting, "Gas!"

The *Tennessee*, the other inboard battleship, had more

trouble. Seaman J. P. Burkholder looked out a porthole on the bridge just as one of the converted 16-inch shells crashed down on No. 2 turret a few feet forward. The porthole cover tore loose, clobbered him on the head, and sent him scurrying through the door. Outside he helped a wounded ensign, but couldn't help one of his closest friends, who was so far gone he only wanted Burkholder to shoot him.

Another armor-piercing bomb burst through No. 3 turret farther aft. Seaman S. F. Bowen, stationed there as a powder carman, was just dogging the hatch when the bomb hit. It wasn't a shattering crash at all. Just a ball of fire, about the size of a basketball, appeared overhead and seemed to melt down on everyone. It seemed to run down on his skin and there was no way to stop it. As he crawled down to the deck below, he noticed that his shoe strings were still on fire.

Splinters flew in all directions from the bombs that hit the *Tennessee*. One hunk ripped the bridge of the *West Virginia* alongside, cut down Captain Mervyn Bennion as he tried to direct his ship's defense. He slumped across the sill of the signal bridge door on the starboard side of the machine-gun platform. Soon after he fell, Ensign Delano arrived on the bridge, having finally been sent up from central station. As Delano stepped out onto the platform, Lieutenant (j.g.) F. H. White rushed by, told him about the captain, and asked him to do what he could.

Delano saw right away it was hopeless. Captain Bennion had been hit in the stomach, and it took no medical training to know the wound was fatal. Yet he was perfectly conscious, and at least he might be made more comfortable. Delano opened a first-aid kit and looked for some morphine. No luck. Then he found a can of ether and tried to make the captain pass out. He sat down beside the dying man, holding his head in one hand and the ether in the other. It made the captain drowsy but never unconscious. Occasionally Delano moved the captain's legs to more comfortable positions, but there was so little he could do.

As they sat there together, Captain Bennion prodded him with questions. He asked how the battle was going, what the *West Virginia* was doing, whether the ship and the men were badly hit. Delano did his best to answer, resorting every now and then to a gentle white lie. Yes, he assured the captain, the ship's guns were still firing.

Lieutenant Ricketts now turned up and proved a pillar of strength. Other men arrived too—Chief Pharmacist's Mate Leak . . . Ensign Jacoby from the flag radio room . . . Lieutenant Commander Doir Johnson from the forecastle. On his way up, Johnson ran across big Doris Miller, thought the powerful mess steward might come in handy, brought him along to the bridge. Together they tenderly lifted Captain Bennion and carried him to a sheltered spot behind the conning tower. He was still quite conscious and well aware of the flames creeping closer. He kept telling the men to leave him and save themselves.

In her house at Makalapa, Mrs. Mayfield still couldn't grasp what had happened. She walked numbly to a window and looked at Admiral Kimmel's house across the street. The Venetian blinds were closed, and there was no sign of activity. Somehow this was reassuring . . . surely there would be some sign of life if it was really true. It didn't occur to her that this might be one morning when the admiral had no time for Venetian blinds.

By now Captain Mayfield was in his uniform. He took a few swallows of coffee, slopping most of it in the saucer, and dashed for the carport. He roared off as the CINCPAC official car screeched up to the admiral's house across the street. Admiral Kimmel ran down the steps and jumped in, knotting his tie on the way. Captain Freeland Daubin, commanding a squadron of submarines, leaped on the running board as the car moved off, and Captain Earle's station wagon shot down the hill after them.

In five minutes Admiral Kimmel was at CINCPAC Headquarters in the sub base. The admiral thought he was there by 8:05; Commander Murphy thought it was more like 8:10. In either case, within a very few minutes of his arrival, the backbone of his fleet was gone or immobile— *Arizona*, *Oklahoma*, and *West Virginia* sunk . . . *California* sinking . . . *Maryland* and *Tennessee* bottled up by the wrecked battleships alongside . . . *Pennsylvania* squatting in drydock. Only the *Nevada* was left, and she seemed a forlorn hope with one torpedo and two bombs already in her.

Nor was the picture much brighter elsewhere. On the other side of Ford Island the target ship *Utah* took a heavy list to port as her engineering officer, Lieutenant Commander S. S. Isquith, pulled his khakis over his pajamas. The alarm bell clanged a few strokes and stopped; the men trooped below to take shelter from bombing. Isquith sensed the ship couldn't last, and he had the officer of the deck order all hands topside instead.

The men were amazingly cool—perhaps because they were used to being "bombed" by the Army and Navy every day. When Machinist's Mate David Gilmartin reached the main deck, he found the port rail already under water. Twice he crawled up toward the starboard side and slid back. As he did it a third time, he slid by another seaman who suggested he throw away the cigarettes. To Gilmartin's amazement he had been trying to climb up the slanting deck while holding a carton of cigarettes in one hand. Relieved of his handicap, he made the starboard rail easily.

As the list increased, the big six-by-twelve-inch timbers that covered the *Utah's* decks began breaking loose. These timbers were used to cushion the decks against practice bombing and undoubtedly helped fool the Japanese into thinking the ship was a carrier unexpectedly in port. Now they played another lethal role, sliding down on the men trying to climb up.

As she rolled still further, Commander Isquith made a last check below to find anyone who might still be trapped—and almost got trapped himself. He managed to reach the cap-

tain's cabin where a door led to the forecastle deck. The
timbers had jammed the door; so he stumbled into the captain's bedroom where he knew there was a porthole. It was
now almost directly overhead, but he managed to reach it by
climbing on the captain's bed. As he popped his head
through the porthole, the bed broke loose and slid out from
under him. He fell back, but the radio officer, Lieutenant
Commander L. Winser, grabbed his hand just in time and
pulled him through. As Isquith got to his feet, he slipped
and bumped down the side of the ship into the water. Half
dead with exhaustion, harassed by strafers, he was helped by
his crew to Ford Island.

Others never left the ship—Fireman John Vaessen in the
dynamo room, who kept the power up to the end; Chief Watertender Peter Tomich in the boiler room, who stayed behind to make sure his men got out; Lieutenant (j.g.) John
Black, the assistant engineer, who jammed his foot in his
cabin door; Mess Attendant Smith, who was always so afraid
of the water.

Of the other ships on this side of Ford Island, the *Tangier*
and *Detroit* were still untouched, but the *Raleigh* sagged
heavily to port. Water swirled into No. 1 and 2 firerooms,
flooded the forward engine room, contaminated the fuel oil,
knocked out her power. In the struggle to keep her afloat, no
one even had time to dress. As though they went around that
way every day, Captain Simons sported his blue pajamas . . .
Ensign John Beardall worked the port antiaircraft guns in
red pajamas . . . others toiled in a weird assortment of skiv-
vies, *aloha* shirts, and bathing trunks. Somehow they didn't
seem even odd: as Signalman Jack Foeppel watched Captain
Simons in the admiral's wing on the bridge, he only marveled
that any man could be so calm.

Ford Island, where all these ships were moored, was itself
in chaos. Japanese strafers were now working the place
over, and most of the men were trying to make themselves
as small as possible. Storekeeper Jack Rogovsky crouched un-

der a mess hall table nibbling raisins. The men in the air photo laboratory dived under the steel developing tables. Some of the flight crews plunged into an eight-foot ditch that was being dug for gas lines along the edge of the runway. This is where Ordnanceman Quisdorf's unit was hiding when he and another airman arrived in the squadron truck. But they didn't know that—they thought they had been left behind in a general retreat. They decided their only hope was to find a pair of rifles, swim the north channel, and hole up in the hills until liberation.

Nor was there much room for optimism in the Navy Yard. On the ships at the finger piers, the stern gunners had a perfect shot at the torpedo planes gliding down Southeast Loch, but most of them had little to shoot with. The *San Francisco* was being overhauled; all her guns were in the shops; most of her large ammunition was on shore. The repair ship *Rigel* was in the same fix. The *St. Louis* was on "limited availability" while radar was being installed; her topside was littered with scaffolding and cable reels; three of her four five-inch antiaircraft guns were dismantled.

The little *Sacramento* had just come out of drydock, and in line with drydock regulations most of her ammunition lockers had been emptied. The *Swan* plugged away with her two three-inch guns, but a new gun earmarked for her top deck was still missing. A pharmacist's mate stood on the empty emplacement, cursing helplessly. The other ships were having less trouble, although there was little power on the *New Orleans,* and to Seaman L. A. Morley on the *Honolulu* just about everything seemed to be "secured for the week end."

On all these ships the men had more time for reflection than their mates along Battleship Row. On the *New Orleans* the ship's gambler and "big operator" sat at his station, reading the New Testament. (Later he canceled his debts and loans; threw away his dice.) A young engineer on the *San Francisco*—with nothing to do because her boilers were dismantled—appeared topside, wistfully told Ensign John E. Parrott, "Thought I'd come up and die with you." Machinist's Mate Henry Johnson on the *Rigel* remarked that now he knew how a rabbit felt and he'd never hunt one again. A few minutes later he lay mortally wounded on the deck.

Their very helplessness turned many of the men from fear to fury. Commander Duncan Curry, strictly an old Navy type, stood on the bridge of the *Ramapo* firing a .45 pistol as the tears streamed down his face. On the *New Orleans* a veteran master at arms fired away with another .45, daring them to come back and fight. A man stood near the sub base, banging away with a double-barreled shotgun.

A young Marine on 1010 dock used his rifle on the planes, while a Japanese-American boy about seven years old lit a cigarette for him. The butt of his old cigarette was burning his lips, but he never even noticed it. As he fired away, he remarked aloud, "If my mother could see me now."

Ten-ten dock itself was a mess, littered with debris from the *Helena* and *Oglala* alongside. In the after engine room of the torpedoed *Helena*, Chief Machinist's Mate Paul Weisenberger fought to check the water that poured aft through the ship's drain system. The hit had also set off the ship's gas alarm; its steady blast added to the uproar. Marine Second Lieutenant Bernard Kelly struggled to get ammunition to the guns. In keeping a steady supply flowing, it was a tossup whether he had more trouble with the damage or with conscientious damage control men, who kept shutting the doors.

Topside was a shambles. The *Helena's* forecastle, which had been rigged for church, looked as if a cyclone had passed. The *Oglala*, to starboard, listed heavily; her signal flags drooped over the *Helena's* bridge. Across the channel, Battleship Row was a mass of flames and smoke. Above the whole scene, a beautiful rainbow arched over Ford Island.

Just below 1010 dock, the *Pennsylvania* and destroyers *Cassin* and *Downes* sat ominously unmolested in Drydock No. 1. Likewise the destroyer *Shaw* in the floating drydock, which was a few hundred yards to the west. Aboard the *Pennsylvania* the men waited tensely. Lieutenant Commander James Craig, the ship's first lieutenant, checked here and there, making sure they would be ready when the blow came —or at least as ready as a ship out of water could be. He told Boatswain's Mate Robert Jones and his damage control party to lie face down on the deck. He warned them that their work was cut out, and to be prepared for the worst.

On deck, the gunners were getting in a few licks in advance. For Gunner's Mate Alvin Gerth, captain of one antiaircraft gun crew, it was already hard, dangerous work. The electrical system had gone haywire, and he could fire by percussion only. On top of that, the ammunition was so old, he had a lot of misfires. Normally he could throw them over the side, but the ship was in drydock, so that was out of the question. He piled them on deck behind the mount, gradually transferring the area into a little arsenal wide open to the sky. Not very safe to do, but he figured his time was up anyhow.

It was much the same on the ships anchored in the harbor. Radioman Leonard Stagich sat by his set on the destroyer *Montgomery* writing prayers on a little pad. In the transmitter room of the aircraft tender *Curtiss,* Radioman James Raines sat with three other men listening to the steady booming outside. No orders, so they just waited. With the doors and portholes dogged down and the ventilators off, it grew hotter and hotter. They removed their shirts and took turns wearing the heavy headphones. Still no orders. They kept moving about the room, squatting in different places, always wondering what was going on outside. From time to time the PA system squawked meaningless commands to others on the ship, which only made them wonder more. Still no orders.

But the most exasperating thing to those at anchor was just sitting there. It took time to build up enough steam to move—an hour for a destroyer, two hours for a larger ship.

Meanwhile, they could only fire their guns manually, dodge the strafers, and watch (to use their favorite phrase) "all hell break loose."

The destroyer *Monaghan* had a slight edge on the others. As the ready-duty destroyer, her fires were already lit; and then of course she had been getting up steam since 7:50 to go out and contact the *Ward*. Commander Bill Burford would be able to take her out in a few minutes now, but at a time like this, that seemed forever.

At the moment the destroyer *Helm* was still the only ship under way. Twenty minutes had passed since Quartermaster Frank Handler genially waved at that aviator flying low up the channel. After the first explosion Commander Carroll quickly sounded general quarters . . . swung her around from West Loch . . . caught Admiral Furlong's sortie signal . . . and was now ready to get up and go. Turning to Handler, he said, "Take her out. I'll direct the battery."

Handler had never taken the ship out alone. The channel was tricky—speed limit 14 knots—and the job was always left to the most experienced hands. He took the wheel and rang the engine room to step her up to 400 rpm. The engine room queried the order and he repeated it. The ship leaped forward and raced down the channel at 27 knots. To complicate matters, there wasn't a single compass on board; everything had to be done by seaman eye. But Handler had one break in his favor—the torpedo net was still wide open. So the *Helm* rushed on, proudly guided by a novice without a compass breaking every speed law in the book.

By this time Handler was game for anything; so he took it in his stride when at 8:17 he came face to face with a Japanese midget sub. He saw it as the *Helm* burst out of the harbor entrance—first the periscope, then the conning tower. It lay about 1000 yards off the starboard bow, bouncing up and down on the coral near the buoys. The *Helm's* guns roared, but somehow they never could hit the sub. Finally it slid off the coral and disappeared. The *Helm* flashed the news to headquarters: "Small Jap sub trying to penetrate channel."

Signal flags fluttered up all over Pearl Harbor, telling the ships of the fleet. From the bridge of the burning *West Virginia*, Ensign Delano read the warning and sighed to himself, "Oh, my God—that too!"

As the *Helm* began patrolling off the harbor entrance, Quartermaster Handler noticed several big Army bombers circling Hickam Field, trying to land. Japanese planes nipped at them from all sides—Handler could see the bullets ripping off big chunks of metal—but the pilots went about their business as though it happened every day.

The B-17s were coming in from the mainland—12 planes in the 38th and 88th Reconnaissance Squadrons under Major Truman Landon. It was a long flight for those days—14 hours' flying time. To save gas, the planes were flying separately instead of in formation. They also were stripped down—no armor or ammunition, their guns in cosmoline.

Even so, some of the B-17s barely made Oahu. On Lieutenant Karl Barthelmes' plane one of the crew accidentally flicked a switch, which threw the plane north of its course, and by the time they figured out why, the gas needle wobbled at zero. Barthelmes turned hard south, and as he approached Oahu around 8:00 A.M., he was suddenly overtaken by 12 to 15 light planes marked with large red circles. They flew above, under, and alongside the B-17, apparently escorting the big plane in. The bomber's crew sighed with relief, removed the lifebelts they had put on while the plane was off course. They waved their thanks, but the pilots of the other planes were apparently too preoccupied to respond.

About the same time Major Landon was also flying in from the north. He had let one of his crew practice navigation most of the way, and they were heading west 150 miles north of Oahu when Landon finally took over. As he turned southward and approached the island, a flight of nine planes came straight at him, flying north. For an instant he too

thought it was a reception committee. Then a burst of gunfire, a quick glimpse of the red circles told him the truth. He
pulled up into the clouds and shook off any pursuit.

Most of the B-17s had no advance notice. Major Richard
Carmichael flew in over Diamond Head, pointing out the
sights to his West Point classmate Colonel Twaddell, the
weather officer. As they passed along Waikiki Beach, they
could see the smoke over Pearl, but assumed the Navy was
practicing. Other pilots saw the smoke too—Lieutenant
Bruce Allen thought there was an unusual amount of cane
burning . . . Lieutenant Robert Ramsey thought it was
some sort of big celebration.

They drew closer, and the devastation spread below them.
Sergeant Albert Brawley gazed at the blazing rows of planes
at Hickam and wondered whether some hot fighter pilot had
crashed, setting them all on fire. Lieutenant Charles Bergdoll
still thought it was a drill, complete with smoke pots and
mock bombing, until he saw the remains of a smashed B-24
burning beside the runway. He knew the Army would never
wreck anything so expensive.

Now the planes were asking for landing instructions from
the tower. A calm, flat voice gave wind direction, velocity,
the runway on which to land, as though it were any other
day. Occasionally the voice observed without emotion that
the field was under attack by "unidentified enemy planes."

Lieutenant Allen was the first to land. Then came Captain Raymond Swenson's plane. As it circled in, a Japanese
bullet exploded some magnesium flares in the radio compartment, which set the whole plane on fire. It bounced down
heavily . . . the blazing tail section broke off . . . and the
forward half skidded to a stop. Lieutenant Ernest Reid, the
copilot, reacted to habit and set the parking brakes as usual.
The crew all reached shelter except Flight Surgeon William
Schick. A Zero riddled him as he ran down the runway.

Now it was Major Landon's turn to come in. The same
nasal voice in the tower told him to "land from west to east"

and added laconically that there were three Japanese planes on his tail. With this encouraging news he came on in, landing safely at 8:20.

As the planes rolled to a stop, the men jumped out and raced for the boondocks on the Honolulu side of the field. Sergeant Brawley lay in the keawa bushes, listening uneasily as the bullets thudded around him. Lieutenant George Newton picked a swamp, Lieutenant Ramsey a drainage ditch. Lieutenant Allen tried to disappear into grass three inches high. Lieutenant Homer Taylor ran the opposite way, winding up in some officer's house under a couple of overturned sofas. The officer's wife and children huddled there too, and every time a Japanese plane roared by, a small boy tried to get out from under the sofa and look outside. He would nearly get to the end of the sofa, then Taylor would grab an ankle and drag him back just in time. This duel continued until the end of the raid.

Taylor had the right idea—nothing was immune. Even the Snake Ranch, the new beer garden for enlisted men, exploded in a shower of glass and lumber. The only thing saved was a recording of "San Antonio Rose"—when the place was later rebuilt, it was the only record the old-timers allowed.

The base fire department was now in action, but no firemen ever operated under greater handicaps. Bombs blasted the water mains, then the fire house itself. As Hoseman Howard King manned one of the engines, his crew chief, Joe Clagnon, suddenly yelled to look out. Before King could move, there was a blinding flash and something that felt like a ton of bricks. Lying in the smoke, he saw dimly the twisted engine, Clagnon dying, his own leg shattered. He begged a passing GI to put a tourniquet around his leg; the man said dazedly that he was sorry but he didn't have a handkerchief.

Through it all Fire Chief William Benedict calmly directed his men, munching an apple. Soon he was hit but the wound was minor. Then he was hit worse, but he got up again and continued supervising the work. The third time he stayed down, but as they carried him away badly injured, he was still munching the apple.

Some of the casualties were needless. One first sergeant, in a well-meaning attempt to organize his unit, lined them up on the edge of the parade grounds just outside the big barracks. The target was too inviting to miss—a couple of Zeroes peeled off and strafed the men.

Perhaps it didn't make much difference—the strafers seemed just as interested in individuals. One Zero caught a lineman up a telegraph pole. He yanked out his spurs and slid down the pole, as the wood splintered around him. Another strafer stitched up Hangar Avenue, sawed right through the cab of a swerving truck. Searching out targets, the planes swooped unbelievably low. Completely absorbed in his work, one pilot forgot about flying. As he skimmed along the parking ramp, his propeller tips flecked the asphalt . . . his belly tank scraped off and went scooting down the ramp. He finally pulled up—hitting the hills beyond the field, according to one man . . . crashing into the sea, according to another . . . getting away with it completely, according to a third.

It's a wonder anybody noticed. The dive bombers were concentrating on the hangars, and most men were trying to get out of the area. A pack of men headed across the ball field for the post school building. A strafer caught up with them as they crossed the diamond—Private J. H. Thompson got two bullet holes in his canteen, one of his buddies in the bill of his cap, and others got off far worse. Corporal John Sherwood joined 200 others in a wild dash from the big barracks, which were perilously close to the hangars. They headed across the parade grounds for the post exchange, encouraged along by the inevitable Zero. Sherwood, a compact little man, was clad only in undershorts and must have been a spectacular figure. His sergeant, Wilbur Hunt, still recalls how he paused in his work and wondered how anybody that short could run that fast. Today Sherwood denies he ran. but says he passed at least a hundred who did.

From the shelter of the PX, Corporal Sherwood watched a master sergeant pedal furiously by on a bicycle. Head down, feet pumping hard, all the time shooting a .45 pistol in the air, he seemed curiously like a cowboy in a Wild West movie. Perhaps there was something of that spirit in the air, for out in the open near the married men's quarters a group of small children were leaping up and down shrieking, "Here come the Indians!"

Gradually, fear and panic gave way to anger. A wounded man outside Hangar 15 kept shaking his fist at the sky in helpless rage. Sergeant George Geiger was bitterly mad, searched for a gun—any gun. He found one in the barracks supply room, but there was no ammunition. Then he heard there was a supply of arms at the main gate. When he got there, everything was gone except a .45 pistol holster. He took it, later gave it to a man who had a pistol but no holster.

Guns began to appear. Sergeant Stanley McLeod stood on the parade ground, hammering away with a Thompson submachine gun . . . Staff Sergeant Doyle King fired another from under a panel truck . . . Technical Sergeant Wilbur Hunt set up 12 .50-caliber machine guns in fresh bomb craters near the barracks. His gunners turned up from an unexpected source. A bomb had blown off a corner of the guardhouse, releasing everybody. The prisoners dashed over to Hunt and said they were ready to go to work. It was just as he thought—the ones who are always in trouble are the ones you want with you when the going gets tough. He put them on the guns right away.

Wheeler had its guardhouse heroes too. All the prisoners were turned loose, and two of them helped man a machine gun on the roof. At the main barracks men broke down the supply room doors, and three guns were firing from the narrow back porch. Somebody had set up another out in the open, toward the main road. Pfc. Arthur Fusco helped set one up in front of a hangar, but by now all the smoke made it useless. At one point he took cover in the hangar office, and was surprised to hear the phone ringing. He automatically picked up the receiver. A post wife was on the other end, asking what all the noise was about.

Most of the men had no idea what to do or where to go. Staff Sergeant Francis Clossen, like the men at Hickam, was at least sure the hangar line was a poor choice. He ran toward the road, fell down, limped on. Then a solicitous chaplain stopped him, thinking he was wounded. That out of the way, he climbed a fence . . . lost his shoes . . . and plunged into some keawa bushes. At least a dozen others had reached the patch before him.

Pfc. Carroll Andrews was one man with a definite objective. A sergeant told him to hit for Schofield. He and a buddy started off through the noncom housing area, running in short spurts between the strafing. Once they ducked into the kitchen of an empty house. Bullets ripped the stove, and they marveled at the splintering porcelain—it was the first time they realized how the stuff could shatter.

On they ran, and then another interruption. This time it was a soldier who had seen Andrews playing the organ for Catholic services. He asked Andrews to help him say the Catholic's Act of Contrition. He explained he hadn't been to mass or confession for years and needed to make an emergency peace. Andrews stopped and repeated the words with him.

They dashed on. Soon a Filipino woman ran up with a tiny baby. She too had seen Andrews in Church, wanted him to baptize the baby. By now mildly exasperated, Andrews asked her why she didn't do it herself. She said she wasn't sure how. So he went in another empty house, tried the kitchen faucets (they didn't run), found a bottle of cold water, and baptized the baby. The mother burst into tears and ran off.

They finally reached Schofield about 8:30. At this point it was an odd place to go for protection. The planes were gone now—they were finished with this whole area by 8:17

—but the post was in enormous confusion. The various antiaircraft units were trying to get going to their assigned positions, but there were often difficulties. The men in Battery B, 98th Coast Artillery, couldn't get trucks to tow their guns to Wheeler Field until the raid was all over. When they were issued machine-gun ammunition, they found it was 1918 stuff—so old the belts came to pieces in the loading machine. With the Japanese likely to return any minute, Private Lester Buckley—back safely from his compost heap—opened the gates of the corral, so that at least his mules would have a chance.

At Wahiawa, a small town next to Wheeler and Schofield, Mr. and Mrs. Paul Young listened to the explosions nearby. The Youngs were Koreans and ran a small laundry in a shed attached to their house. They had just put in a big night at mah-jongg, and Mr. Young was all for staying in bed. But Mrs. Young was curious and finally walked down to the Wheeler gate to find out what was going on. The sentry had a quick answer: "Get back home. Don't you know there's a war on?"

Mrs. Young ran back, calling out the news. Mr. Young and his brother, Sung do Kim, then got up and came down to watch the show. Suddenly they saw a plane flying up the road from Pearl Harbor, looking for something to strafe. Mrs. Young sensed trouble, and they all took cover, except for their old Chinese hired man. He stayed outside, nonchalantly rolling some Bull Durham. The plane got him before he could finish making the cigarette.

They ran out and dragged the old man in. Mrs. Young scolded him like a naughty child, asked him why he didn't come inside with them. He replied he couldn't talk because it hurt so much.

Now a dogfight began. Stray bullets whined about the house—one smashed a window; another nicked the washing machine; another bored a hole through the door where Mrs. Young was peeking out. The family, crouched under the ironing table, caught occasional glimpses of the planes through the skylight. Suddenly there was an ear-splitting roar. A Japanese plane sheared off the top of the eucalyptus tree in their yard, crashed in a pineapple field just beyond. The American fighter that shot it down disappeared off toward the mountains. Mrs. Young, of course, couldn't know it, but Lieutenants Welch and Taylor had reached Haleiwa, taken off in their P-40s, and were now in business.

At Haleiwa, eight miles away, there was now plenty of other action. Two B-17s had lumbered up from the south and were circling above. Captain Chaffin and Major Carmichael had given up trying to land in the shambles at Hickam. After rejecting Wheeler and Ewa for the same reasons, they finally decided on Haleiwa, which the Japanese apparently didn't know about. The little strip was only 1200 feet long—certainly not inviting—but they were almost out of gas and there was no other choice. Down they came, somewhat surprisingly, to perfect landings.

They taxied as close as they could to a clump of trees, but they were already too late. A Zero had seen them land and came over to investigate. Somebody yelled a warning, and Major Carmichael and his classmate, Colonel Twaddell, dived under a big rock on the beach. The Zero was probably low in ammunition—he gave Haleiwa a perfunctory burst and flew off. But a Pacific comber took care of Carmichael and his friend. It rolled in, completely drenching them. It even ruined Carmichael's watch.

At Kaneohe on the windward side, a strafing Japanese plane cost Ordnanceman Homer Bisbee his watch too, but much more indirectly. As he dived for cover off the seaplane ramp, he noticed he was swimming with his good watch on. At first he held his arm up out of the water; next, he put the watch in his white cap and laid it on the ramp. When he came out from under a few minutes later, the cap was still there, but the watch was missing.

Almost anything could have happened to it—the ramp was

an inferno. Again and again the dive bombers strafed the 26 PBYs lined up in neat rows, the four others moored in the bay. Several small boats servicing the planes at anchor were riddled too, and one man had to swim all the way across Kaneohe Bay to reach safety. Only one gun was firing back—Chief Aviation Ordnanceman John Finn had mounted a machine gun on an instruction stand far out on the ramp. He hammered away at the strafers in a shower of blazing gasoline from the planes parked around him. A bullet clipped him in the heel, but he kept on firing.

The pilots and flight crews struggled to salvage what was left. Ensign C. S. Malwein got a tractor, and with two other men struggled to save a plane that wasn't burning yet. A Japanese fighter swooped down to stop them, and the wing fabric was soon a mass of flames.

Another Zero cut down Aviation Machinist's Mate Robert Ballou as he ran out on the ramp with a rifle. Two of his buddies put him on a cot and set off for a truck being used as an ambulance. They were spotted right away. Flat on his back, Ballou watched the tracer bullets smoke by; he found it especially disconcerting when he realized the men had set the cot down and were running for cover. He jumped up and outran them both.

About 8:15 A.M. the planes flew off to the north. The quiet was anything but restful. So far there had been no bombing, and everyone sensed that this was what would happen next. Sure enough, around 8:30—Ensign Reese remembered glancing at his watch—nine horizontal bombers appeared, flying in close formation. Dirt, metal, cement, glass flew in all directions as they dropped their load. Then another formation appeared but saved their bombs perhaps for a better target—Kaneohe's two new hangars were wrecked by now.

All was still serene at Bellows Field, the Army's fighter base only six miles down the coast. Captain John P. Joyce, the officer of the day, was shaving in the officers' club just before 8:30, when a single plane buzzed the field once, firing about

50 rounds. A private of the medical detachment was hit in bed in the tent area. A messenger drove off to tell Major L. D. Waddington, the base commander, who lived about a mile away, but even this rather startling event didn't seem to stir much excitement. Certainly not enough to keep Private Raymond McBriarty from going to church as usual at 8:30. Like everybody else, he hadn't paid much attention to the strafing plane. But then as he sat in the pew with more time to meditate, he began to think how strange it was.

Outside, a big B-17 was coming in downwind on the short 2600-foot strip. Lieutenant Robert Richards was another of the bomber pilots who wanted no part of Hickam—three of his crew had been wounded already. So on the tower's advice, he was now trying Bellows. With a damaged plane almost out of gas, he decided to get down as quickly as possible, and got away with a downwind landing.

At this point Hickam finally notified Bellows about the attack. Major Waddington hurried on over to get the defense organized, and about the same time nine Japanese planes—apparently attracted by Richards' B-17—dropped by and shot up the field.

Other enemy planes kept on top of Ewa, the Marine air base west of Pearl. There were no antiaircraft guns, no planes that could fly, no chance to do anything. Lieutenant Colonel Larkin, the base commander, watched from under a truck, and most of his men were pinned down just as effectively.

Up above, Lieutenant Yoshio Shiga raked Ewa with his Zero fighter. He noticed a Marine standing beside a disabled plane and charged down, all guns blazing. The man refused to budge . . . kept firing back with a pistol. Shiga still considers him the bravest American he ever met.

Lieutenant Shiga was also impressed by the B-17. He watched one of the big bombers shake off a swarm of Zeroes and lumber on safely to Hickam. He made a mental note that in the days ahead the Flying Fortress was going to be a hard plane to knock out.

Perhaps the visitors' biggest surprise was the antiaircraft fire, which was now coming to life. As Commander Fuchida's 50 horizontal bombers approached Battleship Row in a long, single line from the south, he felt they looked entirely too much like ducks in a shooting gallery. If he were doing it again, they would come in some other way.

As they neared the target, Fuchida traded positions with the lead bomber in his squadron. This plane had a specially trained bombardier, and when he released his bombs the other planes would follow suit. All the squadrons operated the same way.

Everything depended on perfect timing. When Fuchida saw the third plane in his group get out of line and prematurely drop its bomb, he was thoroughly annoyed. The man had a reputation for carelessness anyhow. Fuchida scribbled, "What happened?" on a small blackboard and waved it at the culprit. The pilot indicated that he had been hit, that the bomb lines had been shot away, and Fuchida was filled with remorse.

The squadron flew on. The *Nevada* was its particular target, and everybody waited for the lead plane to release. It never did. They ran into clouds at the crucial moment and had to try again. Next time around there was too much smoke over the *Nevada*, so Fuchida picked the *Maryland* instead. This time there was no trouble. The lead plane released and the others followed suit. Fuchida peeked down and felt sure he had two hits.

Lieutenant Toshio Hashimoto, leading one of the rear squadrons, had an even more difficult time. The backwash of the planes in front kept throwing his group off. Then the lead plane miscalculated its range and signaled the others to hold everything. As they circled for another run, the expert bombardier Sergeant Umezawa bowed his apologies.

There were other errors over which the planes had no control. Their map of the area was made in 1933, and the efforts to up-date it hadn't been too successful. The new Navy tank farm was noted, but a 1936 artist's conception of Hickham had been accepted as gospel, so that the map showed eight pairs of hangars instead of the five actually built. The map also put the underground gasoline system where the baseball field was—at one time it had indeed been planned for there. Also, the administration building—a vital center—was labeled the officers' club and hence not touched. This mistake arose because dances were held there while the permanent club was being built. Whatever the other successes of Japanese agents, apparently they weren't invited to dances at Hickam.

But all in all, Fuchida had good reason to be satisfied. As the first attack wave wound up its work around 8:30, he could weigh what had been done to the fleet and the airfields against his own losses: five torpedo planes . . . one dive bomber . . . three fighters.

Admiral Nagumo was also taking stock of the striking force, now hovering about 200 miles north of Oahu. Brief radio flashes from the planes gave a pretty good picture: 8:05 A.M., torpedoes successfully dropped . . . 8:10 A.M., 30 planes hit, 23 on fire . . . 8:16 A.M., large cruiser hit . . . 8:22 A.M., battleship hit . . .

Once again everyone went into ecstasy. In the *Akagi's* engine room Commander Tanbo's firemen hugged each other with joy as the news filtered down. Up on deck, Seaman Iki Kuramoti shouted in glee. But tough Commander Hoichiro Tsukamoto, navigation officer of the *Shokaku,* lived in fear of being caught by American planes. He knew the carriers were easy targets; he didn't know how little was left to hit them.

Admiral Yamamoto was also serious as he waited for results in the operations room of his flagship *Nagato* back at Kure. The minutes ticked away on the large nautical clock that hung on the wall. Yamamoto had almost finished his second cigarette when the first word came in. As the results piled up, the rest of the room buzzed with excitement, but Yamamoto rarely changed expression. One intercepted U. S. message spoke of ships operating around the harbor. "Good!" exclaimed Rear Admiral Matome Ugaki, "that means our midget subs are getting through!" Yamamoto merely nodded. Actually he still felt the midget submarines were a mistake, that it was a waste of manpower to sacrifice men at the outset of war.

He may have been right—certainly Ensign Sakamaki was getting nowhere. Coming in for another try at the harbor entrance, he got close enough to a patrolling destroyer to see the white uniforms of the crew. It apparently picked him up too, for several depth bombs thoroughly shook up the sub. One of them stunned Sakamaki and filled the sub with fumes and a thin white smoke. When he came to, he withdrew to check his damage. Nothing seriously wrong, so he tried again. According to Sakamaki, he made three separate attempts to get by charging, depth-bombing American destroyers before ending up briefly on the coral reef just outside the harbor entrance.

American memories and records suggest no such spirited engagement. Between the *Ward's* contact at 6:45 and the time the *Helm* saw the midget on the coral at 8:17, there was only one sub report—the sound contact made by the *Ward* at 7:03.

If Sakamaki was confused or mistaken, it's quite understandable. The air in the sub was vile, the batteries were leaking, the smoke getting worse. And there is certainly no question about one thing he recalls seeing. Once, as he twisted his periscope toward Pearl Harbor, he saw columns of black smoke towering toward the sky. "Look! Look!" he cried.

Seaman Inagaki was completely overjoyed: "Just look at that smoke!"

They clasped each other's shoulders and solemnly pledged, "We'll do the same!"

Chapter IX

"You Don't Wear a Tie to War"

THE *Breese* SAW IT FIRST. From her anchorage off Pearl City, the old destroyer-minecraft sighted a conning tower turning up the west side of Ford Island just after 8:30. The *Medusa* and *Curtiss* saw it a few minutes later, and signal flags fluttered from all three yardarms.

The *Monaghan* caught the warning right away. The ready-duty destroyer had now cleared her nest and was heading down the west channel, the first ship to get going. A signalman turned to Commander Bill Burford: "Captain, the *Curtiss* is flying a signal that means, 'Submarine sighted to starboard.' "

Burford explained it was probably a mistake . . . such a thing could easily happen in all the confusion of gunfire and burning ships.

"Okay, Captain—then what is that thing dead ahead of us that looks like an over-and-under shotgun?"

The skipper squinted through the smoke and was amazed to see a small submarine moving toward them on the surface several hundred yards ahead. In its bow were two torpedo tubes, not side by side as usual, but one directly above the other. They seemed to be pointed directly at the *Monaghan*.

By now everybody was firing. The *Curtiss* pumped a shell right through the conning tower at 8:40—decapitating the pilot, according to her gunners; clipping off his coat button, according to *Monaghan* men. The *Medusa* was firing too, but at the crucial moment the powder hoist broke on the gun that had the best shot. The *Monaghan's* own guns were blazing as she rushed at the sub, but the shot missed and hit a derrick along the shore.

The midget missed too. It failed to get the *Curtiss* with one torpedo; the other whisked by the charging *Monaghan* and exploded on the Ford Island shore. The *Monaghan* rushed on, and everybody else held their fire as Burford tried to ram. He grazed the conning tower, not really a square blow, but hard enough to spin the sub against the *Monaghan's* side as she surged by. Chief Torpedoman's Mate G. S. Hardon set his depth charges for 30 feet and let them go. They went off with a terrific blast, utterly destroying the sub and knocking down nearly everybody on deck. Fireman Ed Creighton thought the ship had at least blown up its own fantail.

But she hadn't. Instead, the *Monaghan* rocketed on, now too late to make her turn into the main channel leading to sea. She drove ashore at Beckoning Point, piling into the derrick already set on fire by her guns. Fireman Creighton ran to the bow and manned a hose; others wrestled the anchor free. Burford backed off, turned, and steamed out to sea while the nearby ships rang with cheers.

The whole harbor was on the upsurge. A trace of jauntiness —even cockiness—began to appear. Three men in a 50-foot launch hawked .30 and .50-caliber ammunition off the foot of Ford Island as if they were selling vegetables. A bomb hit a mobile "gedunk" wagon on 1010 dock, and men from the *Helena* dashed ashore to gather up the free pies, ice cream, and candy bars. A number of seamen sneaked away from their regular stations on the *Whitney* to take a turn at the machine guns—like patrons of a shooting gallery. When a gun crew on the *Blue* winged a plane, everyone stopped work, danced about shaking hands with one another.

A strange exhilaration seized the men at the guns. Not knowing of war, they compared it to football. Marine Gunner Payton McDaniel on the *Nevada* sensed the tingle of going onto the field at game time. Ensign Martin Burns on the *Phoenix* felt the excitement of the scrimmage. When the *Honolulu* and *St. Louis* winged a plane, Machinist's Mate Robert White could only compare the cheers to Navy scoring against Army. And in fact, when the Marine gunners on the *Helena* knocked down a plane, Captain Bob English shouted from the bridge, "The Marine team scored a touchdown!"

In their excitement men performed astonishing feats. Woodrow Bailey, a sailor on the *Tennessee,* chopped a ten-inch hawser in half with one stroke. Gun Captain Alvin Gerth and two other men did the job of 15 men at one of the *Pennsylvania's* five-inch guns. Kenneth Carlson ran up vertical ladders on the *Selfridge* with a bandoleer of .50-caliber machine-gun shells slung over each shoulder—normally he could handle just one of the 75-pound belts. A man on the *Phelps* adjusted a blue-hot 1.1 gun barrel by twisting it with his hands—didn't even notice the heat.

There were fiascoes too. When an old chief on the *St. Louis* cleared some Navy Yard rigging from the ship's foremast, other crew members paused to watch with delight a Mack Sennett classic—he was chopping away the scaffold he stood on. The *Argonne* gunners shot down their own antenna, then almost got the Fourteenth Naval District signal tower. Next a hole appeared in the powerhouse smokestack. Seaman Don Marman says the *Helena* fired the shot; Marine Gunner McDaniel of the *Nevada* also claims the honor. Other shells —with the fuses defective or not set at all—whistled off toward downtown Honolulu.

Little matter. At the moment all anybody cared about was keeping the guns going. The *Tennessee's* five-inch guns fired so fast that paint hung from the overheated barrels in foot-long strips. On the *Pennsylvania* Gunner's Mate Millard Rucoi was busy ramming shells when a man at the next five-inch gun began waving his arms, as though describing a shapely woman. Rucoi was too busy for frivolity and there was too much noise for conversation, so he just shook his fist and went on ramming. Finally the man came over and shouted to come and look at his gun barrel—it was so hot it was wavy. He asked Rucoi whether he should keep shooting. The answer was easy: "Hell, yes, keep her going."

Nothing was allowed to interfere. At 1010 dock, tugs towed the sinking *Oglala* clear of the *Helena* to a new berth farther astern. As the lines between the two ships were cast off, Admiral Furlong appeared on the *Oglala's* bridge and wandered into the line of fire of a *Helena* five-incher. A very young boatswain's mate stuck his head out of the gunport: "Pardon me, Admiral, sir! Would you mind moving from the wing of the bridge so we can shoot through there?"

Lieutenant Commander Shigekazu Shimazaki got a real reception when he arrived with the second attack wave at 8:40. There were no torpedo planes this time—just 54 high-level bombers, 80 dive bombers, and 36 fighters. The level bombers would concentrate on Hickam and Kaneohe, but the dive bombers screamed down on Pearl, searching for targets that hadn't been plastered.

The *Maryland* and *Helena's* newly installed 1.1 guns now swung into action and bagged three planes right away. On the *Castor*, Quartermaster William Miller listened with clinical interest to the new weapon. It wasn't a bark like the three-inch guns, or an ear-blasting crack like the five-inchers— just a muffled, persistent pom-pom that was somehow very reassuring. On the *West Virginia*, Ensign Ed Jacoby was more surprised than reassured; these guns had been a constant headache in practice—they were always breaking down—but this morning they worked like a charm.

A dive bomber crashed near Ford Island, just off the dock normally used by the *Tangier* . . . another into the main channel near the *Nevada* . . . another off Pearl City, not far from the destroyer-minecraft *Montgomery*. Chief Machinist's Mate Harry Haws sent Seaman D. F. Calkins in the destroyer's whaleboat to investigate. The pilot was sitting on the wing, but refused to be rescued. As the gig drew along-side, he pulled a pistol. He had no chance to use it—Calkins shot first.

In their anger and excitement the men shot at anything that flew. This had already been learned by the B-17s coming into Hickam. Now it was discovered by 18 planes flying into Ford Island on a routine scouting mission from the carrier *Enterprise*.

The big ship had been due back at 7:30 A.M. from her trip to Wake, but heavy seas held up the refueling of her destroyers, and at 6:15 she was still some 200 miles west of Oahu. So the early-morning scouting flight took off as usual—13 planes from Scouting Squadron 6; four from Bombing Squadron 6; one additional reconnaissance plane. They were to sweep the 180-degree sector ahead of the ship, then land at Ford Island. Ensign Cleo Dobson and the other married pilots were delighted—they couldn't go ashore until the *Enterprise* docked, but they could at least call their wives.

The planes droned off. It must have been about 8:00 A.M. when they all heard Ensign Manuel Gonzales yell over the radio, "Don't shoot! I'm a friendly plane!" No one ever saw him again.

Lieutenant (j.g.) F. A. Patriarca's patrol took him north to Kaui, and as he swung back toward Oahu shortly after eight, he noticed planes orbiting northward in the distance. It looked like the Army on maneuvers. When he reached Oahu, he learned the truth and gunned his plane out to sea, calling again and again over the radio: "White 16—Pearl Harbor under attack. Do not acknowledge." He headed back for the *Enterprise,* but the carrier—now under radio silence—had changed course and disappeared. Running out of gas, Patriarca finally crash-landed in a pasture at Kauai.

The warning was too late for some of the pilots. Japanese fighters racked up Ensigns Bud McCarthy, John Vogt, and

Walter Willis; only McCarthy escaped alive. Navy antiaircraft fire took care of Ensign Edward Deacon; he crashed into the sea, but both he and his rear-seat man were saved. Then a Zero caught Lieutenant (j.g.) Clarence Dickinson's plane. The rear-seat man was shot, but Dickinson bailed out. Landing in a dirt bank just west of Ewa Field, he stumbled to the main road. He hoped at least to catch a ride to Pearl.

The rest of the pilots somehow squeaked into Ewa or Ford Island. Lieutenant Earl Gallaher arrived over Pearl about 8:35, decided it was hopeless and made for Ewa instead. Ensign Dobson happened along and decided that was a good idea too. They touched down, and a Marine ran up shouting, "For God's sake, get into the air or they'll strafe you too!" Taking off again, they circled about for a few minutes, finally headed into Ford Island when it looked like a lull.

As Dobson dropped his wheels to land, every gun in the Navy seemed to open up on him. Tracers flew by. A pom-pom shell burst under his right wing, throwing the plane on its side. He dropped his seat down . . . hid behind the engine . . . and dived for the runway. At 50 knots extra speed, he shuddered to think that his tires might be shot. But he made it all right, scooted the whole length of the runway, ground-looped to a stop just short of a ditch.

There was nothing dazed or stunned about Ford Island now. Some of the men were dragging damaged planes clear of the burning hangars. Others were salvaging the guns and setting up pillboxes. One ordnanceman had to improvise his mount out of some sewer pipe. There still weren't enough guns to go around, and Chief Storekeeper Bonett—a quiet, unassuming man who was supposed to know nothing about weapons—was busy assembling .30-caliber machine guns in the paint storage building.

Others rallied around the oil-soaked men who struggled ashore from Battleship Row. Many of them headed for a spot near the gas dock, where the beach shelved off gradually. Chief Albert Molter dragged in a tall ensign, still wearing binoculars, who had passed out just short of the beach. As he tugged away, he saw another man swimming in, using only one arm. Molter thought he must be using a cross-chest carry on someone else, and helpfully called out that the water was shallow. The man murmured his thanks and stumbled to his feet—he was carrying a large canned ham.

The wounded were quickly taken in tow—some to the tennis courts, which had been turned into a receiving station; others to the mess hall, where they lay on tables yet to be cleared of breakfast. Seaman Thomas Malmin, who drove the bus that ran around the island, took the worst hit to the dispensary. Once he picked up an ensign—no apparent wounds but in a state of complete shock. He couldn't speak, couldn't hear, fought desperately to stay in the bus when it reached the building. Another time he gave four colored men a lift. They were all badly hurt but wouldn't let anybody touch them or aid them in any way. They kept together in the bus and helped each other out at the end—still going it alone.

The dispensary was quickly swamped, and the men piled up in the patio—sprawling, sopping bundles that looked completely out of place on the bright, clean tiles. A young girl, perhaps 14, went around trying to get their names, but she just couldn't bear to look.

The service families opened their larders and wardrobes for the men who weren't wounded. An officer walked about in seaman's jumpers; a sailor with him wore a T-shirt, swallow-tailed coat, and full-dress "fore and aft" admiral's hat. Like the other good Samaritans, Mrs. Pat Bellinger had raided her husband's trunk.

Off Ford Island, a weird flotilla dodged Japanese strafers, darted in and out of the burning oil, picking up the men still swimming. Boatswain's Mate A. M. Gustchen maneuvered Admiral Leary's barge with all the professional polish an admiral's coxswain should have. Musician Walter Frazee, who had never steered a boat before, handled a launch from the *Argonne*. Chief Jansen brought his honey barge in close, fighting fires on the *West Virginia*. A water barge turned up to redeem a mildly tarnished past. For some time it had been the crew's custom to give any ship more than its quota of fresh water—if the ship made it worthwhile. A suggested rate of exchange was 10,000 gallons for a big dressed turkey, sixty dozen eggs, with a few extra items to sweeten the deal. Just the day before, such a transaction was worked out with the *Curtiss;* in fact, the turkey was in the oven at the very moment the Japanese struck. Now, all thoughts of a Sunday feast were forgotten, as the barge rushed to help the swimmers.

They were all types. When Seaman Albert Jones idled his motor for a second to spread sand for better footage, a sailor in the water screamed hysterically—he was sure he would be forgotten. Another man swam over and did his best to help. It wasn't easy, for he had just lost his own arm.

Ensign Maurice Featherman of the *West Virginia* lay exhausted on the deck of a harbor tug and didn't care whether he lived or died. His shipmate, Ensign John Armstrong, appeared from nowhere in starched whites—looking as if he had just stepped out of the Harvard Club. Kneeling at Featherman's side, he set about injecting his friend with the will to live: "Mo, history is being made now, and you and I are in the middle of it, and our actions might affect the outcome."

Few men thought in such terms, but more and more acted as if they did. Chief Radioman Thomas Reeves hung on alone in a burning passageway of the *California*, trying to pass ammunition by hand, until he fell unconscious and died. The ship had taken a bad hit around 8:25, and flames raged along the second deck. As Ensign Herbert Jones lay wounded in their path, he calmly explained to two friends that he was done for anyhow and they must leave him.

On the bridge of the tanker *Neosho*—lying between the *California* and the rest of Battleship Row—Commander John Phillips prepared to move his ship from the area. As her engineers lit off the boilers and the blowers cut in, Aviation Machinist William Powers jumped with fright—that rising whine sounded just like bombs in the movies. By 8:35, some of the *Neosho's* crew had joined air station personnel in the job of chopping the lines. Slowly she cleared the dock and backed up Battleship Row to the fuel depot on the other side of the channel.

Actually the Japanese weren't interested in the *Neosho*. When one strafer flew down Battleship Row, he even held fire while passing the tanker—just a waste of good bullets. He might have cared more had he known she was still half loaded with high-octane aviation gas.

Next up the line, the *Oklahoma* lay bottom-up, but her men were by no means out of the fight. Marine Sergeant Thomas Hailey reached Ford Island, volunteered for a mission in a small unarmed plane. They gave him a rifle and sent him up. The mission: locate the Japanese fleet. The plane had no luck and returned five hours later. For Hailey it was an especially uncomfortable trip because he still had on only the oil-soaked underwear he wore from the *Oklahoma*.

Most of her survivors settled for the *Maryland*. A seaman covered with oil tagged after Chief Gunner's Mate McCaine, calling, "What can we do, Chief?" Marine Sergeant Leo Wears found a shorthanded gun on the main deck, appointed himself a member of its crew. Ensign Bill Ingram took over another gun that seemed to need help. As he worked away, someone on the bridge hollered down, telling him that on the *Maryland* an officer was expected to wear his cap when he fought. There were plenty of them lying around, so Ingram put one on, paused long enough to wave cheerfully in the general direction of the bridge.

The *Maryland's* own crew were just as busy. Mess Attendant Arvelton Baines, who had been in the brig for fighting with civilians, worked to get ammunition topside until he passed out from exhaustion. A hulking Marine sergeant—

nicknamed "Tiny," as usual—rammed a five-inch antiaircraft gun with his hand when the hydraulic hammer got stuck. The men sweated away, oblivious of the flames blown toward them, above them, in fact all around them from the burning *West Virginia* and *Arizona*. Under the circumstances, Chief George Haitle was mildly astonished when an officer drew a gun and threatened to shoot the first man caught lighting a cigarette.

Men on the *West Virginia* were even more surprised when they too were chewed out for smoking. The ship was now a sea of flames—ammunition exploding everywhere, bullets and shells flying all over the place. Everything aft of the fore-mast was lost in choking smoke. Abandon ship had been ordered, and her port bow was level with the water, when Ensign Thomas A. Lombardi arrived from shore leave around 8:50. He stepped aboard and stood rooted in his tracks—could this litter of clothing, bedding, bodies, and debris be the same neat deck he had left the night before?

It was no weirder a picture than the one he made himself. As he pitched in to help the wounded, he was still wearing his white dinner jacket, black tie, and tuxedo pants. They didn't matter, but he needed something far more effective than the black evening pumps he still wore. Then a miracle—he stumbled over a pair of rubber boots lying on deck. And an even greater miracle (for Lombardi was an old Syracuse football player with frame and feet to match)—they were size 13, a perfect fit.

On the signal bridge, Ensign Delano also had an unexpected windfall in the way of apparel—he picked up the only helmet he ever found that fitted. He clapped it on and checked two idle machine guns mounted forward of the conning tower. They seemed in good shape, so he recruited a young officer, a seaman, and Mess Attendant Doris Miller to get them going. The first two would do the firing; Miller would pass the ammunition. Next time Delano looked, Miller had taken over one of the guns and was happily blazing away

The big steward had no training whatsoever in machine guns, and at least one witness felt he was a bigger menace than the Japanese. But there was nothing wrong with his heart, and it was the only time Delano had ever seen him smile, except the day he won that big fight as the *West Virginia's* heavyweight boxer.

As fast as men could be spared, Delano packed them off to help the *Tennessee* alongside. Others thought of it themselves and crawled across on the ten-inch hawsers. When a *Tennessee* gun captain asked one *West Virginia* ensign what fuse setting to use, he got an impatient reply: "To hell with fuse settings —shoot!" More shells sailed off for downtown Honolulu.

Everyone at least agreed there was no time for technicalities. Captain Charles E. Reordan fought the *Tennessee* in his Panama hat. Crew members gladly recruited Private Harry Polto, a soldier who happened to be visiting aboard, and assigned him to a five-inch gun. Men tossed scores of empty shell cases overboard with carefree abandon, forgetting completely the swimmers struggling alongside. But through all the scorn for details, the seaman's prerogative to gripe was carefully preserved. Few seemed to mind Yeoman Duncan grumbling that his new whites had been ruined by a broken steam pipe.

Even the twisted, burning *Arizona* still showed signs of fight. Boatswain's Mate Barthis and most of those still living stood on the fantail, dropping life rafts to the men in the water. Coxswain Forbis gave a hand until Barthis said nothing more could be done. Then he dived in—his watch stopped at 8:50. Radioman Glenn Lane was already in the water, had been swimming ever since the big explosion blew him overboard. He could have reached the shore easily but wanted some more interesting way to stay in the fight.

Suddenly he saw it right before his eyes. The *Nevada* was swinging out . . . getting under way . . . moving down the harbor. He paddled over to meet her. Someone tossed him a line, yanked him aboard. Two other *Arizona* seamen were hauled up the same way, and all three were assigned to a five-inch gun on the starboard side. The *Nevada* steamed on down the channel, gliding past the burning wrecks, proudly heading for the sea.

It seemed utterly incredible. A battleship needed two and a half hours to light up her boilers, four tugs to turn and pull her into the stream, a captain to handle the whole intricate business. Everybody knew that. Yet here was the *Nevada*—steam up in 45 minutes, pulling away without tugs, and no skipper at all. How could she do it?

She had certain advantages. It might normally take two and a half hours to get up steam, but two of her boilers were already hot. One was the boiler that normally provides power for a ship at her mooring. Ensign Taussig had lit the second during that last peacetime watch, planning to switch the steam load later. Now his efficiency paid off. Both boilers had plenty of steam—giving the *Nevada* some 90 minutes' jump in getting away. Hard work in the fire room made up the difference.

And four tugs might normally be needed to ease the ship out, but in a pinch their role could be filled by a good quartermaster. The *Nevada* had a superb one—Chief Quartermaster Robert Sedberry.

It was the same with leadership. Captain Scanland and his executive officer might be ashore, but the spark was supplied by Lieutenant Commander Francis Thomas, the middle-aged reservist who was senior officer present. As damage control officer, Thomas was down in central station when he heard that the engine room was ready. He put a yeoman in charge of central station, vaulted up the tube to the conning tower, and took over as commanding officer.

Chief Boatswain Edwin Joseph Hill climbed down to the mooring quay, cut loose an ammunition lighter alongside, and cast off. The *Nevada* began drifting away with the tide, and Hill had to swim to get back on board. But after 29 years in the Navy, he wasn't going to miss this trip.

In the wheelhouse Sedberry backed her until she nudged a dredging pipeline strung out from Ford Island. Then ahead on the starboard engines, astern on the port, until the bow swung clear of the burning *Arizona*. Now ahead on both engines, with just enough right rudder to swing the stern clear too. She passed so close, Commander Thomas felt he could almost light a cigarette from the blazing wreck.

So she was on her way—and the effect was electric. Photographer J. W. Burton watched from the Ford Island shore . . . Lieutenant Commander Henry Wray from 1010 dock . . . Quartermaster William Miller from the *Castor* in the sub base—but wherever men stood, their hearts beat faster. To most she was the finest thing they saw that day. Against the backdrop of thick black smoke, Seaman Thomas Malmin caught a glimpse of the flag on her fantail. It was for only a few seconds, but long enough to give him an old-fashioned thrill. He recalled that "The Star-Spangled Banner" was written under similar conditions, and he felt the glow of living the same experience. He understood better the words of Francis Scott Key.

It was less of a pageant close up. All kinds of men compose even a great ship's crew, and they were all there on the *Nevada*. As the Japanese planes converged on the moving ship, Seaman K. V. Hendon spied a pot of fresh coffee near the after battle dressing station; he paused and had a cup. A young seaman stood by one of the five-inch casemate guns, holding a bag of powder close to his chest—he explained that if he went, it was going to be a complete job. One officer beat on the conning tower bulkhead, pleading, "Make them go away!" Ensign Taussig, his left leg hopelessly shattered, lay in a stretcher near the starboard antiaircraft director. Turning to Boatswain's Mate Allen Owens, he remarked, "Isn't this a hell of a thing—the man in charge lying flat on his back while everyone else is doing something."

As the *Nevada* steamed on, all the Japanese planes at Pearl Harbor seemed to dive on her. At 1010 dock, Ensign

David King watched one flight of dive bombers head for the *Helena,* then swerve in mid-attack to hit the battleship instead. Another group shifted over from Drydock No. 1. Soon she was wreathed in smoke from her own guns . . . from bomb hits . . . from the fires that raged amidships and forward. Sometimes she disappeared from view, when near-misses threw huge columns of water high in the air. As Ensign Delano watched from the bridge of the *West Virginia,* a tremendous explosion erupted somewhere within her, blowing flames and debris far above the masts. The whole ship seemed to rise up and shake violently in the water.

Another hit on the starboard side slaughtered the crew of one gun, mowed down most of the next group forward. The survivors doubled up as best they could—three men doing the work of seven. It was all the more difficult because Chief Gunner's Mate Robert E. Linnartz—now acting as sight-setter, pointer, and rammerman—had himself been wounded.

In the plotting room far below, Ensign Merdinger got a call to send up some men to fill in for the killed and wounded. Many of the men obviously wanted to go—it looked like a safer bet than suffocating in the plotting room. Others wanted to stay—they preferred to keep a few decks between themselves and the bombs. Merdinger picked them at random, and he could see in some faces an almost pleading look to be included in the other group, whichever it happened to be. But no one murmured a word, and his orders were instantly obeyed. Now he understood more clearly the reasons for the system of discipline, the drills, the little rituals, the exacting course at Annapolis, the gold braid—all the things that made the Navy essentially autocratic but at the same time made it work.

The *Nevada* was well beyond Battleship Row and pretty far down 1010 dock when she encountered still another obstacle. Half the channel was blocked by a long pipeline that ran out from Ford Island to the dredge *Turbine,* lying squarely in midstream. Somehow Quartermaster Sedberry snaked between the dredge and the shore. It was a fine piece of navigation and a wonderful arguing point for Captain August Persson of the dredge. The Navy had always made him unhook the pipeline every time the battleships came in or out, claiming there wasn't enough room to pass. Captain Persson had always claimed they could do it if they wanted. Now he had his proof.

The Japanese obviously hoped to sink the *Nevada* in the entrance channel and bottle up the whole fleet. By the time she was opposite the floating drydock, it began to look as though they might succeed. More signal flags fluttered on top the Naval District water tower—stay clear of the channel. Still lying in his stretcher near the starboard director, Ensign Taussig was indignant. He was sure they could get to sea. In fact, he felt the ship was all right—she looked in bad shape only because someone down below was counterflooding her starboard bow instead of stern. Sitting by his five-inch casemate gun, Marine Sergeant Inks had different ideas. He had been in the Corps forever and knew trouble when he saw it. He was gloomily muttering that the ship would never get out.

In any case, orders were orders. Thomas cut his engines and nosed her into Hospital Point on the south shore. The wind and current caught her stern and swung her completely around. Chief Boatswain Hill, who had cast off a long 30 minutes before, now went forward to drop anchor. Then another wave of planes dived on the *Nevada* in one final, all-out fling. Three bombs landed near the bow. Hill vanished in the blast—the last time Thomas saw him, he was still working on the anchor gear.

It was now nine o'clock, and the hour had come for the ships in drydock—the flagship *Pennsylvania* in Drydock No. 1, with the destroyers *Cassin* and *Downes* lying side by side just ahead of her; the destroyer *Shaw* in the new floating drydock a few hundred yards to the west.

The three ships at the main drydock fought under a special

handicap. The water had been pumped out, dropping their decks to a point where the high sides of the drydock blocked most of the view. This was noticed right away by George Walters, a civilian yard worker operating a traveling crane that ran on rails along the side of the dock. From his perch 50 feet up, Walters saw the first planes dive on Ford Island. Like everybody else he thought it was a drill and caught on only when he saw the PBYs crumble.

He looked down and realized that the men lolling in the sun on the *Pennsylvania, Cassin,* and *Downes* were aware of none of this. He yelled but nobody paid attention. He threw a wrench, but that only made them angry. As the attack spread all over the harbor, they finally understood.

When the Japanese turned their attention to the *Pennsylvania,* Walters decided to capitalize on the ship's predicament. He devised a unique defense. He ran his crane back and forth along the ship, hoping to protect it and ward off low flying planes. A forlorn hope perhaps, but after all this was a crane taking on an air force.

At first, Walters' contribution infuriated the *Pennsylvania* gunners, who felt he was only spoiling their aim. Gradually they learned to use him. They discovered that, sitting in their trough, they couldn't see the planes soon enough anyhow. The crane's movements at least gave them a lead on where a plane might next appear. Then they could set their guns and be ready when it came. Walters was just completing his transition from goat to hero when a Japanese bomb blasted the dock, putting him out of business.

It, of course, made no real difference: planes were swarming on the drydock from every direction. On the *Pennsylvania,* Gun Captain Alvin Gerth pumped out shells directly over the heads of the next gun crew forward. He had adjusted the gun to shoot a little below the safety cutout, and every time he fired, the blast would knock down the other gun captain. He in turn would jump up, run back, and kick Gerth in the seat of his pants. This went on and on.

On the *Pennsylvania*, too, there was a new jauntiness in the air. Electrician's Mate James Power took time out for a quick glance at his home-town paper, the Odessa, Texas, *Times*. He just had to know the score of the big Thanksgiving game between Odessa High and Midland. When he saw that Odessa had won for the first time in ten years, he jumped and hollered with joy.

More bombs rained down, and Captain Charles Cooke of the *Pennsylvania* began to worry about the drydock gate. He realized that a direct hit would let in a rush of water, pushing his ship into the destroyers lying ahead. To guard against this, he ordered the drydock partially flooded and sent Lieutenant Commander James Craig to tighten up the mooring line. Craig carried out the job in nimble, skillful fashion . . . paying no attention to the bullets that whipped the ground around him. He seemed to live a charmed life. At 9:06 he stepped back on board, just in time to be killed by a 500-pound bomb that shattered the starboard casemate he was passing through.

Boatswain's Mate Robert Jones rushed up to help the men hit by the blast. He gently pulled a blanket over one seaman who was obviously dead. The man thrashed out with both hands, yanked the blanket from his face: "I've got to breathe, ain't I?"

The dock was flooding fast when yard worker Harry Danner suddenly realized he had left his lunch tin down in the pit. He started back but was too late. It was sailing away into the *Cassin* and *Downes*, carried along by the inrush of water, just the way Captain Cooke figured a loosely moored battleship might do. When Danner finally reached the top of the dock, the *Pennsylvania* was still smoking from her bomb hit. He decided she could use some help and rushed up the gangplank. After a brief encounter with the duty officer, who couldn't grasp the idea of a civilian manning a gun, he got on board and joined one of the five-inch antiaircraft crews.

As the *Pennsylvania* fought on, a record player could be

heard in one of the ship's repair shops. It had apparently
been on when the attack started, and no one bothered to
turn it off. Now, in the midst of this early-morning nightmare,
it repeated over and over again the pleasant strains of Glenn
Miller's "Sunrise Serenade."

Up ahead the *Cassin* and *Downes* seemed to catch everything that missed the *Pennsylvania*—a bad hit at 9:06 . . .
another at 9:15. By the time the drydock was flooded, both
destroyers were heavily on fire. Explosions racked their decks,
and a big blast ripped the *Cassin* at 9:37. She sagged heavily
to starboard and rolled slowly over onto the *Downes*. Seaman
Eugene McClarty got out from under just in time, and as he
streaked onto the drydock, another bomb crashed behind
him, shaking the gangway loose. It fell into the drydock as
McClarty pulled one sailor to his feet; but two other shipmates were too late, and plunged on down into the blazing
caldron.

On the quarter-deck of the *Downes* a single sailor hung on,
manning a .50-caliber machine gun. Watching from the
Pennsylvania, Gunner's Mate Millard Rucoi wondered how
long any man could stand that kind of heat. He soon had
his answer. As the flames swept closer, the sailor seemed to
have a harder and harder time keeping his head up. Finally
he dropped to his knees, head down, but with one hand still
hanging on the trigger of the gun. That's the way Rucoi last
saw him when the flames and smoke closed off the view.

The *Shaw* was having just as much trouble in the floating
drydock to the west. A bad hit around 9:12 . . . fire spreading toward her forward magazine . . . a fantastic explosion about 9:30. It was the Fourth of July kind—a huge
ball of fire ballooned into the air; bits of flaming material arched and snaked across the sky, trailing white
streamers of smoke behind. Once again the whole harbor
paused to take in the scene. Seaman Ed Waszkiewicz watched
from the Ford Island seaplane ramp, nearly half a mile
across the bay. At this distance he knew he was at least safe

—until he looked up at the sky. One of the *Shaw's* five-inch shells was tumbling end over end, arching directly at him. He dived behind a fire truck as the shell hit the concrete ramp several feet away. It didn't explode, merely bounced a hundred yards along the ramp and clanged into one of the hangars.

Ensign David King also took in the show from his station on the *Helena.* The gun mounts, mattresses, and bodies flying through the air reminded him strangely of the dummies and clowns fired from a gun in a circus. Only this time, he mused, no one would land in a net.

By now many of the planes were shifting over to the seaplane tender *Curtiss,* lying off Pearl City on the other side of Ford Island. A little earlier the *Curtiss* had clipped a bomber, which crashed into her starboard seaplane crane—perhaps the war's first kamikazi. In any case, it started bad fires, and these may have attracted the pilots hungry for a new kill.

Sealed in the transmitter room, the *Curtiss'* four radiomen couldn't see any of this, but they could hear the bombs coming closer and they could feel the ship shudder from near-misses. Radioman R. E. Jones was on the battle phones and couldn't move, but the other three could and did. James Raines squatted between the transmitters; on his left crouched Dean B. Orwick; right in front of him, Benny Schlect—three men packed together in a space 30 inches wide.

Raines never really noticed any noise—the incredible thing was the hole that suddenly appeared in the deck right in front of him and no hole above. How could a bomb do this without coming through the overhead?

Then he noticed his left shoe was missing . . . then that Schlect was dead and Orwick hurt. The room filled with smoke as Jones ran over to help. Together they got Orwick to the door, undogged it, and laid him outside. Jones went back to try to move Schlect, and Raines stayed with Orwick. There was little he could do—a shot of morphine . . . a tourniquet . . . a few comforting words. Orwick asked quietly, "My foot's gone, isn't it?" Raines said yes it was, but everything would be all right. Corpsmen were there now, and they carried Orwick away. To his deep sorrow, Raines later learned that Orwick didn't pull through. Also, he was quite surprised to hear that he had broken his own back.

On the beleaguered *Raleigh*, Captain Simons watched the bomber crash into the *Curtiss* around 9:10, saw another plane in the same formation let go two bombs at his own ship. The first missed; the second was a perfect strike. It landed aft between a couple of gun crews . . . grazed an ammunition ready box . . . passed through the carpenter shop . . . through a bunk on the deck below . . . through an oil tank . . . through the bottom of the ship . . . and exploded in the harbor mud.

The *Raleigh* took a bad list to port, and from then on the battle was to keep from capsizing. The first step was to get rid of all topside weight. The planes went off on a scouting trip; everything else went over the side—catapults, torpedo tubes, torpedoes, booms, ladders, boat skids, chests, stanchions, anchors, chains, rafts, boats, everything. All the time Captain Simons kept a yeoman busy with pencil and paper, carefully plotting where everything fell, so it could be recovered later. Then he got some pumps from the Navy yard, another from the *Medusa* . . . stuffed life belts into the holes . . . borrowed four pontoons . . . warped a lighter alongside. He also found time to send Carpenter R. C. Tellin with an acetylene torch to help Commander Isquith investigate some mysterious tappings coming from inside the hull of the overturned *Utah*.

While this work was getting under way, the *Raleigh* never stopped firing. Captain Simons thought his 1.1 guns had a lot to do with the plane that struck the *Curtiss* . . . another that crashed north of Ford Island . . . two more that fell near Pearl City . . . and a fifth that blew to bits in mid-air.

But there always seemed to be more—Simons watched another plane bomb the *Dobbin,* moored with her destroyers off the northern end of Ford Island. The bomb just missed the big tender, exploding off her starboard side. But a near-miss could do a lot of damage. Shrapnel slashed across her afterdecks, gouging the mainmast and smokestack . . . ripping a whaleboat to splinters . . . wrecking a refreshment stand . . . cutting down the crew at No. 4 gun.

Twenty-two-year-old Fireman Charles Leahey watched the blood trickle around the corner of the gun mount, and he thought about the Navy planes that drowned out the sound track every night there was a movie: "They always come around when we're having a show; where in the hell are they now?"

Just east of the *Dobbin,* the hospital ship *Solace* was getting ready for a busy day. In the main operating room, Corpsman T. A. Sawyer was breaking out drapes, getting the sterilizers started. Near him a nurse stood by, occasionally peeking through an uncovered porthole at the battle raging outside. Heavily influenced by the movie comedian Hugh Herbert, she would exclaim, "Woo-woo, there goes another one!" whenever a Japanese plane was hit. Another nurse was tearing long strips of adhesive for holding dressings in place after surgery; a near-miss rocked the ship, hopelessly entangling her in the tape. Out on the promenade deck a chief petty officer, clearly all thumbs, was hard at work rolling bandages.

A steady stream of launches began unloading the injured, sometimes escorted by shipmates and friends. Seaman Howard Adams of the *Arizona* helped carry a buddy to the operating room. He took one look, turned to the rail, and was sick. But he came back, asking if he could help. It was a big decision, for that day he chose his career—medical work.

A few hundred yards north of the *Solace,* the destroyer *Blue* cast off and moved slowly down the east channel toward the harbor entrance. As she passed Battleship Row,

Machinist's Mate Charles Etter helped toss lines to the men still swimming in the water. Some were hauled aboard, but others couldn't hang on and fell back into the thick oil that spread over the channel. There was no time to stop for a second try.

The men on the blazing wrecks cheered the *Blue,* and the other destroyers, too, as one by one they glided by. As fast as they built up enough steam to move, they got under way— no waiting for skippers who still were on shore. The *Blue* sailed under Ensign Nathan Asher—his complement of officers was three other ensigns. *Aylwin* was handled by Ensign Stanley Caplan, a 26-year-old University of Michigan chemistry graduate in civilian life.

Outside the harbor, Quartermaster Frank Handler watched and waited on the bridge of the *Helm.* For 40 long minutes she and the *Ward* had been out there alone. For all anyone knew, the whole Japanese Navy might be just over the horizon. When would help come?

The first destroyer burst out of the channel just about nine o'clock. It was the *Monaghan,* fresh from her brush with the midget. Then the *Dale*. . . the *Blue* . . . the *Henley* . . . the *Phelps* . . . men soon lost track. Perhaps not much to start a war on, but there would be more to follow.

With a splintering crash Admiral Leary's special mahogany gangway sailed over the side of the cruiser *Honolulu* and broke in half on the dock. It was the first thing 30 men headed for, when word was passed to strip the ship of unnecessary equipment and prepare to sortie.

The *Honolulu* was warped alongside the *St. Louis* in one of the Navy Yard's finger piers, and as the men cast off the lines between the two ships, a dive bomber charged down on them. Seaman Don Marman ducked under the narrow space between the Number 1 turret overhang and the deck— there was about a two-foot clearance. He never knew so many men could get in so small a spot at one time. The bomb plunged through the concrete pier on the port side and exploded next to the ship. It holed her oil tanks, pushed in the armor plating, and made any sortie impossible. Perhaps she couldn't have gone anyhow, for in the excitement of casting off, one man chopped away the power line to the dock. Since the *Honolulu* didn't have enough steam yet to supply her own power, this knocked out her lights and all the electrical gear for operating the guns.

The same thing happened on the *New Orleans* at the next pier. Hot cables danced on the decks, the lights went out, the ammunition hoists ground to a halt. So the men formed human chains to pass the shells and powder from the magazines to the guns. As they sweated away in the dark, Chaplain Howell Forgy did his best to encourage them. He passed out apples and oranges . . . stopped and chatted with the gun crews . . . patted Seaman Sam Brayfield on the back . . . told him and the others that they couldn't have church this morning, but "praise the Lord and pass the ammunition."

Nobody chopped the cables that gave the *St. Louis* power, but nothing else was spared. A shopfitter dropped down over the starboard side and burned off the gangway with an acetylene torch. Somebody else chopped loose the water hose, leaving a 12-inch hole in the side of the ship; Shopfitter Bullock welded a plate over it in ten minutes. Up on the bridge, Captain George Rood signaled the engine room, and the *St. Louis* began backing out at 9:31 A.M.—the first cruiser under way.

As she pulled out, Captain Rood called down to the wardroom and requested some water. The strafing was especially heavy, but Pharmacist's Mate Howard Myers took pitcher and glass up the exposed ladder and served it properly. For the men on the *St. Louis,* nothing was too good for Captain Rood.

As the ships began pulling out, the men caught on shore raced to get back in time. Admiral Anderson tore through red lights in his official car. Admirals Pye and Leary got a

lift from Richard Kimball, manager of the Halekulani. When
Admiral Pye noticed one of the B-17s circling above, Kimball
recalls him exploding: "Why they've even painted 'U. S.
Army' on their planes!"

Ensign Malcolm of the *Arizona* drove his overnight host,
Captain D. C. Emerson, and as the car hit 80, the old captain
tapped Malcolm on the shoulder: "Slow down, kid; let's
wait'll we get to Pearl to be killed."

Commander A. M. Townsend of the *St. Louis* chugged
along as best he could in a '29 jalopy. Entering the main
gate, he gradually overhauled a man running toward the
fleet landing. It was a friend he hadn't seen for ten years.

Yeoman Charles Knapp of the *Raleigh* and eight other
sailors piled into a taxi at the YMCA. Hundreds of others
caught in town did the same. Manuel Medeiros' Pearl Harbor Drivers' Association kept at least 25 cabs shuttling back
and forth—Driver Tony Andrade alone took six loads.

There were no taxis on the dusty country road where
Lieutenant (j.g.) Clarence Dickinson stood after parachut-
ing from his burning plane. He resorted to an old American
expedient—hitchhiking. After a while a pleasant middle-aged
couple drove up in a blue sedan. Mr. and Mrs. Otto F. Heine
were on their way to breakfast with friends at Ewa, completely unaware of any battle. It took a few minutes to grasp
that this hitchhiker was different—that he had just been shot
down from the sky. At first Mrs. Heine said politely that there
really wasn't time to help him, that their friends were already
waiting. But when the facts sank in, she bubbled with solici-
tude. Mr. Heine drove on toward Pearl without saying much.
As they rounded the closed end of the harbor, strafers raked
the car in front of them. He took one hand from the wheel
and gently pushed Mrs. Heine's head under the dashboard.

The strafing planes were doing their best to paralyze the
traffic now converging on Pearl Harbor. Radioman Frederick
Glaeser wasn't convinced it was a real attack until a dive
bomber gave his car a burst about three miles from the main

gate. Jack Lower, a civilian electrician, was a little closer
when the planes got interested in him. He was with a group
of other workers, riding in the back of an open truck. Every
time a plane approached, the men would hammer on the cab
roof, the truck would stop, and everybody would scatter—
behind palm trees, in the bushes, under the truck, anywhere.
When the plane was gone, they would jump back in and
start off again. It took 20 minutes to go two miles.

Even more snarls resulted from the average American's
knack of creating his own traffic jams. A vegetable truck
stalled and tied everybody up for a while. Word spread that
a Fifth Columnist did it, but more likely some frightened
farmer was trying to get to safety. About a mile from the
gate everyone was held up by cross-traffic slanting off to
Pearl City and Ewa. Two columns of cars sat bumper to
bumper. In one line Commander Jerry Wiltse, skipper of the
Detroit, waited in his station wagon. The car opposite him
in the other line contained an old chief and his wife. When
Wiltse's line began to move, it was too much for the chief.
He jumped out and got in the commander's car, as his abandoned wife screamed, "But you know I don't know how to
drive!"

Near the gate Commander Wiltse stopped again, this time
picked up an aviator running alongside the road. It was
Lieutenant Dickinson, who had left the Heines' sedan at the
Hickam turn-off rather than involve them in the Pearl Harbor jam. When Wiltse reached the officers' club landing,
Dickinson hopped out and eventually found still another ride
to the landing opposite Ford Island.

Out on the main road, more jams developed. Finally Captain A. R. Early, commanding Destroyer Squadron One,
jumped from his car and told a traffic cop to throw all cars
without Pearl Harbor tags into the cane fields. To his surprise, the officer did it. There had been a feud between the
Navy and the local police for years, and ordering that cop

around was the only pleasure Captain Early got from the day.

When he finally reached the Navy Yard, Captain Early methodically put his car in its assigned parking space, carefully locked it, and then went on to the officers' landing. It was full of men trying to get rides to their ships . . . trying to find where their ships were . . . and, in some cases, trying to grasp the fact that their ships were gone forever. Commander Louis Puckett, supply officer of the *Arizona*, sat in the grass near the landing with four or five other officers from the ship. They just didn't know what to do.

A steady stream of launches ferried the men out to the ships and Ford Island. Commander McIsaac, skipper of the *McDonough*, gave Admiral Anderson a lift to the *Maryland* in his launch. The admiral marveled at the fearless, debonair spirit of the men in the launch; Commander McIsaac was pretty impressed by the admiral's own poise—he even had the little bag he liked to carry ashore.

It wasn't always possible to show such poise. A dive bomber screeched down on Seaman P. E. Bos' launch, and it was a tossup whether to dive overboard or stay in and take a chance. Bos was one of the ones who stayed—the machine gun missed them by inches. Shrapnel holed the crash boat taking Seaman Joseph Smith to the *Dale*, and the men abandoned it by the old coal docks. They all switched to another boat and chased the *Dale* out to sea. They never caught up with her. Nor did Lieutenant Commander R. H. Rogers, skipper of the *Aylwin*, who pursued Ensign Caplan in a motor launch.

It was all right with Captain Early, the squadron commander. He only wanted to get his destroyers out, and he was quite satisfied as he stood on the shore at 9:30 and saw that he now had on his hands more unemployed skippers than ships.

Pearl Harbor had no monopoly on hectic efforts to get back to duty. The men who pulled on their clothes, gulped coffee, kissed their wives, and dashed off to Hickam were just as frantic. Master Sergeant Arthur Fahrner couldn't find any collar insignia, and Mrs. Fahrner didn't help—she was forever handing him a tie.

"We're at war," he kept telling her; "you don't wear a tie to war."

First Lieutenant Warren Wilkinson meticulously pinned on all his insignia but started his car too abruptly. His chin banged against the horn button and it stuck. For a few seconds he drove on toward his squadron hangar, then couldn't stand it any longer. In the midst of the bombing and strafing he got out, raised the hood, and disconnected the horn.

By the time Wilkinson reached the hangar area, the dive bombing had tapered off and the field seemed strangely quiet. Sergeant H. E. Swinney wandered out from Hangar 11 and joined a group of men looking at a big bomb crater nearby. Sidewalk superintendents appeared everywhere, inspecting the damage, taking uneasy sidelong glances at the bodies that sprawled on the grass.

Near the barracks across the street, Sergeant Robert Hey put down his Tommy gun for a breather; then about nine o'clock he got word that the high-level bombers were coming. At first he couldn't see them at all. Then he saw antiaircraft bursts to the south above Fort Kamehameha. Soon he could make out the planes themselves—tiny specks far above the puffs of smoke. They were flying in a perfect V, never had to break formation. As he watched the planes pass over, he heard a faint rustling sound which kept getting louder. He yelled a warning, dived across the sidewalk into the dirt next to the barracks. Two of the bombs hit less than 50 feet away, and the fragments whizzed by, just over his head.

There was no warning in Hangar 15. Sergeant Swinney had returned from his inspection tour and was checking a damaged B-18. Under the plane some men were changing a bullet-riddled tire. Nearby the crew chief was explaining how

Official U.S. Navy Photo

A wall of antiaircraft fire meets the second Japanese attack wave as it arrives over Pearl Harbor.

Courtesy of Brigadier General Kendall Fielder

The *Nevada* starts her famous sortie. At top, she pulls out from her berth at the north end of Battleship Row. In the middle, she glides by the blazing *Arizona*. At bottom, she heads on down the channel. These pictures are believed never before published.

The *Nevada* ends her sortie aground at Hospital Point. The current has swung her around, so that she now faces back up the channel; but the flag still flies from her fantail—reminding at least one witness of Francis Scott Key and "The Star-Spangled Banner."

After the raid the *Nevada* pulled clear of Hospital Point and backed across the harbor, where she is shown beached on the firm sand of Waipio Peninsula.

Late in the attack, bombs rained down on the destroyers *Cassin* and *Downes* in Drydock No. 1, wrecking both ships. Some of their machinery was later salvaged.

Drydock No. 1 after the raid, showing the *Cassin* rolled over on the *Downes*, with the battleship *Pennsylvania* just astern. At the right is Crane 51, which civilian yard worker George Walters ran back and forth alongside the *Pennsylvania*, trying to ward off low-flying planes.

Toward the end of the attack the destroyer *Shaw* exploded in the floating drydock. Debris sailed through the air, and one five-inch shell arched half a mile across the channel, landing on Ford Island a few feet from where this picture was taken.

The cruiser *St. Louis* passes the upturned hull of the *Oklahoma*, on her way to sea around 9:40 A.M. She was the only large ship to get out during the attack. To the left, burning oil from the *Arizona* drifts down toward the torpedoed *California*.

The burning oil engulfs the *California's* stern at ten o'clock. "Abandon ship" has just been sounded, and the men are swarming down her side, making their way to Ford Island.

Official U.S. Navy Photo

Photo by Andrew Kirk

Four American participants: (*top left*) Captain Mervyn Bennion of the battleship *West Virginia,* who died on his bridge; (*top right*) Bandleader Oden McMillan of the battleship *Nevada,* who led his men in "The Star-Spangled Banner" as the attack began; (*below, left to right*) Lieutenants Kenneth Taylor and George Welch, who together bagged seven of the eleven planes shot down by Army pilots.

United Press Photo

Four Japanese participants: (*top left*) Commander Mitsuo Fuchida, who led the attacking planes; (*top right*) Commander Shin-Ichi Shimizu, who organized the necessary supplies: (*lower left*) Commander Takahisa Amagai, who was flight deck officer on the *Hiryu;* and (*lower right*) Rear Admiral Ryunosuke Kusaka, who made a key decision that led to Japanese withdrawal after the raid.

Official U.S. Navy Photo

Ten-ten dock after the attack, showing the capsized mine layer
Oglala. Her seams were sprung by the torpedo that holed the cruiser
Helena (*at left*), but there are men who still claim that the ancient
mine layer really "sank from fright."

Official U.S. Navy Photo

The torpedoed *Raleigh*. In his successful battle to stay afloat, Captain Simons jettisoned everything movable, wangled extra pumps,
stuffed life belts into the leaks, borrowed four pontoons and the
lighter that can be seen alongside. Astern is the capsized *Utah*.

Pearl Harbor from Admiral Kimmel's lawn. It was here the admiral stood, watching the first blows fall on Battleship Row in the background. Photographed around noon by a neighbor, Mrs. Hall Mayfield.

During the attack forty Navy shells, but only one Japanese bomb, fell on Honolulu proper. This scene shows one of the areas hit by accident.

U.S. Army Photograph

While barracks burn in the background, the American flag—shredded
by machine-gun fire—still flies at Hickam.

Courtesy of Roger Pineau

At top, Japanese painting commemorates the heroes of the midget submarine attack. Missing from the picture is Ensign Kazuo Sakamaki, the only member of the group who survived. He beached his sub after the raid and became U. S. Prisoner of War No. 1. Ensign Sakamaki's photo appears at the left.

Ensign Sakamaki's midget sub lies beached off Bellows Field, where it was discovered the morning after the raid.

The midget sub rammed by the *Monaghan* was also recovered. It was eventually dredged up from the harbor bottom and is shown here, about to be used as filling for a new sea wall. The bodies of its two crewmen are still inside.

Long after the raid was over, rescuers clambered about the hull of the upturned *Oklahoma,* cutting through to the crew members trapped inside. Thirty-two men were ultimately pulled out alive—the last some thirty-six hours after the big ship rolled over into the Pearl Harbor mud.

the wheel was assembled to some mechanic who had chosen this particular moment to learn his trade a little better.

The bomb plunged through the roof with a deafening roar. The hangar went totally dark, and Swinney thought to himself that this was the end. Then the smoke and dust cleared, and an encouraging shaft of sunlight streamed through the hole. So he was alive after all—but he now had the terrifying feeling that everyone else had completely disintegrated. It was an illusion, however, for after he had groped his way out—alive but unhurt—he saw several dead lying where he had stood.

Corporal John Sherwood was working outside Hangar 15 when the high-level attack began. For some reason he headed for Hangar 13—a poor choice, since it had not yet been damaged. But he found a good corner in the engineering office, lay down, and waited. For the first time that morning he even had a chance to pray. As the bombs thundered closer, two young lieutenants—both crying like children—ran in and tried to dislodge him. Sherwood told them to go find their own corner. The hangar took several hits, and Sherwood realized he was in the wrong place after all. He ran out, leaving the lieutenants free to take any corner they liked.

At the base hospital Nurse Monica Conter also had to fight for her cover. Lying on the floor with other nurses, doctors, and patients, she had seized the galvanized lid of a brand-new garbage can and was holding it over herself. Someone kept tugging, trying to get it, but she managed to hang on.

Once again, good shelter was at a premium. Private Bert Shipley joined four men in a manhole who were firing at the planes with rifles. They knew they wouldn't hit anything, but it made them feel better. Some cooks in the bombed-out mess hall holed up in the freezer. More bombs hit the building, and they were all killed by concussion. Private John Wilson dived under the edge of a one-story frame building. He was glad to find the shelter, but it was even better to be there with his buddy Stan Koenig. He kept thinking if he was going to be killed, he wanted some friend to know about it.

Hickam couldn't do much about the high-level attack, but when the dive bombers returned around 9:15, the men fought bitterly with what was left. One airman manned a .30-caliber machine gun in the nose of a damaged B-18 and kept firing until the plane burned out from under him.

As fast as men fell at the machine guns on the open parade ground, others rushed out to take their place, and then they too would fall. Old-timers, like Sergeant Stanley McLeod . . . young recruits, like Corporal Billy Anderson of Virginia, lay there side by side. A few men somehow survived. Staff Sergeant Chuck Middaugh, a burly 235-pound roughneck always in trouble, grabbed a .30-caliber machine gun in his hands and fired away until he got a plane.

On the ball diamond two men set up a machine gun on a tripod between home plate and some trees along the edge of the field. It looked like a pretty safe spot with a good field of fire. Suddenly a wave of planes roared out of the sky, saturating the field with bombs . . . scoring a direct hit on the gun . . . killing both men instantly. They had no way of knowing that the Japanese were sure the ball diamond was clever camouflage for Hickam's underground gasoline system.

Other bombs did put the system briefly out of action. They hit a water main near its real location, and since it worked by water, it could no longer operate. The damage was serious, but Staff Sergeant Guido Mambretti, the Petroleum Section's maintenance man, bet Major Robbins a bottle of cognac he could get the thing working again. He did too, but he still hasn't collected.

While Mambretti toiled away, volunteers rushed up and moved several loaded tank trucks out of the storage area. Other volunteers turned up who had no connection at all with Hickam. Major Henry Sachs, an ordnance specialist passing through on his way to the Middle East, dashed to the Hickam cargo pier and took on the job of unloading the SS *Haleakala*, a munitions ship full of dynamite and hand grenades. A Hawaiian motorcycle club appeared, on the hunch they might be useful. One of the members, a huge, fat native, attached himself to Captain Gordon Blake, who was trying to disperse the B-17s. They made quite a pair bouncing along the runway—the Hawaiian resplendent in *aloha* shirt and rhinestone-studded cyclist belt; Blake seated behind, hanging on for dear life.

In between motorcycle trips, Blake tried to guide the B-17s still in the air to someplace where they could land. One put down on Kahuku Golf Course; another suddenly turned up at Wheeler. As the pilot climbed out, Colonel William Flood, Wheeler base commander, told him dead-pan to get back up and find the Japanese fleet. The pilot looked depressed: "You know, Colonel, we just came over from California."

"I know, but, son, there's a war on."

"Okay," the pilot sighed, "if I can just get a cup of coffee, we're off."

Flood couldn't bear to keep the joke going any longer, told the pilot to get some sleep and he'd use him tomorrow.

It's hard to say how many planes really did get up from Wheeler. General Howard Davidson, commanding all the fighters, thought about 14. Air Force records indicate no P-40s and only a handful of worthless P-36s. Perhaps the general was counting in Welch and Taylor, who landed three different times for ammunition and then took off again.

These two were having a busy morning. After reaching Haleiwa, they had rushed straight for their planes. No briefing or checking out—Major Austin, the squadron commander, was off deer hunting, and they didn't bother with Lieutenant Rogers, the acting CO. They just took off.

First they flew down to Barbers Point, where the Japanese

were said to be rendezvousing. Nobody there. Just as well—
there hadn't been time to belt up enough ammunition. So
they dropped by Wheeler to get some more. By nine o'clock
they were almost ready to take off again when seven Japanese
planes swept in from Hickam for one last strafing run. Welch
and Taylor gunned their P-40s and flew straight at them.
Both men were up and away before the Japanese could give
chase. Instead, the P-40s managed to get into the Japanese
flight pattern and shot two down—one was the plane that
grazed the eucalyptus tree behind Mr. Young's laundry.

Then Welch and Taylor headed for Ewa, where they had
seen some dive bombers at work. It was a picnic. Between
them, they got four more before Taylor had to land with a
wounded arm. Welch stayed on and picked off another.

They had plenty of cooperation from the ground. Ewa,
like the other airfields, was bounding back. Sergeant Emil
Peters and Private William Turner manned a machine gun
in one of the disabled planes; Sergeant William Turrage
manned another; Sergeant Carlo Micheletto was firing too,
until a low-flying strafer cut him down.

A piece of shrapnel nicked Lieutenant Colonel Larkin, the
base commander, and Captain Leonard Ashwell became another casualty when he sped off on a bicycle to check some
sentries. He forgot about a barbed-wire fence, careened into
it, and arose somewhat the worse for wear. As Pharmacist's
Mate Orin Smith treated the wounded, he himself was hit in
the leg. He patched it up and rejoined his ambulance, which
eventually accumulated 52 bullet holes.

On the windward side of the island, Bellows tried to
fight back too, but a group of Japanese fighters gave the men
little chance. Lieutenant George Whitman took up the first
P-40 about nine o'clock, and six Zeroes got him right away.
Next they pounced on Lieutenant Hans Christianson before
he could even get off the ground. Then they caught Lieutenant Sam Bishop just after he took off. He managed to

crash-land into the ocean and swim to safety. The attack was over before anybody else tried his luck.

None of the planes could even fly at nearby Kaneohe. The horizontal bombers took care of everything the strafers missed. Then there was a lull, and the bull horn bellowed for all hands to fight the hangar fires. Aviation Ordnanceman Henry Popko joined a wave of men who surged forward to answer the call. Halfway there, the strafers met them, and the men had to scatter. Seaman "Squash" Marshall raced for cover with the bullets snapping at his heels. It was another of those classic dashes that seemed to catch everyone's fancy. He actually outran a Zero for 100 yards, according to one man, then zagged to one side as the bullets plowed straight on. The men who watched set up a huge cheer—just as if someone had hit a home run at a ball game.

By 9:30 the dive bombers were back, but now everybody seemed to have some kind of gun. Ensign Hubert Reese and his friend Joe Hill sat in their clump of weeds, popping away with rifles. Others had mounted machine guns on water pipes, on tail-wheel assemblies, on anything. Big, friendly Aviation Machinist's Mate Ralph Watson cradled a .30-caliber weapon in his arms, kept it going long after he was hit.

Suddenly all guns began to concentrate on one fighter. Everyone had the same idea at once—it seemed like telepathy. Smoke began pouring from the plane. It kept on diving, motor wide open. Ensign Reese wondered if the pilot was crazy—it was hard to believe they were actually shooting one down. But it was true. The pilot never pulled up. As he hit the hillside, there was a cloud of dirt, a burst of fire in the air, and the plane completely disintegrated.

It wasn't the gunfire or bombing; it was the door that swung to and fro from the concussion that bothered Lieutenant Commander McCrimmon as he operated on his third patient at the Kaneohe dispensary. The man had a bad stomach wound, and Commander McCrimmon just couldn't concentrate. Finally he had a sailor hold the door steady so he could finish the operation.

He was scrubbing up for the next patient, when he suddenly realized what he had done. The door had distracted him so much he had sewed the wrong parts of the stomach together. Before the man came out of ether, McCrimmon had him back on the table, reopened the wound, corrected the error, and sewed him back up.

Three miles away, Mrs. McCrimmon stood in the yard beside the house, watching the planes dive on Kaneohe. The McCrimmons lived on the beach, and pretty soon 27 Japanese planes came flying down the coast, so low overhead she could see the white scarves worn by some of the pilots. Her two little boys waved and waved, but none of the pilots took any notice.

The Navy families on Ford Island had no time to watch and wave. The war surged all around them. Some huddled in the strong, concrete Bachelor Officers' Quarters. Others brought Cokes and cigarettes for the men swimming ashore. Chief Albert Molter turned his home into a first-aid station. He had about 40 there—all soaking wet, all covered with oil, most suffering from shock, some burned very badly. He borrowed a first-aid kit from the big crate the Boy Scouts used as a clubhouse. He broke open the canned fruit and juice he was keeping in case of emergency. He raided the linen closet for sheets, towels, blankets. He gave away all his civilian clothes—he didn't expect to wear them soon again anyhow.

At the senior officers' housing quarters on Makalapa, Mrs. Mayfield and her maid Fumiyo went next door, to sit out the raid with Mrs. Earle. They were soon joined by Mrs. Daubin, the only other wife on the hill. In the Earles' living room the women built a makeshift shelter by turning over two big bamboo sofas and piling all the cushions on top. In the course of this construction work Fumiyo whispered: "Mrs. Mayfield, is it—is it the *Japanese* who are attacking us?"

Mrs. Mayfield told her yes, as kindly as she could.

The shelters and defensive measures varied from house to house. Mrs. Mary Buethe, a young Navy wife, grabbed her children and hid in a clothes closet every time she heard a plane. At the Hickam NCO quarters, Mrs. Walter Blakey preferred her bathtub. Mrs. A. M. Townsend filled her tub with water and some pails with sand at her house in the "Punchbowl" section of town. Mrs. Claire Fonderhide, whose husband was at sea in a submarine, sat with a .45 automatic and waited. Mrs. Joseph Cote's little boy Richard used his gun too—he filled a water pistol with green paint and fired it all over the place.

Mrs. Carl Eifler, wife of an infantry captain, couldn't find her little boy. He had completely disappeared, the way little boys will. She busied herself, packing a suitcase, filling jugs with water, emptying the medicine cabinet, all the time wondering where her child could be. He finally sauntered home, but things looked so black by now, her thoughts were following a new channel: "Do I allow myself and my boy to be taken or do I use this pistol?" While she tried to make up her mind, she washed the bathroom woodwork.

Mechanically, other wives also went about their daily chores. Mrs. William Campbell, whose husband was in the Navy, carefully washed his whites and was hanging them on the line when an amazed Marine sentry saw her and chased her to cover.

Mrs. Melbourne West, married to an Army captain, did her ironing. She had this incessant feeling that her husband would need a lot of clean shirts if there was going to be a war.

As the service families numbly adjusted to war, much of Honolulu carried on as usual. The people in close touch with the Army and Navy knew all too well by now; but for the thousands with little contact—or perhaps out of touch for the week end—the world was still at peace.

Mrs. Garnett King called her local garage: could they wash the family car? They said they were pretty busy right now, but could take it in the afternoon. While explosions boomed in the distance, civilian Arthur Land helped transfer 20 gallons of salad from a caterer's truck to his own car—this was the day of the Odd Fellows Picnic. As the noise gradually subsided later in the morning, Mr. Hubert Coryell remarked to another civilian friend, "Well, that was quite a show." Then he went off to archery practice.

People somehow ignored the most blatant hints. Second Lieutenant Earl Patton, off duty for the day, was out with friends in a chartered fishing boat when a plane plunged into the sea nearby. Assuming it was an accident, they headed for the spot to help the pilot. Then another plane swooped by, strafing them with machine guns. One of the party was even nicked, but Patton charitably assumed the second plane was just attracting their attention to the first.

Walking home from church, Mrs. Patrick Gillis saw the side of a house blown in . . . figured someone's hot-water heater had exploded. Mrs. Cecilia Bradley, a Hawaiian housewife, was in the yard feeding her chickens when she was wounded by a piece of flying shrapnel. She thought it was somebody deer hunting in the hill behind her house. Mrs. Barry Fox, living on Kaneohe Bay, awoke to the sound of explosions, looked out, and saw strange-looking planes circling the base, flames boiling up, a wall of smoke. She decided it was a smoke-screen test. She didn't become really alarmed until she turned on the radio at 9:30 and didn't hear the news. That was the time she always listened to the latest bulletins, and this morning there was only music.

One by one they gradually learned. Stephen Moon, a Chinese 12-year-old, was at early mass on Alewa Heights—he planned to go on to the school club picnic at Kailua. Near the end of the service his mind began to wander, and his eyes strayed out the window. Right above Alewa Heights two planes were in a dogfight. But that was common, and he thought nothing of it. He glanced a little to the left and saw black puffs of smoke in the sky. That was strange—he knew the practice ammunition always left white smoke. As his attention drifted back to church, he became aware of a completely changed atmosphere. Right in the middle of the service, parents were slipping in and hurriedly taking their children out. He knew there was something wrong now, for the grownups were whispering and acting very mysteriously. The mass ended, and instead of the regular hymn, everyone stood and sang "The Star-Spangled Banner."

But it was all too deep for Stephen. Still thinking about the picnic, he strolled off toward a friend's house. Then a plane roared down from the sky and shot at a car driving toward Pearl. He spun around and ran home as hard as he could. His mother was glad to see him too; she had been looking for him everywhere.

Captain Walter Bahr, one of Honolulu's crack harbor pilots, also noticed the black puffs of smoke as he went out to meet the Dutch liner *Jagersfontein*, inbound from the West Coast. The pier watchman explained it was probably the Navy practicing. But he had a curious sense of urgency when he boarded the ship at 9:00 A.M. No one told him anything, but he sensed danger in all that noise and smoke. He brought her in fast. They were about at the harbor entrance when bombs began to fall, and columns of water shot up around them. Since Holland was already at war, the *Jagersfontein* was armed and the Dutch crew knew exactly what to do. They peeled the canvas covers from their guns and began firing back—the first Allies to join the fight.

A scrappy young flyweight boxer named Toy Tamanaha listened to the gunfire as he walked down Fort Street to the Pacific Café for breakfast around 9:30. He didn't think much of it—there was always shooting going on. Somebody in the café said it was war, but Toy remained unconvinced. Then somebody said all carpenters had been called to their jobs. Toy's close friend Johnny Kawakami was a carpenter, so Toy advised him to get going, and sauntered off himself to the Cherry Blossom Sweet Shop on Kukui Street for a popsicle. He was just inside when it happened—a blinding blast hurled him right out into the street. Vaguely he heard yells of help. He noticed his left leg was missing. He thought, "Maybe I only lost one leg." He was wrong—the other was gone too—but just before he blacked out, it was nice to hear someone come up and say, "Toy, you'll be all right."

There were explosions all over Honolulu—the Lewers and Cooke Building in the heart of town . . . the Schuman Carriage Company on Beretania Street . . . Kuhio Avenue near Waikiki Beach . . . a Japanese community out McCully Street. Four Navy Yard workers were blown to pieces in their green '37 Packard at the corner of Judd and Iholena. The same blast killed a 13-year-old Samoan girl sitting on her front porch watching the gunfire.

Many of the people in Honolulu later believed the explosions were bombs. (Some of them still do: in the words of one witness, "As the years pass, the bombs keep dropping closer.") But careful investigation by ordnance experts revealed that antiaircraft shells caused every one of the 40 explosions in Honolulu, except for one blast near the Hawaiian Electrical Company's powerhouse.

In their excitement, gunners on the *Tennessee, Farragut,* and probably other ships forgot to crank in fuses. Other ships like the *Phoenix* had trouble with bad fuses. Others like the *Nevada* fired some shells that exploded only on contact. As one *Nevada* gunner explained, if the shell missed, it still had to come down somewhere.

But even the shells didn't do a complete job of waking up Honolulu. At Police Headquarters, Sergeant Jimmy Wong's blotter reflected a good deal of consternation about the explosions—the first was a complaint phoned in at 8:05 by Thomas Fujimoto, 610 E Road, Damon Tract, that a bomb had interrupted his breakfast. But there were also more familiar entries, indicating normalcy far into the morning: "10:50 A.M. A man reported to be drunk and raising trouble at Beretania and Alapai."

As the uproar increased, Editor Riley Allen of the *Star-Bulletin* gallantly struggled to get out an extra. He was a fast, if unorthodox, typist. This morning he was at his best— one hand punching madly, the other rooting out the keys that piled up in a hopeless snarl. The papers were on the street by nine-thirty; the headline: WAR! OAHU BOMBED BY JAPANESE PLANES.

At her home on Alewa Drive, Mrs. Paul Spangler heard the newsboys shouting "Extra!" She had no ready change and debated whether to raid the money she set aside for church collection. She finally did.

Back at the *Star-Bulletin* office, Editor Allen got a call from an exasperated policeman. Would he recall his newsboys—they might get hurt. They had gone to Pearl Harbor to sell their papers.

Anyone still in doubt learned by radio. At 8:04 KGMB had interrupted a music program with the first word—a call ordering all Army, Navy, and Marine personnel to report to duty. The call went out again at 8:15 and 8:30. By then KGU was on the air too, calling doctors, nurses, defense workers to report for emergency duty. The first explanation came at 8:40—"A sporadic air attack has been made on Oahu . . . enemy airplanes have been shot down . . . the rising sun has been sighted on the wingtips." This only confused many listeners, who thought "sporadic" meant "simulated."

It took time to sink in, even if a person understood "sporadic." Some people tuned in between bulletins, heard only a gospel service or the incidental music that was used to fill in. Reassured, they turned off their sets again. Others harked back to Orson Welles' broadcast of the Martian invasion . . . they weren't going to bite on this one.

Webley Edwards was at KGMB by now and did his best to gear the station to the crisis. But it was hard to drop some peacetime practices that were done almost by instinct. The records played between the bulletins sometimes seemed hideously incongruous. Once the song was "Three Little Fishes," a popular melody of the time that began:

"Down in the meadow in the iddy biddy poo
    Thwam thwee little fishies and a mama fishie too."

As people continued to phone, continued to ask questions, continued to be doubtful, Edwards grew more and more exasperated. Finally a call came from Allan Davis, a prominent businessman and member of the station's Board of Directors. When he too asked if it wasn't really a maneuver, Edwards burst out, "Hell, no, this is the real McCoy!"

Davis sounded really shocked . . . mumbled "Oh, oh," and hung up.

The effect was so impressive that Edwards decided to use the same words on the air. That might be the way to get people to really believe the news. Starting about 9:00 A.M., he repeated again and again that the attack was the "real McCoy" —so often that most people who listened to the Honolulu radio that day remember little else.

As they sat by their sets, many of the listeners found themselves paying special attention to the tone in Edwards' voice. They seemed to be searching for some extra clue that would tell them how serious the situation was. Mrs. Mayfield thought he sounded hoarse with suppressed excitement. Joan Stidham thought he was terse.

Edwards had at least one very disappointed listener. Sitting in the wardroom of the Japanese carrier *Akagi*, Commander Shin-Ichi Shimizu tuned in the radio to see how the Americans would react to the attack. Soon the announcer began breaking in with orders for different units to report to duty, but his voice was calm, and in between times the station continued to play music. It was a big anticlimax. The announcer wasn't nearly as excited as Shimizu.

Chapter X

"I Want Three Volunteers: You, You, and You"

HIGH ABOVE PEARL HARBOR, the last raiders wheeled off to the west, vanishing as mysteriously as they had appeared. On the *Nevada*, Commander Thomas moved off the mud of Hospital Point, and with the aid of tugs backed across the channel to the hard, sandy bottom of Waipio Peninsula. Word was passed releasing the men from battle stations, and Musician C. S. Griffin began groping his way up from the third deck forward. When he finally stepped into the bright morning sun, he glanced at his watch—it said 10:00 A.M.

For the first time men realized what a strain it had been. Boatswain's Mate K. V. Hendon ran into one of his best friends, who had been working a five-inch gun all morning. The man was so dazed he couldn't recognize anybody—all he could still see were planes. The men in the antiaircraft gun shack passed cigarettes around, omitting as usual the clean-cut member of the team, who, as far as they knew, didn't smoke or drink or even take coffee. Shakily he said, "I think I'll have one of those."

Ensign John Landreth emerged from the port antiaircraft director, felt a curious numbness. Training and discipline had seen him through, but in the back of his mind the question kept revolving, "What is this really? A dream, perhaps, or is it really me shooting at other men and they shooting at me? What is this really?"

Perhaps indeed it was a dream, thought Pfc. John Fisher, a young MP at Fort Shafter. And when no one was looking, he even pinched himself, hoping he would wake up and find everything was all right. As Staff Sergeant Frank Allo surveyed Hickam's smoldering wreckage, he felt like a small boy looking at his dog lying in the road after it had been hit by a car: it was simply unbelievable that such a thing could have happened.

But there was little time for reflection. A man had to think fast just to stay alive on the burning, sinking ships. When the *Oglala* finally rolled over on her port side at ten o'clock, Admiral Furlong slid down toward the low side of her deck. He showed the timing of a trapeze artist, hopping nimbly ashore as the side of the deck rolled flush with the edge of 1010 dock. Officially, it was said the *Oglala's* seams had been sprung by the torpedo that holed the *Helena;* but there are men who still claim the old Fall River boat really "sank from fright."

Across the channel, it was time to abandon the *West Virginia* too. Fires raged out of control around the conning tower and foremast, igniting the paint work, trapping Lieutenant Ricketts and the others still on the bridge. Ensign Lombardi got a hose going, and a seaman played it on the little group. Then Ensign Hank Graham tossed up a line, and the men came down hand over hand to the deck. Ensign Delano was cut off from the rest; he finally crawled forward on the searchlight platform and used the turrets as a giant stepladder to reach the deck. He jumped overboard and swam for Ford Island, trying to keep ahead of the oil burning on the water.

"Help! Help! I can't swim any farther," called a familiar voice somewhere behind. It was an old chief petty officer, known to be a poor swimmer. Delano was now too weak to do any towing, but at least he could encourage the man. As he turned his head, the old chief thrashed by, arms and legs flying through the water, still yelling that he couldn't swim any longer. He reached shore five minutes before Delano.

Ensign Jacoby plunged off the *West Virginia's* forecastle, still wearing shoes, uniform, and even cap. He swam under the burning oil, emerged beyond it, and headed for a launch from the *Solace*. But his waterlogged clothes dragged him down, and the burning oil crept after him faster than he could swim. A sailor in the launch dived in to help—apparently forgetting that he couldn't swim at all. They were rapidly drowning each other when someone else in the launch knotted some sheets together, tossed out the improvised line, and dragged them both in. It was close—as they were hauled aboard, the bow of the launch was already starting to burn.

Ensign Vance Fowler, the *West Virginia's* disbursing officer, abandoned ship far more stylishly. He pushed off in a raft and moved swiftly to shore, using his cash ledger as a paddle.

Seaman George Murphy had no use for a paddle, trapped in the dispensary of the overturned *Oklahoma*. He and some 30 others were in a triangular-shaped air space with about a three-foot ceiling. Carpenter John A. Austin had a flashlight, and they played it around, trying to figure out where they were. None of them yet understood that the ship had turned over . . . that the tile overhead was really the deck.

For over an hour they didn't even try to get out. They could cling to a coaming around the tile without constant swimming, and it seemed best just to wait. They all assumed help was on the way—never dreaming they were far below the surface of Pearl Harbor.

Time went on, and they began to wonder. Eventually someone kicked a porthole under the water, and the men took turns ducking down and investigating it. They were still reluctant to dive through, because many of the ship's portholes led only to void space, and nobody wanted to get trapped that way.

Finally there was no choice. The air grew foul, and it was

clear they couldn't live in the compartment. One by one they began squeezing through. It was a slow process. The porthole hung the wrong way (that's how they learned the ship was upside down), and every time anybody tried it, one man had to go under water and hold it open for the other to escape.

Nothing could help the man who first found the porthole. He was simply too big for the 14-inch opening. He bobbed back up, completely broken. Several others began shouting and calling out prayers.

Seaman Murphy barely made it. He had to try three times before he finally squeezed through and kicked out from the ship. He popped to the surface and was picked up by a launch from the *Dobbin* shortly after ten o'clock. The thing that really amazed him was not his escape but the scene in the harbor. The men in the compartment had all assumed that the *Oklahoma* was the only ship damaged.

There was no problem abandoning the *California*. As the burning oil drifted down the harbor, engulfing her stern, Captain Bunkley gave the order at 10:02 A.M., and the men swarmed ashore. But the wind blew the burning oil clear, and by 10:15 Captain Bunkley was trying to get everybody on board again to fight the fires. Yeoman Durrell Conner abandoned his efforts to evacuate some files, and watched an officer appeal to the men on shore. He gave quite a pep talk, saying that the *California* was a good ship, and if they would all come back and fight the fire, he thought they could save her.

The men seemed a little slow, and Conner had an inspiration. Noting the flag had not been raised, he grabbed a seaman and together they hoisted the colors on the fantail. A big cheer went up, and men began streaming back.

The upturned *Utah* was of course beyond hope, but the banging within her hull told Commander Isquith that he might at least save someone trapped inside. So he worked away with Machinist Szymanski, who knew all about weld-

ing . . . Watertender H. G. Nugent, who knew the structure
of the ship's hull . . . and Chief Motor Machinist Terrance
MacSelwiney, who wanted so much to help. Strafers bothered
them at first, but then the raid died down, and cutting outfits
arrived from the *Raleigh* and *Tangier*. They traced the noise
to the dynamo room and went to work. After an hour they
had an 18-inch hole and yelled to whoever was inside to
stand clear so they could pound the plating in. When they
finished, out popped Fireman John Vaessen, who had kept
the lights going until it was too late to get out.

Unlike the men in the *Oklahoma* dispensary, Vaessen
knew right away that the ship was upside down. He set out
for the bottom with a flashlight and an open-end wrench for
tapping signals. When he reached the double bottom, he had
to undo 20 bolts to get through to the outer skin of the ship.
Here he enjoyed a stroke of the incredible luck that sometimes helps a brave man in danger. His wrench just happened to fit the bolts.

Down in the plotting room of the *Nevada*, Ensign Merdinger wasn't yet trapped, but his agile mind began thinking
along those lines. The room was five decks down. The regular lights were out, and the emergency system cast a weird
green glow. The ventilation was gone, and to save their
breath, the men lay down, phones strapped to their heads.
Some were stripped to the waist; others still wore their shirts.
Merdinger noted the beads of sweat glistening in the pale
green light and thought what a dramatic movie it would
make of men trapped in a submarine.

His thoughts passed through various phases, taking the
form of silent prayers. At first he hoped he wouldn't be
wounded. As things grew worse, he hoped that, if wounded,
he at least wouldn't be permanently crippled. Finally, he
reached the point where he was completely prepared to give
his life. He prayed only that he might die—and he knew he
was guilty of a cliché—like an officer and a gentleman, an
inspiration to his men.

Certainly there was nothing to encourage him in the reports drifting down from above. The plotting room was a sort of clearinghouse for information, and all the news seemed bad. He heard about the *Oklahoma*—and the *Nevada* started to list. The *Arizona* blew up—and fire spread close to the *Nevada's* magazines. Every disaster on the other ships seemed to stalk his own. And now, to top it off, the bridge was calling for anyone who could speak Japanese. That suggested even more unpleasant possibilities.

Topside, Ensign John Landreth heard the radio say the Japanese were landing on Diamond Head. Radioman Peter La Fata of the *Swan* picked up even worse news: they had taken Waikiki.

The danger lay not to the east but to the west, according to rumors heard by the *Arizona* survivors at the Navy receiving station—in fact, 40 Japanese transports were off Barbers Point. It was worse than that; they were already landing men at Waianae Beach, someone told Gunner's Mate Ralph Carl on the *Tennessee*.

Others claimed the Japanese were really landing to the north. At the Navy Yard, civilian worker James Spagnola heard that the entire north shore was lost. At Schofield, Lieutenant Roy Foster got word that a major assault would be launched on Schofield and Wheeler within 30 minutes to an hour. Marine Sergeant Burdette Odekirk heard that Schofield had fallen.

As if seaborne invasion wasn't enough, other reports spread that Japanese paratroopers were raining down from the skies—at Nanakuli Beach to the northwest . . . in the sugar-cane fields southwest of Ford Island . . . in the Manoa Valley, northwest of Honolulu. A man could spot them by the rising sun sewed on their backs . . . or by the red patch on the left breast pocket . . . or by the rising sun shoulder patch. In any case, they were wearing blue coveralls.

At Kaneohe, Mess Attendant Walter Simmons lost no time taking off his own blue dungarees. Orders were to change to

khakis, but Simmons and most of the others had none. So they
boiled vats of strong coffee, dipped in their whites, made
khakis that way. Next report—the Imperial Marines landing
on the west shore were in khaki. All hands change to whites.
Later, the force landing to the east was in white. Back to blues.

These were not men who had lost their heads—they were
acting on the best information available. An official Army
circuit monitored at Kaneohe reported sampans landing
troops at the Navy Ammunition Depot . . . transports to
the north . . . eight enemy battleships 70 miles away. The
Navy's harbor circuit was just as active. On the *Vestal* Radioman John Murphy logged in messages that Japanese troops
were landing on Barbers Point . . . paratroopers dropping
in Nuuanu Valley . . . Honolulu's water supply had been
poisoned.

Later, some radiomen felt the Japanese must have used
Army and Navy frequencies, filling the air with false reports.
But the outgoing logs of the various official message centers
show that most, if not all, of the traffic was authentic:

1146. From Patwing. Enemy troops landing on north
shore. Blue coveralls, red emblems.

1150 COM14 to CINCPAC. Parachutists landing at Barbers Point.

In the present frame of mind, small incidents were easily
misinterpreted and then exaggerated. The *Helm* firing at
the midget quickly became a Japanese task force bombarding
the shore. When Fort Kamehameha, under the same illusion,
began firing at the *Helm*, that just proved it.

It was the same with the paratroopers. Lieutenant Dickinson and Ensign McCarthy bailing out of their flaming planes
were quickly spotted as two . . . 20 . . 200 enemy soldiers. And once the idea was planted, the power of suggestion
did the rest. Honolulu Police Headquarters got a frantic
call that parachutists were landing on St. Louis Heights. Sergeant Jimmy Wong called for a National Guard Company

and sent up Patrolman Albert Won. The Guard never arrived, but Won got there, armed with a .38. Luckily, all he found was a kite dangling from a tree.

Even more frightening reports were now pouring in. The local Japanese were rising, it was said, and Fifth Columnists were on the loose. Sergeant Wong got a call at 10:08 A.M. that two Japanese with a camera were on Wilhelmina Rise. He sent a squad car, found only a couple out walking. McKinley High School reported saboteurs—two pedestrians happened to be passing the ROTC building. But the stories spread faster than they could possibly be disproved or checked.

On the seaplane tender *Swan*, Radioman Peter La Fata heard that Japanese drivers were making milk deliveries at Pearl Harbor with radio transmitters concealed in the cans to beam in the raiding planes. Mrs. McCrimmon heard that it happened at Kaneohe. Private Sydney Davis heard that it was Hickam where the milk trucks went, and that they drove up and down the hangar line knocking the tails off planes. Lieutenant George Newton also heard it was Hickam, and that a warrant officer shot the milkman when he boasted, "Well, I guess we Japanese showed you." Radioman Douglas Eaker heard that the sides of the truck dropped down and Japanese machine-gunners sprayed the field.

Other rumors described how the local Japanese had ringed Oahu with white sampans—presumably to show the pilots that they had the right island. Additional reports told of arrows cut in the cane fields, helpfully pointing out the last 20 miles to Pearl Harbor. Under the circumstances, Corporal Maurice Herman wasn't surprised when all communications failed at his infantry outfit's command post. Along with everybody else, he supposed Japanese saboteurs had cut the wires. A careful check uncovered the break right next to the command post itself. A soldier pitching a pup tent had needed a piece of line and cut it out of the unit's radio coil.

Worst of all was the report that Fifth Columnists were

poisoning the water. At Ewa the post dentist spread a canvas cover over the base water tower, hoping to frustrate the saboteurs. Others heard that it was too late for preventive measures—the water was already contaminated. Mrs. Arthur Gardiner, a Navy wife, tried in vain to find a way of explaining the development to her thirsty two-year-old. Fifteen-year-old Jackie Bennett ordinarily didn't drink much water—now she was never thirstier. Storekeeper H. W. Smith heard the rumor after he had already quenched his thirst. He became violently ill and thought what an inglorious way to die for his country. They were quite clinical at the Hickam dispensary. Lieutenant Colonel Frank Lane had Saliva, the hospital's mascot dog, nailed up in a crate, then gave him a pan of water to see what would happen. The experiment failed when Saliva wouldn't drink. As the day wore on, people grew too thirsty to care . . . drank the water anyhow and, of course, with no aftereffects.

In all the excitement over spies and Fifth Columnists, almost everybody forgot about Japanese Consul General Kita. Soon after the attack started, Reporter Lawrence Nakatsuka of the *Star-Bulletin* went up to the consulate to get Mr. Kita's comments, but had little luck. The consul simply said he didn't believe there was an attack. Nakatsuka returned to the office, and as soon as the *Star-Bulletin's* extra was run off, he went back to the consulate with a copy. If it wasn't adequate evidence, it might at least be a conversation piece.

Meanwhile AP Correspondent Eugene Burns tipped off the police that the consulate might be worth checking. Robert Shivers, the local FBI man, was urging the same thing, having failed to interest the Army or Navy in the matter. It was around eleven o'clock by the time Lieutenant Yoshio Hasegawa—the ranking officer of Japanese ancestry—got under way. He arrived with two carloads of men, to find Consul General Kita lounging around the back yard in slacks, with Reporter Nakatsuka still trying to get his story.

Hasegawa and Kita entered the consulate, and other police

trailed along. Smoke was coming from behind a door, and somebody asked if there was a fire. "No," Kita replied vaguely, "there is just something in there."

The police opened the door and found two men burning papers in a washtub on the floor. They stamped out the fire and managed to salvage one brown Manila envelope full of documents. The tour continued, and behind another door they found three or four men getting ready to burn five burlap bags of torn papers.

Hasegawa posted guards around the place, confined the staff to one room, arranged for the files to be turned over to the FBI and the Navy. He also asked Kita and the other Japanese the same question that Reporter Nakatsuka had found so fruitless: did they know there was a Japanese attack on? No, they said solemnly, they didn't know.

By now there was time for some of the formalities of war. At 11:15, 72-year-old Governor Joseph E. Poindexter read his Proclamation of Emergency over KGU. His voice trembled badly, but perhaps with good reason. One antiaircraft shell had already exploded in his driveway; another pursued him to his office, bursting in a corner of the Iolani Palace grounds. As the governor wound up his address, a phone call came through from the Army—get off the air; another attack was expected. The Governor's aides complied with startling vigor—seizing him the instant he finished, rushing him down the stairs, into his car and away. The bewildered old man thought he must have done something very wrong on the broadcast and was under arrest.

In line with the Army's order, both KGU and KGMB went off the air at 11:42. This was done, of course, to prevent enemy planes from beaming in on either station— undoubtedly a sound precaution, considering how useful Commander Fuchida had found the local radio. But the silence only added to the misery of the service wives, huddled in their homes, lonely and afraid, longing for any news Most of them kept their radios on—listening for the occasional orders that still came over the regular stations, or to the harrowing Fifth Column rumors that poured out over the police radio.

Many of the wives were more than ready when formal evacuation of the Hickam and Pearl Harbor areas began at noon. The plan had been worked out long in advance—buses and car pools would take everyone to the University of Hawaii, the various public schools, the YWCA; from there the evacuees would eventually move in with families in safe areas who had volunteered to take them. Now the plan was under way—loud-speaker cars rolled up and down the post streets, bellowing out instructions to get ready.

At Hickam, Mrs. Arthur Fahrner struggled to load her five children into the family car. But as fast as she packed them in, they would squirm out and run back to the house for some favorite toy. Finally she was ready, but just as she started off, ten-year-old Dan came running out—nearly left behind when he made a last trip back for his swimming medal.

At Schofield, Major Virgil Miller's family faced a different problem. A Chinese GI had been sent to their house to tell them where to go, and the Millers weren't taking any chances. Fearing he was a Japanese soldier in American uniform, they made him shout his instructions through the locked front door.

Some didn't wait for formal evacuation. When the planes strafing Pearl City discouraged 11-year-old Don Morton from searching for his brother Jerry, their mother lost no time. She just scooped Don up in the family car and set off for the landing where the boys had been fishing. There was no traffic, but she kept honking the horn anyhow. It finally stuck, adding to the general din. Near the landing, Jerry emerged from the algarroba bushes and climbed aboard—a Marine corporal had pushed him to safety just before getting hit himself.

The boys' mother, Mrs. Thomas Croft, now turned the

car around and headed for Honolulu. Huge explosions mush-roomed up on their right. Thoroughly frightened, they stopped the car and ran into a cane field. There they sat for the next two hours . . . hands over their ears, heads be-tween their knees. Whenever a plane flew by, Mrs. Croft would ask one of the boys to peek up and see if it was Ameri-can. It never was.

Everyone had a different idea of safety. Mrs. Gerald Jacobs, another Pearl City Navy wife, stopped her car and stuck her head in a roadside bush—literally like an ostrich. Mrs. James Fischer stayed indoors, just as her husband told her to do. But for only so long. She suddenly put on her winter coat, ran out of Navy Housing Unit 1, and began hitchhiking to Hon-olulu. A family friend saw her and gently led her back to shelter. Mrs. E. M. Eaton joined a group of friends who zigzagged madly down back roads to the Mormon church.

They took along the things they thought would come in handy. Mrs. Joseph Cote picked up a loaf of bread, a can of tuna, but no can opener. Mrs. Arthur Gardiner carried a blanket, a can of orange juice, a butcher knife, and *Pinocchio*. She and her two children then joined several other families in a small railroad ravine behind the junior officers' duplex quarters. *Pinocchio* proved a good idea, and the mothers took turns reading. Occasionally there were interruptions—cheers when a plane crashed, or an uneasy glance at some low-flying strafer—then back to the book again. As they read, they all did their best to keep a calm voice.

Once some Hawaiian-Japanese cane-field workers came running down the railroad track toward the little group. Everyone was sure the local Japanese had captured the island and this was the end. Mrs. Gardiner grabbed her butcher knife, ready to fight for her children's lives. But the field hands veered off and hid in the cane, equally terrified that they were going to be massacred by an aroused white popula-tion.

The local Japanese had heard some rumors too. Early in

the day the story spread that the Army planned to kill them all. Later this was modified—the Army would kill only the men, leave the women to starve.

There had already been some close calls. Five Japanese civilians had an especially narrow escape walking down a peaceful country road far from the fighting. They were spotted by Seaman George Cichon and several shipmates, who were bringing a truckload of ammunition from Lualualei Depot to Pearl Harbor. The driver stopped the truck, and one of the sailors wanted to shoot them all. At first the others more or less agreed, but suddenly someone said, "We are not beasts; these people had nothing to do with the attack." The men sheepishly got back in the truck and drove on. During the entire incident not a word was spoken by the five Japanese.

It was in this atmosphere that a young Japanese named Tadao Fuchikami, wearing a green shirt and khaki pants, chugged up to Fort Shafter on a two-cylinder Indian Scout motorcycle at 11:45 A.M.

Fuchikami was an RCA messenger, and this morning his day had started as usual. He punched in around 7:30, killed a little time, then picked up a batch of cables waiting for delivery. The cables had been put in pigeonholes, according to district, and Fuchikami just happened to take Kalihi, which included Fort Shafter. He thumbed through the envelopes to plan his best route—one of his first stops should be the doctor on Vineyard Street. The one for Fort Shafter would come later—there was nothing on the envelope that indicated priority; it just carried the two words "*Commanding General.*"

As he started off, he was already aware of the war. The operator had said something about planes dogfighting; he could see the antiaircraft burst over Pearl; he knew it was the Japanese. But war or no war, he still felt he had his regular job to do.

This morning it was slow going. The traffic was a nightmare. Then as he headed toward Shafter, he ran into a National Guard roadblock. They advised him to go home, told him they almost mistook him for a Japanese paratrooper. This was quite a jolt—Fuchikami hadn't realized how much his messenger's uniform resembled what the parachutists were supposed to be wearing. From now on he felt very conspicuous.

Next he hit a police roadblock on Middle Street. Only defense workers could get through. He rode his motorcycle on the sidewalk up to the barrier, showed the police his Shafter message, and they finally let him pass. When he got to Fort Shafter itself, he surprisingly had no trouble at all. A sentry waved him right on in. He drove straight to the message center and delivered the cable.

The message was decoded and delivered to the adjutant at 2:58 P.M. He saw that it reached General Short right away, who in turn sent a copy to Admiral Kimmel. It was a cable from General Marshall in Washington, filed at the Army Signal Center for transmission via Western Union at 12:01 (6:31 A.M., Hawaii time) and received by Honolulu RCA at 7:33 A.M., just 22 minutes before the attack. It said that the Japanese were presenting an ultimatum at 1:00 P.M., Eastern Standard Time (7:30 A.M. in Honolulu) and helpfully explained, "Just what significance the hour set may have we do not know, but be on the alert accordingly . . ."

Admiral Kimmel told the Army courier that it wasn't of the slightest interest any more and threw it in the waste basket.

He could have better used a message saying what the Japanese were up to now. They had disappeared completely. No one seemed to have the slightest idea where they had come from or where they had gone.

At first Kimmel thought they probably came from the north. He had always felt there was more possibility of an attack from the north than from the south. At 9:42 A.M. he even radioed Halsey on the *Enterprise* that there was "some indication" of enemy forces to the northwest.

But soon all the information ran the other way. At 9:50 A.M. CINCPAC reported two enemy carriers 30 miles southwest of Barbers Point. Already maneuvering in the area, the *Minneapolis* knew it wasn't so, tried to scotch the report by radioing, "No carriers in sight." The message came through, "Two carriers in sight."

At 12:58 P.M. four Japanese transports were reported to the southwest . . . at 1:00 P.M. an enemy ship four miles off Barbers Point. A bearing on a Japanese carrier, which had briefly broken radio silence, could be read as coming from either directly north or directly south. The interpreter figuratively tossed a coin, called it directly south.

Recalling that two Japanese carriers had recently been detected at Kwajalein, Admiral Halsey played a hunch that fitted in nicely with the meager intelligence available—he began concentrating his search to the south and southwest.

The ships emerging from Pearl Harbor did their best to chase down the leads. When a message arrived reporting the enemy off Barbers Point, Admiral Draemel hoisted the signal "concentrate and attack." There weren't many ships to "concentrate"—just the *St. Louis, Detroit, Phoenix,* and a dozen destroyers—but they all dashed bravely forward. They, of course, found nothing, and as they steamed on to join Halsey, they were themselves identified as the enemy by an *Enterprise* scouting plane. This generated more reports pointing to the southwest, some of which were relayed to Admiral Draemel. Without realizing it, his ships were at one point searching for themselves.

The air search was having no better luck. At first the only planes available were some old unarmed amphibians based on Ford Island. They belonged to Utility Squadron One, which performed chores like carrying mail, towing targets, and photographing exercises. Nothing else could fly, so they had to be used; but it wasn't an appealing assignment—even after rifles were provided for protection.

"I want three volunteers—you . . . you . . . and you," Chief G. R. Jacobs told three of the squadron's radiomen. Aviation Radioman Harry Mead soon found himself airborne in one of the planes. They had no luck, but they did establish that the Japanese weren't lying off Oahu. It made no difference; the rumors rolled on.

The Army couldn't get up any search planes in the early stages, but by mid-morning Major General Frederick Martin called Patwing 2 to put some bombers at the Navy's disposal. That was what he was meant to do under the Army-Navy plan for "cooperation." Nobody would give him a mission.

But General Martin heard somewhere that two carriers were south of Barbers Point, so he sent out four light bombers at 11:27 A.M. They found nothing. Then he sent some other planes a few miles to the north. They didn't find anything either. That afternoon he made one more try—this time at the Navy's request. He sent six B-17s to look for a carrier that was rumored to be 65 miles north of Oahu. They too found nothing.

On Ford Island, nine of the planes just in from the *Enterprise* were still undamaged, and Ensign Dobson rushed to get them in shape. Each one was loaded with a 500-pound bomb, and tank trucks stood by to gas them up.

The pilots waited at the command center, swapping experiences and joyfully greeting late-comers who trickled in from forced landings all over the island. Lieutenant Dickinson arrived, having hitched one last ride—this time in a launch from the Navy Yard. He was surprised at the way men who had never been particularly close now fell on one another's shoulders. One senior officer, who had always seemed a crotchety martinet, threw an arm around Dickinson and even produced a nickel, calling, "Somebody go and get this officer a cup of coffee . . ." (It was great while it lasted, but Dickinson also noted that within a couple of days relationships were back to normal.)

By 12:10 the planes were ready, the pilots climbed in, and Lieutenant Commander Halstead Hopping led them on a flight that scouted a wide sector 200 miles to the north. The right direction, but by now just a little too late.

As they returned to Pearl late that afternoon, the sun blazed unmercifully in Ensign Dobson's face. He was dead tired, and it made him so very sleepy. He tried to concentrate, but his mind kept drifting off. Could it be, he wondered, that this day was just a dream . . . that when he got back to Ford Island, he could go home to his family after all?

As the search dragged on, the best clues lay untouched. Major Truman Landon couldn't interest anybody in the Japanese planes he saw flying north when he was bringing in his B-17. Lieutenant Patriarca had seen Japanese planes flying north too, but he was so concerned about alerting the *Enterprise* that he didn't think of anything else. The Opana radar plot had quite a story to tell, but when the Navy asked the Army radar people whether they had any information on the Japanese flight in, nobody knew anything. And everyone forgot that radar not only can track planes in but also track them out. Opana carefully plotted the planes returning to the north—and the information center was manned by now—but in the excitement no one did anything with this data.

It made no difference to Commander Fuchida. The Japanese leader didn't even try to cover his tracks on the flight back to the carriers. There just wasn't enough gas for deception. As fast as the bombers finished their work, they rendezvoused with the fighters 20 miles northwest of Kaena Point, then flew back in groups. The fighters had no homing device and depended on the larger planes to guide them to the carriers.

Fuchida himself hung around a little while. He wanted to

snap a few pictures, drop by all the bases, and get some idea of what was accomplished. The smoke interfered a good deal, but he felt sure four battleships were sunk and three others badly damaged. It was harder to tell about the airfields, but there were no planes up, so perhaps that was his answer.

As he headed back alone around eleven o'clock, a fighter streaked toward him, banking from side to side. A moment of tension—then he saw the rising sun emblem. One of the *Zuikaku's* fighters had been left behind. It occurred to Fuchida that there might be others too, so he went back to the rendezvous point for one last check. There he found a second fighter aimlessly circling about; it fell in behind, and the three planes wheeled off together toward the northwest— last of the visitors to depart.

At his end, Admiral Kusaka did his best to help. He moved the carriers to within 190 miles of Pearl Harbor. He wasn't meant to go closer than 200 miles, but he knew that even an extra five or ten miles might make a big difference to a plane short of gas or crippled by enemy gunfire. He wanted to give the fliers every possible break.

Now everything had been done, and Admiral Kusaka stood on the bridge of the *Akagi* anxiously scanning the southern horizon. It was just after 10:00 A.M. when he saw the first faint black dots—some flying in groups, some in pairs, some alone. On the *Shokaku*, the first plane Lieutenant Ebina saw was a single fighter skimming the sea like a swallow, as it headed for the carrier. It barely made the ship.

Gas was low . . . nerves were frayed . . . time was short. In the rush, normal landing procedures were scrapped. As fast as the planes came in, they were simply dragged aside to allow enough room for another to land. Yet there were few serious mishaps. As one fighter landed on the *Shokaku*, the carrier took a sudden dip and the plane toppled over. The pilot crawled out without a scratch. Lieutenant Yano ran out of gas and had to ditch beside the carrier—he and his crew were hauled aboard, none the worse for their swim.

Some familiar faces were missing. Twenty-seven-year-old Ippei Goto, who this morning had donned his ensign's uniform for the first time, failed to get back to the *Kaga*. Baseball-loving Lieutenant Fusata Iida didn't reach the *Soryu*. Artistic Lieutenant Mimori Suzuki never made the *Akagi*—he was the pilot who crashed into the *Curtiss*. In all, 29 planes with 55 men were lost.

But 324 planes came safely home, while the deck crews waved their forage caps. The men swarmed around the pilots as they climbed from their cockpits. Congratulations poured in from all sides. As Lieutenant Hashimoto wearily made his way to his quarters on the *Hiryu*, everyone seemed to be asking what was it like . . . what did he do . . . what did he see.

Now that it was all over, many of the pilots felt a curious letdown. Some begged for another chance because they missed their assigned targets. Others said they were dissatisfied because they had only "near-misses." Commander Amagai, flight deck officer of the *Hiryu*, tried to cheer them up. He assured them that a near-miss was often an effective blow. Then he had an even brighter idea for lifting their spirits: "We're not returning to Tokyo; now we're going to head for San Francisco."

At the very least, they expected another crack at Oahu. Even while Commander Amagai was cheering up the pilots, he was rearming and refueling the planes for a new attack. When Lieutenant Hashimoto told his men they would probably be going back, he thought he detected a few pale faces; but, on the whole, everyone was enthusiastic. On the *Akagi*, the planes were being lined up for another take-off as Commander Fuchida landed at 1:00 P.M.—the last plane in.

When Fuchida reported to the bridge, a heated discussion was going on. It turned out another attack wasn't so certain after all. For a moment they postponed any decision, to hear

Fuchida's account. After he finished, Admiral Nagumo announced somewhat ponderously, "We may then conclude
that anticipated results have been achieved."

The statement had a touch of finality that showed the way
the admiral's mind was working. He had always been against
the operation, but had been overruled. So he had given it
his very best and accomplished everything they asked of him.
He had gotten away with it, but he certainly wasn't going to
stretch his luck.

Commander Fuchida argued hard: there were still many
attractive targets; there was virtually no defense left. Best
of all, another raid might draw the carriers in. Then, if the
Japanese returned by way of the Marshalls instead of going
north, they might catch the carriers from behind. Somebody
pointed out that this was impossible—the tankers had been
sent north to meet the fleet and couldn't be redirected south
in time. Fuchida wasn't at all deterred; well, they ought to
attack Oahu again anyhow.

It was Admiral Kusaka who ended the discussion. Just
before 1:30 P.M. the chief of staff turned to Nagumo and announced what he planned to do, subject to the commander's
approval: "The attack is terminated. We are withdrawing."

"Please do," Nagumo replied.

In the home port at Kure, Admiral Yamamoto sensed it
would happen. He sat impassively in the *Nagato's* operations
room while the staff buzzed with anticipation. The first attack was such a success everyone agreed there should be a
second. Only the admiral remained noncommittal. He knew
all too well the man in charge. Suddenly he muttered in almost a whisper: "Admiral Nagumo is going to withdraw."

Minutes later the news came through just as Yamamoto
predicted. Far out in the Pacific the signal flags ran up on
the *Akagi's* yardarm, ordering a change in course. At 1:30 P.M.
the great fleet swung about and headed back home across the
northern Pacific.

South of Oahu, Ensign Sakamaki was still trying. But despite all the vows he exchanged with Seaman Inagaki their midget sub was no nearer Pearl Harbor. A brief encounter with a reef had damaged one torpedo tube beyond repair. About noon they ran on another reef and smashed the other tube. They worked clear again, but now they had no weapon left.

"What are we going to do, sir?" asked Seaman Inagaki.

"We're going to plunge into an enemy battleship, preferably the *Pennsylvania*. We're going to crash against the ship and if we're still alive, we're going to kill as many as we can."

To Sakamaki's surprise, Inagaki bought the idea. He tightened his grip on the wheel and shouted, "Full speed ahead!" But it was no use. The afternoon turned into a jumbled series of frustrations. Sakamaki was dimly aware of trying and trying but just not getting anywhere. The sub wouldn't steer . . . the air pressure was more than 40 pounds . . . the hull reeked with the smell of bitter acid. He choked for air; his eyes were smarting; he was only half-conscious. Occasionally he could hear Inagaki sobbing in the dark, and he was crying too.

"Let's make one more try," he gasped, but the next thing he knew he saw Diamond Head off to port. It was dusk and he had wandered a good ten miles from Pearl Harbor. He was beaten and he knew it. With his last strength he set his course for the rendezvous point off Lanai Island, where he was to meet the mother sub *I-24*. Then he passed out.

Chapter XI

"Chief, My Mother and Dad Gave Me This Sword"

SUNDAY AFTERNOON, Pearl Harbor was sure of only one thing
—wherever the Japanese were, they would be back.

The *Pennsylvania*, still squatting in Drydock No. 1,
trained her big 14-inch guns down the channel mouth. Fireman H. E. Emory of the *California* teamed up with an officer
who had found an old Lewis machine gun. They made a
swivel mount from the wheel of an overturned cart and
established themselves on a mooring quay. On Ford Island,
Seaman James Layman joined a working party filling and
loading sandbags. He skinned his knuckles on the burlap,
got blisters shoveling the sand; but the situation was desperate and he worked until it was too dark to see.

At the Navy Yard a Coxey's Army of servicemen, civilian
yard workers, and 100 per cent amateurs struggled to get the
undamaged ships in condition to fight. An officer of the
Pennsylvania asked civilian yard worker Harry Danner to
help find extra men to load ammunition. There were a number of yard hands around, but even on December 7 a vestige
of protocol remained—the officer didn't feel he could give
orders to a civilian. So the two men went around together,
Danner serving as ambassador. They soon had enough volunteers, and a human chain was formed between three
loaded whaleboats and the *Pennsylvania's* ammunition hoist.
They transferred over a thousand bags of powder.

Danner next headed for the *Honolulu* to help get her engines reassembled. He had banged up a foot and thrown away his shoes, but he hobbled across the Navy Yard as fast as he could with another worker. They might as well have been the Japanese invasion force. Trigger-happy sentries were now stopping anybody not in uniform, and it took a lot of persuading to get through. But the work was finished by 10:30 that night.

At the next pier other yard workers struggled to install the *San Francisco's* antiaircraft batteries. James Spagnola clambered around the guns, still sporting the golf shoes he wore when the attack began. It was a job that normally took two weeks, but this time it was done in one day.

Through all the pounding and hammering and the clatter of pneumatic drills, a juke box blared away at the pier canteen. Most of the time it played "I Don't Want to Set the World on Fire."

There was music on the *Maryland* too—her band tooted bravely on the quarter-deck while her gunners got ready for the next attack. The *Tennessee* was just as ready, but the rest of Battleship Row—once the core of the fleet's strength—was now out of the game.

The *Arizona* sprawled twisted and burning. A small boat eased alongside her fantail; Lieutenant K. S. Masterson climbed aboard and hauled down the torn, oil-stained colors still flying from her stern. He felt they should be saved as a war memento. Quartermaster Edward Vecera replaced the *West Virginia's* battle colors with a fresh flag borrowed from another ship. He asked an officer what to do with the dirty, ragged bunting just hauled down. The officer replied that normally all battle colors were sent to Annapolis, where they would be displayed in a glass case, but this time—well, maybe it would be better to burn them. Vecera carried out the suggestion.

On the *West Virginia's* quarter-deck a devoted band of officers still fought the fires that raged throughout the ship.

Lieutenant Commander Doir Johnson looked at the melted porthole glass and thought of the limp watches painted by Salvador Dali. Against fire that hot, nothing could be done. The group was finally forced off about five o'clock. But men still lived on the *West Virginia*. Far below decks three sailors sat, hopelessly trapped in the pump room. They clung to life until the day before Christmas Eve.

It was a different story on the upturned *Oklahoma*. Little knots of men swarmed over her bottom—tracing the steady tapping that came from within . . . pounding back signals of encouragement . . . calling for more cutting equipment. Teams from the *Maryland*, the salvage ship *Widgeon*, the *Rigel*, the *Solace*, the Navy Yard, the *Oklahoma* herself worked at half a dozen different places along the huge hull.

The job wasn't just a matter of cutting a hole and pulling somebody out. The tapping echoed and reverberated through the hollow space along the keel until nobody could say where it really came from. The cutters had to make an educated guess and, once inside the hull, search out the source. They had to stumble back and forth through a dark, eerie, upside-down world . . . tapping and listening for answering taps . . . until they could pinpoint the right spot. Then more cutting to get finally through to the trapped men.

There were bitter disappointments. The first two men located were asphyxiated because the acetylene torch ate up all the oxygen. A call went out for pneumatic cutting equipment—slower but perhaps less dangerous. Julio DeCastro, a Navy Yard foreman and expert chipper, took out a crew of 21 yard hands, went to work with drills and air hammers. But a new danger arose—this slower cutting method let the trapped air escape faster than the hole could be made. As the air hissed out, the water would rise, threatening to drown the men before they could be freed. The cutters used rags, handkerchiefs, anything to keep the air from escaping too fast. They weren't always successful.

The teams lost all track of time. At one point the *Mary-*

land sent over some stew, and Fireman John Gobidas of the *Rigel* paused long enough to grab a bite. There were no spoons or plates; he just dipped his hands—foul with oil and muck—into the stew and spread it on some bread. He thought it tasted very good.

Inside the *Oklahoma* the trapped men waited. Eight seamen buried in the steering engine room set up a curious democracy. Every move or decision affecting their lives was decided by vote. Their first step was to pool their clothing and their mattresses—the room was where they always slept —and plug an air vent that spouted a steady stream of water. Next, they investigated possible routes of escape, but water gushed through every door they tried, so they voted to sit back and wait. They found some tools and banged the sides of the ship, but most of the time they just sat. They had plenty of chance to meditate, and 17-year-old Seaman Willard Beal thought of all the mean things he had ever done to anyone.

Just forward, in the passageway off the handling room of No. 4 turret, 30 other men were also waiting. They sat in their shorts, covered with oil, with one flashlight between them. The only hope seemed to lie in an escape hatch that led to the top deck, which now, of course, was straight down. Conceivably, a man might hold his breath . . . pull himself 30 feet down the hatch . . . cross the deck . . . and come up into the harbor outside the ship. But it was a very long shot. Several tried and came back, unable to do it. One succeeded—a nonswimmer, nonathlete from Brooklyn named Weisman. He told the rescue crews where to look, and a cutting team was organized.

The men in the handling room passageway had no way of knowing this. They only knew that the air was growing worse and the water was slowly rising as the air was used up. By late afternoon there were just ten men left, and Seaman Stephen Young bet money they would suffocate before they drowned. His friend Seaman Wilber T. Hinsperger took up the bet.

They had by now lost all hope of ever getting out. Still, no one cracked. Instead, they opened a door into the "Lucky Bag" (the ship's lost and found locker) . . . got out pea coats and mattresses . . . and lay down to await the end.

More hours passed. Then suddenly—incredibly—they heard distant banging and hammering echo down from above. At first it would come and go; then it drew closer. Young picked up a dog wrench and pounded back "SOS." The banging grew steadier until finally it was right outside. A voice yelled through the bulkhead, asking the men if they could stand a hole being drilled. Everyone shouted back yes, but it was a close thing. The air rushed out, the water surged up, and as the plate was twisted off, the men scrambled out just in time. Grinning Navy and civilian workers boosted them up through the ship's bottom; and they emerged into the cool, fresh air to find it was—Monday.

Rescuers rushed up with oranges and cigarettes, and a few minutes later Commander Jesse Kenworthy, the *Oklahoma's* executive officer, came by to see if they were all right. He had been on the ship's bottom directing rescue work ever since the attack. He would still be there at 5:30 Monday afternoon when Willard Beal emerged from the steering engine room; in fact, he wouldn't leave until the last of 32 survivors was pulled from the *Oklahoma's* hull some 36 hours after she rolled over into the Pearl Harbor mud.

But all this lay in the future. That Sunday afternoon the survivors were just starting to emerge. Three men were hauled out of a cofferdam, one of them clutching a basketball. He clung to it fiercely, wouldn't give it up even after reaching the *Maryland's* sick bay. Speculation ran wild—some said he had saved it as a reserve supply of oxygen . . . others that he planned to use it as a lifebuoy . . . others that he was just a typical basketball player. Ensign Charles

Mandell heard that, while waiting for rescue, he had even shot a few baskets through a hole in the cofferdam beam.

Men were also trapped on the listing *California*. About three o'clock a rescue party cut into a compartment that was flooded with oil, hauled out two hospital corpsmen. They slumped on deck, looking like two bundles of sodden, oil-soaked rags. Pharmacist's Mate William Lynch walked by, calling the names of men still missing from his unit. One of the bundles suddenly popped up, crying "That's me!"

Other crew members waged a losing fight to keep the *California* afloat. The tender *Swan* drew alongside, con- tributed some pumps, and Radioman Charles Michaels helped drag up mattresses in a futile effort to plug some of the leaks. It was hopeless. A diver from the salvage ship *Widgeon* reported a hole as big as a house. Someone asked him if a collision mat would help, and he gloomily replied, "I don't believe they make them that big."

Later more salvage experts turned up from the *Vestal*, but even their skill was not enough. Finally it was decided that the ship couldn't stay afloat but could be kept in an upright position with planned flooding. Gently the *California* settled to the bottom of the harbor.

The *Nevada* sat on the bottom too, and in the wreckage of the captain's quarters a sword lay twisted and burned behind a charred bureau. Later, when Captain Scanland found it there, he held it out in both his hands and turned to CPO Jack Haley, who happened to be standing nearby: "Chief, my Mother and Dad gave me this sword when I graduated from the Naval Academy many years ago."

Haley could sense all the captain's pent-up emotion and grief at being away from his ship during the attack. The chief understood perhaps better than most, for the *Nevada* meant everything to him too—she was his first and only ship, his home for the past 12 years. He couldn't hold back the tears.

Down in the *Nevada's* plotting room, Ensign Merdinger

stubbornly stuck to his post. He knew from the water dripping into the room that the deck above was flooded. And he knew from the silent phones that few hands were left below decks. There was no longer any need for an information center; still he hated to leave. At three o'clock a rush of water through the seams of the door left no other choice. He phoned topside and was told to come on up. While the water poured in and swirled around the crew's feet, they carefully unplugged the phones, neatly coiled the extension lines, and hung them on their usual hooks.

But the casual approach had its limits. As the men scrambled up the shaft to the conning tower, it occurred to Merdinger that normally some of them might have difficulty making the climb; this time there was no trouble at all.

On deck, preparations were being made for a last-ditch stand. Someone handed Marine Private Payton McDaniel a rifle and two rounds of ammunition. Slender rations, but McDaniel later discovered the rifle had no firing pin anyhow. A Marine detail was sent to the beach to dig emplacements for the World War I machine guns and BARs that had been salvaged. The basic defense plan—hold the ship as long as possible, then take to the hills.

At Hickam, Corporal John Sherwood and Master Sergeant Bonnie Neighbors were also preparing for a last stand. They dragged an old C-33 into the boondocks, dug a good position around it, and set up two machine guns. Private J. H. Thompson joined another man from the 50th Reconnaisance Squadron, who had established a machine-gun nest near the ruined Snake Ranch. The man had taken the trouble to stock it with beer and wine salvaged from the wreckage. Some of the bottles were broken, and the bugs had to be strained out, but this was a minor hardship. The two men cheerfully defended the position all afternoon.

"Help yourself" was also the rule at the officers' club. Everyone expected the Japanese that night, so the food and refreshments might as well be free. At base headquarters

Colonel Cheney Bertholf, the post adjutant, carted out his files and burned them. Even Colonel Farthing, the base commander, was sure the Japanese planned to take over Hickam —that was why they didn't bomb the runways or control tower. Master Sergeant M. D. Mannion felt the place would fall so soon that he might as well pull out and go to Schofield. Up there he might at least be of some service in standing off the enemy.

Actually, Schofield was on the move. Most of the infantry and artillery were now at assigned defense positions around the island—the 98th Coast Artillery at Wheeler . . . the 28th Infantry at Waikiki . . . the 27th farther down the shore . . . other units along the north coast, on the heights above Pearl, and at the bases on the windward side.

As the long column of troops rolled into Kaneohe around 2:30 P.M., Mess Attendant Walter Simmons had only one thought: they had been run out of Schofield. But he too was prepared for a final stand. He now carried an old Springfield rifle and had bandoleers of ammunition strung over his shoulder and around his waist. He felt ready for anything and fancied that he looked just a little like Pancho Villa.

The men shoveled out foxholes—Simmons dug his in the unfinished bottom of the officers' swimming pool—and set up machine guns all over the steep hill in the center of the base. By sundown Kaneohe was prepared for the next attack.

The island's scattered defenses were now being directed by General Short from Aliamanu Crater, three miles west of Fort Shafter. The command post was established in a deep ordnance storage tunnel—ideal for holding out against the coming assault. The general had moved in during the morning, trailed by the usual retinue of staff and communications men.

Lieutenant Samuel Bradlyn was establishing the link with Hickam, and as he set up his code equipment, he watched General Short, General Martin, and other high-ranking officers huddle together. They looked terribly worried, and for the first time Bradlyn realized that even generals were human beings who didn't always know what to do and had to pace back and forth while making decisions.

Of one thing they were certain—there had to be martial law. General Short approached old Governor Poindexter on this shortly after noon. The governor dragged his feet—he thought it was probably necessary, yet he hated to do it. He finally said he wanted to check with the White House first, would give Short his answer in an hour. He put through a call to the President at 12:40 P.M., and it didn't help when the operator—now acting under the Navy censor—kept insisting, "What are you going to talk about?" The governor had been shoved aside already.

The President was properly soothing, agreed that martial law was all for the best. Then Short reappeared to press the point: for all he knew landing parties were on the way . . . the raid was probably the prelude to all-out attack . . . he couldn't afford to take chances. The governor finally signed the Proclamation, and martial law was announced at 4:25 P.M.

The civilians considered themselves in the front lines anyhow. Edgar Rice Burroughs, creator of *Tarzan,* joined a group of men digging slit trenches along the shore. Others rallied to the Territorial Guard, which was hastily built around the University of Hawaii ROTC unit. As the 2nd Battalion mobilized at Wahiawa, a sergeant drove up in a command car with some welcome news—the Army had sent him over from Schofield to help. He was a godsend: the unit had no equipment, and the sergeant knew how to get everything: blankets, mess gear, guns. He proved an ingenious, tireless worker and ultimately stayed with the outfit a whole month. Then one day he commandeered some whisky from a padlocked liquor store, and that proved his undoing. When the proprietor complained, it turned out the man was no sergeant at all—just a prisoner released from the Schofield stockade during the raid. He had immediately stolen a sergeant's uniform . . . then the command car . . . and had been stealing ever since, filling the home guards' desperate needs. He was a sort of military Robin Hood.

Nearly every organized group on Oahu staked out something to do. Boy Scouts fought fires, served coffee, ran messages. The American Legion turned out for patrol and sentry duty. One Legionnaire struggled into his 1917 uniform, had a dreadful time remembering how to wind his puttees and put on his insignia. He took it out on his wife, and she told him to leave her alone—go out and fight his old enemy, the Germans. The San Jose College football team, in town from California for a benefit game the following week end, signed up with the Police Department for guard duty. Seven of them joined the force, and Quarterback Paul Tognetti stayed on for good, ultimately going into the dairy business.

A local committee, called the Major Disaster Council, had spent months preparing for this kind of day; now their foresight was paying off. Forty-five trucks belonging to American Sanitary Laundry, New Fair Dairy, and other local companies sped off to Hickam as converted ambulances. Dr. Forrest Pinkerton dashed to the Hawaii Electric Company's refrigerator, collected the plasma stored there by the Chamber of Commerce's Blood Bank. He piled it in the back of his car, distributed it to various hospitals, then rushed on the air, appealing for more donors. Over 500 appeared within an hour, swamping Dr. John Devereux and his three assistants. They took the blood as fast as they could, ran out of containers, used sterilized Coca-Cola bottles.

All kinds of people went through the line. Navy wife Maureen Hayter was shocked when offered a swig of Old Grand-Dad afterward—it just didn't seem right. Another woman was a well-known prostitute. She couldn't give blood but wanted to do something. Dr. Devereux put her to work cleaning bottles and tubes. She turned out to be his most faithful volunteer.

Civilian doctors and nurses converged on the Army's Tripler Hospital. Among them went Dr. John J. Moorhead, a distinguished New York surgeon who happened to be in Honolulu delivering a series of lectures. Some 300 doctors had attended his first talk Thursday morning, half of them Army and Navy men. Dr. Moorhead had been an Army surgeon in World War I, loved the service, and took great pains to see they were invited. The service doctors accepted with enthusiasm—Dr. Moorhead was a world-famous specialist and, unlike almost everyone else, he could speak from actual battle experience.

On Friday night the doctor was slated to speak on "Back Injuries" but at the last minute the schedule was juggled and he spoke instead on "The Treatment of Wounds." If the Program Committee had known the attack was coming, it couldn't have lined up a better subject.

Dr. Moorhead had Saturday off, but he was to speak on "Burns" at 9:00 A.M. Sunday. As he ate his breakfast, guns boomed in the distance. Walking through the hotel lobby, he heard that Pearl Harbor was under attack. He told Dr. Hill, who was driving him to the lecture, but the local doctor was unimpressed: "Oh, you hear all kinds of stories around this place."

They turned on the car radio and picked up the 8:40 bulletin. That convinced them and they dropped by Dr. Hill's house while he told his wife and children to take shelter. Then they drove on to the Mabel L. Smyth Auditorium so that Dr. Moorhead could give his talk. The two doctors were having the same trouble as everyone else making the lightning adjustment to war . . . realizing that it also affected their own day.

The lecture hall was almost empty—only 50 doctors instead of the usual 300, and no Army or Navy men. As Dr. Moorhead reached the platform shells began landing outside. He cheerily told the audience that the noise reminded him of

Chateau-Thierry. Then he pointed out that this was Sunday, so he would give a sermon with an appropriate text: "Be ye also ready, for in the hour that ye know not . . ."

At this point Dr. Jesse Smith, a local physician, burst into the hall shouting that 12 surgeons were needed at Tripler right away. That did it—speaker and audience bolted from the room together.

Dr. Moorhead and his pickup team of civilian surgeons spent the next 11 hours operating with hardly any break. Once during the afternoon he dropped down to the mess hall for a bite, ran into Colonel Miller, the hospital commandant. The doctor suggested—perhaps a little wistfully—that maybe he should go on active duty. Miller said he would see what he could do, and a little later poked his head into the operating room: "You're in the Army now!" To Dr. Moorhead, this wonderful service was even more wonderful—no forms, questionnaires, or fingerprints; yet he had become a full colonel in two hours.

As he worked away, Colonel Moorhead displayed a mixture of competence and optimism that did wonders for the wounded. "Son," he told one boy, "you've been through a lot of hell, and you're going into some more. This foot has to come off. But there's been many a good pirate with only one leg!"

The wounded needed this kind of cheerfulness. Without it another boy who had lost a leg wanted only to die—he was sure his girl would no longer have him. Private Edward Oveka had a shattered leg too; and after he came out of ether, he was afraid to see if he still had his foot. He finally worked up his courage and took a look—it was still there.

Whatever their feelings, the men were incredibly quiet and uncomplaining. At Queens Hospital, one man lay riddled with shrapnel. When Dr. Forrest Pinkerton began explaining that he would have to delay treating the less serious wounds, the man calmly broke in, "Just do what you can, I know there are other people waiting."

Occasionally the mildest of disagreements would arise. At Hickam, Captain Carl Hoffman thought a drink might buck up a badly wounded major. He was telling someone to measure a shot when the major interrupted, "Don't tell him how much to put in the glass—fill it up." At the Navy Hospital, a seaman with a bad stomach wound wanted orange juice, but the doctor thought this would be fatal and ordered water instead. When the man objected, the doctor finally whispered to the nurse to get the juice—he would probably die anyway. "I heard you, Doctor," called the seaman, "and I still want orange juice." Perhaps due to this sort of determination, a week later the man was doing fine.

Everyone did his best to make the wounded comfortable. Morphine did its work too, and many drifted off to fitful sleep. Radioman Glenn Lane awoke long enough on the hospital ship *Solace* to see an attendant bending over him with some soup. The man was Filipino, and Lane started with fright—he was sure he had been captured by the Japanese.

A man didn't need narcotics to see himself in enemy hands. Dark, dreary thoughts ran through the minds of many still able to fight. Chief Peter Chang saw himself pulling a rickshaw. Fireman John Gobidas expected to be a corpse or a prisoner, but he prayed that Chief Metalsmith Burl W. Brookshire would somehow survive, to inspire others with the courage he had given the men on the *Rigel*. Electrician's Mate James Power thought about those oriental brain tortures, then remembered he was a Texan and decided to make this another Alamo.

Actually, the only Japanese invasion of the Hawaiian Islands was by now well under way. It was just about church time when it all began on Niihau, westernmost island of the Hawaiian chain. Niihau was privately owned by the Robinson family, who operated the island mainly as a sheep and cattle ranch and lovingly preserved it as a pure Polyne·sian paradise—no visitors, no modern conveniences, no West·

ern gadgets like guns, telephones, or radios. Once a week a
boat came over from Kauai, 20 miles away, and left supplies
at Kii Landing on the island's northern tip. There was no
other communication with the outside world. In case of serious trouble, it was arranged that a signal fire would be built
on a mountain in sight of Kauai. Otherwise, it was just assumed that everything was all right.

And this Sunday everything was all right, as the islanders
flocked to the little church in Puuwai, about 15 miles down
the west shore from Kii Landing. Puuwai was the only village on the island—a collection of small houses scattered
among the rocks, cactus, and keawa trees. Everybody lived
there except the Robinsons, who had a homestead at Kie Kie,
two miles away.

But just as everyone was entering the church, two planes
flew overhead. The islanders all noticed that one plane was
sputtering and smoking; they all saw red circles under the
wings. And even though they were just ranch hands and cow-
boys, carefully protected from the problems of the world,
many of them sensed trouble far more quickly than their
sophisticated neighbors on Oahu. Most recognized the Japanese insignia; some even guessed an attack on Pearl Harbor.

About two o'clock one of the planes reappeared, circling low
over the pastures and hedges. The pilot picked out a spot and
bounced to a heavy landing. He bumped over some rocks,
through a fence, and stopped near the house of Hawila
Kaleohano.

There was trouble right away. Hawila ran up and yanked
open the canopy; the pilot reached for a pistol; Hawila
grabbed it first and pulled the aviator from the plane. Then
the pilot began searching inside his shirt; Hawila tore it open
and snatched out some papers and a map.

By now the whole island was crowding around. The villag
ers were shouting questions, and the pilot was shaking his
head, trying to show that he didn't understand English . . .
he could only speak Japanese.

There was just one thing to do—send for Harada, one of the two Japanese on Niihau. He was a 30-year-old Nisei who had come to the island a year ago as a housekeeper, now worked as both the Robinsons' caretaker and an assistant bee-keeper. The head beekeeper was the other Japanese, an old man named Sintani, who had lived on Niihau for many years.

Even with Harada's help, no one got much out of the pilot. He said he flew over from Honolulu; he denied any raid; he was vague about the reason for his trip and all those bullet holes in the plane. Finally the islanders decided to hold him for Mr. Aylmer Robinson himself, who was due in Monday on the weekly boat from Kauai. He would know what to do.

Monday morning they escorted the pilot to Kii Landing and guarded him there all day. But the boat never came.

Tuesday they tried again. Still no boat.

Wednesday and Thursday passed, and by now the island-ers were thoroughly alarmed. Harada came up with a bright idea: Wouldn't it help to move the pilot from Puuwai to his place at Kie Kie; this might calm down the village. Everyone agreed, and it was done.

By Friday it was high time for a signal fire. A group of men went off to build it, and everyone else settled down for another tense day of waiting. At Kie Kie a lone Hawaiian, named Haniki, watched the pilot. In the last day or so the Japanese had opened up a good deal. At first he admitted that he could read and write English, even if he couldn't speak it . . . later that there had indeed been a raid on Pearl Harbor. But, he said, he liked it here and hoped to set-tle down on Niihau after the war was over. He apparently wasn't such a bad fellow after all.

The pilot asked if he could see Harada, and Haniki took him over to the honey house. The two Japanese talked to-gether for a few minutes, then all three men strolled into an adjoining storehouse, where the nets and hives were kept.

Haniki suddenly found himself facing two guns. Harada had stolen a revolver and shotgun from the Robinson house

. . . hidden them in the storehouse until the right moment
. . . and now the battle for Niihau was on.

The two Japanese locked up Haniki in the storehouse and
dashed through the underbrush to the road. They held up a
passing sulky, forcing out a Hawaiian woman and seven children. Then they jumped in, pointed the gun at a young girl
on the horse, made her drive them to Puuwai as fast as she
could. As they neared the village, they jumped off and raced
for Hawila's house to get the pilot's papers. Hawila saw them
coming and bolted for the fields.

Harada and the airman searched the house but found
nothing. After an unsuccessful attempt to recruit Sintani,
Niihau's other Japanese, the two men started searching
through all the houses in the village. Again and again they
shouted for Hawila, threatened to shoot everyone unless
he was immediately produced. But this was an empty threat
because almost all the villagers were now hiding in the fields.
They did find an ancient woman, Mrs. Huluoulani, who
stayed behind reading her Bible. She ignored their threats,
and not knowing quite how to handle her, they left her.

They had a better idea anyhow. They stripped the Japanese plane of its machine guns and once again walked among
the houses. This time they yelled that they would shoot up
the whole place unless they found Hawila. As it grew dark,
they began ransacking the homes in earnest. They ripped
apart Hawila's house and finally discovered the pilot's pistol
and map—but still no sign of his papers. They worked on
through the night, turned the houses inside out, one after
the other. Toward dawn on Saturday the thirteenth, they
were back at Hawila's house, for one last search. Again no
luck. So they burned the place down, hoping to destroy the
papers too.

All this time, except for a brief period around 3:00 A.M.,
curious eyes peeked at the two Japanese from the bushes and
weeds that grew in the rocky fields. The islanders had by no
means accepted the capture of Puuwai, but after all, the

Japanese had the only guns on Niihau. At a strategy meeting in the cactus grove behind the village it was decided to send the women and children to some caves in the hills, then return after dark and try to capture the two men. Somehow this plan fell through, but Beni Kanahali and another Hawaiian did manage to steal all the machine-gun ammunition, and that was a big step forward.

Meanwhile Hawila had hurried up the mountain to tell the men to get the signal fire going. But when they heard the news, they decided the fire wouldn't tell enough of the story. They must go themselves. So six of the men ran to Kii Landing, jumped in a whaleboat, rowed off for help.

After sixteen hours of steady rowing, they reached Kauai at three o'clock Saturday afternoon. They found Aylmer Robinson; he found the military authorities; and a detachment of soldiers, the six Hawaiians, and Mr. Robinson himself were soon racing back to the rescue in the lighthouse tender *Kukui.*

Long before they got there the invasion had reached its climax. About 7:00 A.M. Beni Kanahali, having succeeded in stealing the ammunition during the night, tried his luck again. He sneaked back to the village to see what was going on. His wife came with him, and they both were promptly captured. There were the usual demands for Hawila, but Beni was now tired of the whole thing. He told Harada to take the gun away from the pilot before he hurt somebody. Harada said he couldn't, so Beni jumped the man himself. Then his wife piled in, then Harada on top of her, and for a few seconds the four of them scuffled about.

Harada pulled the woman away. She kicked and clawed as hard as she could. Beni yelled to leave her alone—or it would be Harada's turn next. The pilot jerked his arm free and shot Beni three times—groin, stomach, and upper leg.

According to legend, at this point Beni got mad. As a matter of fact, he was mad already. But he did now think he might die, and he decided to kill the pilot before he could hurt anyone else. With a great heave he picked the man up by his neck and one leg—he had often done it to a sheep—and smashed his head against a stone wall. Harada took one look, let Beni's wife go, pointed the shotgun at himself, and pulled the trigger.

Chapter XII

"We're Leaving Now—Explode Gloriously!"

IT WAS JUST SUNSET when Ensign Ed Jacoby trudged ashore after losing the fight against the *West Virginia's* fires. As he started toward the Ford Island BOQ for a sandwich, a bugle sounded evening colors. He snapped to attention, and the simple ceremony—taking place as always, despite the day's disasters—reminded him that the country lived on . . . that it had survived blows in the past and could do so again.

Nurse Valera Vaubel stood at attention, too, as the flag was lowered at the Navy Hospital. Then she joined some others in a spontaneous cheer. At least this sundown she was still free.

But how much longer no one knew. Certainly not Ensign Cleo Dobson, as he sat on the veranda of the old BOQ, talking over the future with some of the other *Enterprise* pilots. About all they could decide: they were in a real shooting war and right on the front line. Somebody suggested food, and that seemed a good idea, for they had eaten nothing since leaving the *Enterprise* at 6:00 A.M. They raided the deserted kitchen and found some steaks in the refrigerator. The salt and utensils had all disappeared, but they cooked the steaks anyhow on the big range and ate them sitting on the veranda. It was dark now, but they could see well enough by the flickering light of the flames on the *Arizona*.

Farther down Battleship Row, acetylene torches flared on the upturned hull of the *Oklahoma*, but the rest of the harbor was dark. Within the blacked-out ships, men had their first chance to rest . . . and worry. On the *Raleigh* everything had happened so fast during the day that Yeoman Charles Knapp didn't have a chance to be scared. But now he was off watch, and as he lay on a desk for a few minutes' rest, his mind flooded with questions. Would he ever see his mother and sister again, or watch a football game or love a girl or drink a beer or drive a car?

Certainly the outlook wasn't encouraging. Knapp heard that paratroopers were now dropping on Waikiki . . . that more landings were in progress on the north shore . . . and as if the Japanese weren't enough, that Germans were flying the planes. There was no doubt about it—one seaman swore that he had seen one of the captured pilots . . . a big, blond-headed Prussian . . . even heard him talking German.

On the gunboat *Sacramento,* word also spread that one of the pilots was blond, but he was apparently some kind of blond Japanese. Others spoke of huge six-footers, quite different from the Japanese everyone was used to.

Even more terrifying were the stories that the pilots were Hawaiian-born or American-educated. Seaman Frank Lewis of the *Dobbin* heard that the Japanese who crashed on the *Curtiss* was wearing a University of Oregon ring. At the Marine Barracks Private E. H. Robison heard that he was a University of Southern California man—Class of '37 or '39, people weren't quite sure which. At Fort Shafter, Lieutenant William Keogh heard that the pilots were wearing McKinley High School sweaters (they were all apparently lettermen). The cards seemed stacked against the defenders. The men at Fort Shafter could well believe the story that a Japanese admiral boasted he would dine at the Royal Hawaiian next Sunday.

And what was to stop him? Rumors spread that the ships at sea had also suffered. Quartermaster Handler of the *Helm* heard that the whole *Enterprise* task force was sunk; on the *Tangier,* Boatswain's Mate William Land heard that the *Lex-*

ington was gone too. Not just the *Lexington* but the *Saratoga* as well, according to a story picked up by Signalman Walter Grabanski of the *California*.

Nor would there be any help from home, judging from another raft of rumors. The Panama Canal was bombed and blocked, someone told Chief Jack Haley of the *Nevada*, and this of course cut off the Atlantic Fleet. But worst of all, California itself was said to be under attack. On the *Helena* men heard that San Francisco was bombed . . . on the *Tennessee* that an invasion fleet lay off the city . . . on the *Rigel* that the city had been taken and a beachhead established. It might even be a two-prong attack, because word reached the *Pennsylvania* that a Japanese landing force had occupied Long Beach and was working its way toward Los Angeles.

True, there were a few encouraging reports. *California* seamen heard that the Russians had bombed Tokyo, and among the *West Virginia* men word spread that the Japanese had so little steel, they had filled some of the bombs with oyster shells. Perhaps the best news of all circulated among men from the *Oklahoma:* survivors of the attack would get 30 days' leave.

Also, the *Maryland* PA system announced that two Japanese carriers had been sunk, and a more lurid version of this story spread through the Navy Hospital: the *Pennsylvania* had captured two carriers and was towing them back to Pearl. But how could a man believe the good news when even a quick check showed the *Pennsylvania* still sitting in drydock?

About the best that could be believed was the report, spread on the *Nevada*, that the Japanese had landed on Oahu, but the Army was holding its own. The men on the ship were told to be doubly alert for any movement in the cane that ran down to the shore where the ship lay beached. No one remembered to tell them that the ship's own Marine detachment was patrolling the same area. As Private Payton McDaniel crunched through the cane, a man on the ship shouted he saw something move. A spotlight flicked on, and McDaniel froze, praying it wouldn't find him. Other Marines grasped the situation and passed word to the *Nevada* gunners to hold their fire. But it was a terrifying moment, for McDaniel knew that this was a night when men were inclined to fire and ask questions later.

At the sub base, one sentry fired so often at his relief that he ended up with the duty all night. In the Navy Yard, a fusillade of shots erased a small spotlight that was snapped on briefly by the men installing the *San Francisco's* anti-aircraft batteries. Every time such shots were fired, they would set off other guns, until the whole harbor echoed with the shots of men who had no idea what they were shooting at. "You want to get in on this?" yelled a Marine sentry as Pfc. Billy Kerslake dozed off duty in the front seat of a sedan parked near Landing Charley. Kerslake nodded, reached his arm out the window, fired five pistol shots into the air, and fell back to sleep.

The firing quickly spread to nearby Hickam and added to the misery of the B-17 flight crews. It had been a tough day —first the long 14-hour trip from San Francisco . . . then getting the planes in shape . . . bivouacking out in the boon-docks . . . fighting mosquitoes . . . trying to keep dry in the drizzle that began after dark . . . and now this. But the firing couldn't be ignored. During one outburst someone shouted, "The Japs are making a landing!" Tired men poured from their cots as the sky blazed with tracers. Sergeant Nick Kahlefent added to the din when he jumped out of bed on some thorns.

It was an equally sleepless night at Wheeler. Everybody had been evacuated from the barracks area, and no one found a very satisfactory alternative. Private Rae Drenner of the base fire department tossed and turned with 20 other men on the floor of the fire chief's living room. Every time shooting broke out, the men would dash off in their fire truck, dodging the hail of bullets aimed at them by jittery sentries. On the eastern edge of the field the 98th Coast Artillery let go a covering barrage . . . kept it up until the 97th at Schofield telephoned to complain that the shrapnel was ripping their tents.

Schofield got even when the 27th Infantry took pot shots at the 98th's guard detail. Two other Schofield units engaged in a pitched battle across a gully—it ended when one of the GIs, nicked by a ricochet, exploded into language which the other side knew could come from no Japanese. Down near the pack-train corral a sentry challenged three times (showing remarkable forbearance for this night), got no answer, and shot one of his own mules.

The guard at Aliamanu Command Post bagged a deer, and Mess Attendant Walter Simmons figures that in the fields around Kaneohe more mongooses died than on any other night in history. About 1:30 A.M. a small flare burst above Kaneohe —no one yet knows where it came from—and men all over the base began shooting at "parachutists." It made no difference that no one could see them or even hear a plane. A more tangible target was millionaire Chris Holmes' island in the middle of the bay. The story spread first that paratroopers had landed there; later it was only that the Japanese servants had revolted. In any case, a group of men chugged out in one of the few planes that could still taxi and sprayed the place with machine guns.

At Ewa a sentry saw a match flicker and almost shot his base commander, Lieutenant Colonel Larkin, who—against his own orders—was absent-mindedly lighting a cigarette.

As the shooting crackled all over Oahu, sooner or later someone was bound to get hurt. An elderly Japanese fisherman, Sutematsu Kida, his son Kiichi, and two others were killed by a patrol plane as their sampan passed Barbers Point, returning with the day's catch. They had gone out before the attack and probably never knew there was a war. In Pearl Harbor itself, a machine gun on the *California* accidentally cut down two *Utah* survivors while they stood on the deck of the *Argonne* during one of the false alarms.

Lieutenant (j.g.) Fritz Hebel sensed this kind of thing might happen, as he led six *Enterprise* fighters toward Ford Island around 7:30 P.M. They had been searching for a Japanese carrier, arrived back over the *Enterprise* when it was too dark to land, were told to go on to Oahu. Now at last they were coming in.

Cautiously Hebel asked Ford Island for landing instructions. He was told to turn his lights on, "come on over the field and break up for landing." Down in the harbor, Marine Sergeant Joseph Fleck on the *New Orleans* heard the word passed to hold fire—friendly planes coming in. Ensign Leon Grabowski was told too at his 1.1 gun station on the *Maryland;* so was Radioman Fred Glaeser on Ford Island. So, probably, were others.

The planes moved in across the south channel and swung toward the mountains. Somewhere a BAR opened up . . . then two . . . then just about every ship in Pearl Harbor. Tracers criss-crossed the sky—30s . . . 50s . . . 1.1s . . . everything that could shoot. On Ford Island an officer desperately ran up and down the sandbags by Utility Squadron One's position: "Hold your fire! Hold your fire! Those are our planes!"

In the air, Lieutenant Hebel yelled over his radio: "My God, what's happened?" Ensign James Daniels dived for the floodlights at the southwest edge of the field, hoping to blind the gunners. The stunt worked and he swooped off toward Barbers Point. The others weren't as quick or lucky. Ensign Herb Menges plunged down out of control, crashing into a Pearl City tavern called the Palm Inn. Ensign Eric Allen fell near Pearl City too; he managed to bail out, but was riddled by gunfire as he floated down. Lieutenant Hebel tried to land his damaged plane at Wheeler, crashed, and was killed. Ensign Gayle Hermann spun his smashed plane 1200 feet down onto Ford Island, survived. Ensign D. R. Flynn bailed out over Barbers Point, was picked up alive days later by the Army.

Daniels hovered alone off Barbers Point. After about ten minutes the firing died down, and he blandly asked the tower for landing instructions. They were different this time—come in as low and as fast as possible, show no lights. Since he couldn't come in as a friend, he would have to try it like an enemy. He did and landed safely.

On the destroyer tender *Whitney,* crewman Waldo Rathman felt a good deal better: they really showed the Japanese this time. The gunnery was excellent, and it was a thrill to see those planes fall in flames. It made the drubbing of the morning seem a thing of the past.

Watching from her home near Makalapa, Navy wife Jeanne Gardiner couldn't judge the gunnery, but she prayed the antiaircraft fire would get the enemy. As Mrs. Mitta Townsend, another Navy wife, looked on from her home on the "Punchbowl," the moon emerged briefly, bathing Oahu in soft but revealing light. She prayed it would go behind a cloud.

Mrs. Joseph Galloway prayed too, pacing the floor at a friend's house in Honolulu. She had no idea what had happened since her husband left for his ship in the morning. Her portable radio blared occasional alerts about planes, but most of the time it was dead. In the background a distant station faded on and off with dance music from Salt Lake City.

In their desperate search for news other wives made the mistake of tuning in Japanese stations. Mrs. W. G. Beecher heard that her husband's destroyer *Flusser* had been sunk with the entire *Lexington* task force.

Mrs. Arthur Fahrner, wife of Hickam's mess supervisor, didn't need to fish for news. She knew all too well. Someone had told her of the bomb that hit the Hickam mess hall, said no one escaped alive. She took it for granted that Sergeant Fahrner died at his post, and now her job was to get the five children back to the mainland, into school, and find a way to support them.

The Fahrners had been evacuated to the University of Hawaii auditorium, and while the Red Cross performed miracles, there still weren't enough cots for the scores of families that sprawled on the floor. Sunday night Mrs. Fahrner and three other mothers formed a "hollow square" of adults and dumped their ten children in the middle. This at least kept them in one spot, but it still was a night of whimpering . . . of restless tossing . . . of endless trips to the bathroom over and around sleeping people.

Just when everything quieted down, some new disturbance would break out. One little girl lost a kitty with a bell around its neck. Soon it was hard to tell which caused the most commotion—the cat roaming and ringing its bell or the child calling and searching in the dark. The little girl had a way of turning up wherever the kitty had just left.

Slowly the hours dragged by. The children gradually dozed off, but the mothers were wide-eyed all night. Sometimes they talked together; other times they just lay quietly holding one another's hands, waiting for daylight.

The mothers were busier in the Navy storage tunnel at Red Hill, where other families were evacuated. Clouds of mosquitoes swarmed down the air vents, and the women spent most of the night shooing them off so their children could sleep. Then an unexpected crisis arose. One young mother forgot to bring any bottles for her month-old baby. Cups were tried, but of course the baby was too young. Someone suggested a sugar shaker, but the spout was too large. Finally Mrs. Alexander Rowell came up with the solution—she soaked a clean rag in milk and let the baby suck on it. That was what the pioneers did, she explained; she had read all about it in *Drums Along the Mohawk*.

Generous people opened up their homes to other evacuees. One Navy commander's wife at Waipahu took in 20 or 30 women and children, including Don and Jerry Morton and their mother, Mrs. Croft. Everyone made a point of being cheerful, but the rumors were frightening—it was said resistance was weak against the enemy advance from Kaneohe.

Some of the mothers talked as though they were already prisoners, but Don and Jerry vowed to take to the hills and fight to the end.

Here and there a few families stubbornly refused to evacuate. Mrs. Arthur Gardiner had no great faith in the construction of the junior officers' duplex quarters near Makalapa, but it was home, and she wanted to be there when Lieutenant Gardiner returned. She pushed the dining room table against a wall, dragged four mattresses downstairs with the help of five-year-old Keith. She placed them strategically around the shelter and crawled in with Keith and two-year-old Susan. Keith was sick with worry and excitement but tried wonderfully to cooperate; Susan was in open rebellion and went along only when convinced it was part of a new game.

Mrs. Paul Spangler thought it might help to read to her four children as they sat in their blacked-out living room on Alewa Heights. So she rigged her coat over a floor lamp, gathered everybody around her, and picked up a book. Instantly a man was pounding on the door, shouting: "Put out that light!" She gave up and they all went to bed. Navy wife Lorraine Campbell dealt more successfully with the blackout at her home near Pearl Harbor—she turned off all the lights and put a Band-Aid on the radio dial.

Some blackout problems were insurmountable. As Allen Mau, a 12-year-old Hawaiian, tried to make cocoa for the evacuees at his home, he found he couldn't get the milk out of the refrigerator without turning on the automatic light inside. He could get his hand in all right, but not out with the milk bottle too. Finally he went ahead anyhow . . . and almost lost his arm when the whole family dived at the door to shut the light off.

In the darkness many turned their thoughts to the men who had rushed off in the morning. Days would pass before most of the families heard of them again. On Tuesday Mrs. Arthur Fahrner learned that a box of chocolate bars had mysteriously appeared at a friend's house—usually a sure sign that Sergeant Fahrner had been around. Yet she scarcely dared to hope. The following day she found out—the sergeant had been in the bakery getting bread when the Hickam mess hall was hit; he escaped without a scratch. On Wednesday Nurse Monica Conter still had no word of Lieutenant Benning, but she was doing her best to carry on. As she walked down the third-floor corridor of the Hickam Hospital, the elevator door opened and there he was in full combat uniform—looking even dirtier than any soldier she had seen in the movies.

It was Thursday morning when Mrs. Joseph Cote heard the chaplain call her name at the university auditorium. She slipped into the ladies' room and prayed for the strength to bear the bad news. When she emerged, the chaplain told her Chief Cote was fine. Later that day Mrs. W. G. Wallace was back on her civilian job at Pearl Harbor, trying not to look out the window at the charred ships that depressed her so. But a familiar shadow passed the window, and she instinctively looked up—it was her husband, Ensign Wallace, last seen Sunday morning. She threw herself across the desk, halfway through the window and into his arms. Then they slipped into the first-aid shack, where no one could see them, and cried.

It wasn't until Sunday, December 14, that Don and Jerry Morton learned their stepfather had been killed on the seaplane ramp at Ford Island by one of the first bombs to fall.

But the waiting, the gnawing uncertainty, all lay ahead. This black Sunday night the families on Oahu had other worries. In the eerie darkness, Japanese seemed to lurk behind every bush. Betty and Margo Spangler, two teen-age sisters, normally slept out on the *lanai*, but this night they took over their mother's bed. Mrs. W. G. Beecher got her children to sleep, lay awake herself, listening uneasily as the palm trees brushed against the side of the house. Navy wife Reiba Wallace took in a frightened single girl who insisted she heard someone on the roof. Mrs. Wallace spied a rifle in the corner, promised to shoot both the girl and herself if the Japanese came in. This was somehow reassuring; the girl calmed down, and Mrs. Wallace kept it to herself that the gun wasn't loaded. Mrs. Patrick Gillis, a young Army wife, was sure she saw someone skulking outside her apartment house; so did the other five wives who had joined her. The police combed the grounds in vain.

About 4:00 A.M. another alarm went direct to Colonel Fielder in the intelligence office at Fort Shafter: Someone was signaling with a blue light up behind the base. Fielder grabbed a pistol, a helmet, and a sentry. Sure enough, a light was flashing up the mountain. He called for reinforcements, and the squad deployed through buffalo grass . . . crossed a stream . . . surrounded the area . . . and moved in. Two elderly farmers were milking a cow, using a blue light as instructed. A palm frond, swaying in the breeze, occasionally hid the light and made it look like secret code.

Colonel Fielder couldn't know it, but the danger was all over. Oahu was perfectly safe this gusty, squally night.

The Islands' 160,000 people of Japanese blood pulled no sabotage, probably no important espionage. Even Dr. Mori's phone call to Tokyo Friday night—when he talked so mysteriously of poinsettias, hibiscuses, and chrysanthemums—may have been above board. He always claimed it was just an atmosphere piece for the Tokyo newspaper *Yomiuri Shinbun*, and certainly the interview did appear in the paper the following morning—complete with reference to flowers. Actually, Consul General Kita didn't need outside intelligence help— he had more than 200 consular agents, and he himself could get a perfect view of the fleet any time he chose to take a ten-minute drive.

Nor was there any danger from the great Japanese task force north of Oahu. Admiral Nagumo's ships were 500 miles away . . . pounding silently home . . . steaming through heavy mist, slightly south of their outbound course. The crews were strangely quiet. Down in the *Akagi*'s engine room, Commander Tanbo's men didn't even take a ceremonial drink of *sake*. He later learned this was typical—the men whooped it up only over the small, insignificant victories; the big ones always left them sober and reflective.

The Japanese submarines south of Oahu were no threat either. Most of them had lapsed into the role of observers. Commander Katsuji Watanabe casually studied Pearl Harbor from the conning tower of the *I-69*, lying several miles off shore. He watched the flames still licking the *Arizona* and at 9:01 P.M. noted a heavy explosion aboard her. This respite was welcome, for the commander had spent a hard day dodging destroyers. Some of them probably thought they had sunk him, for Watanabe was a master at deception. He would pump out made-to-order oil slicks; and as final, conclusive evidence of his destruction, he liked to jettison Japanese sandals into the sea.

Lieutenant Hashimoto aboard the *I-24* reflected on the change one day had made in the shoreline. The twinkling lights were all gone; Oahu was now just a gloomy shadow. The *I-24* turned east and hurried off for her rendezvous with Ensign Sakamaki's midget. The whole Special Attack Unit was to reassemble at a point seven miles southwest of Lanai, and one by one the mother subs arrived. All night long they waited, riding gently up and down in the ocean swell within easy sight of each other. No midgets ever appeared.

On the *I-24* it was discovered that Sakamaki never expected to come back. His belongings were neatly rolled up; his farewell note (with the fingernail and lock of hair) lay ready to be mailed. There were complete instructions what to do, including some yen for the postage.

But Sakamaki was not dead. After his collapse at dusk, the midget cruised lazily eastward by itself. At some point he must have recovered long enough to surface and open the hatch. In any case, when he finally came to around midnight, he noticed first the moonlight, then a soothing breeze that filtered down from above. He poked his head out the hatch and gulped the cool night air.

Seaman Inagaki woke up and also took a few deep breaths. But he was still groggy and soon fell back to sleep. Sakamaki stayed awake, drinking in the night, letting the sub go where it wanted. The sea wasn't rough, but an occasional wave washed his face. Stars twinkled through the drifting clouds, and moonlight danced off the water. He began having dangerous thoughts for a man on a suicide mission: he got to thinking it was good to be alive.

About dawn the motor stopped, and the midget just drifted. As the light grew brighter, Sakamaki saw a small island to the left. He decided it was Lanai—a remarkable display of faith in the sub's ability to steer itself. Actually, the boat had drifted far off course, rounded the eastern end of Oahu, and was now heading northwest along the windward side of the island.

Sakamaki shook Inagaki awake and pointed out the land— they might still be in time for the rendezvous. He ordered full speed ahead. The sub started and stopped . . . started and stopped again. White smoke poured from the batteries; they were just about shot. Sakamaki waited a few minutes (like a man attempting to start a car on a low battery) and tried again. Nothing happened. Once more. The motor caught, and the midget bolted ahead. Almost instantly there was another jolt . . . a frightful scraping . . . a shuddering stop. They had run her onto a reef again.

This time they were stuck for good. There was nothing to do but scuttle the sub. It carried explosives for just this emergency, and Sakamaki quickly lit the fuse. For a few seconds he and Inagaki watched it sputter, to make sure it didn't go out. Then they scrambled up the hatch.

They climbed out on the cigar-shaped hull, wearing only G-string and loincloth. The moon was sinking in the west, a new day lighting up the eastern sky. Around them the surf foamed and pounded. About 200 yards ahead they could just make out a dark, empty beach. Sakamaki had a final pang of conscience—shouldn't he stay with the midget . . . was this the way of a naval officer? Then he thought, why not try to live; he was not a weapon but a human being. He bade the sub good-by, almost as though it were a person: "We're leaving now—explode gloriously."

He dived into the sea about 6:40 A.M.—his watch, which he had loyally kept on Tokyo time, stopped at 2:10. The water was colder than he expected, the waves higher than they looked. They spun him helplessly about as he struck out for shore. Inagaki had jumped with him but was nowhere to be seen. Sakamaki hailed him, and a voice called back, "Sir, I'm over here." Sakamaki finally spied a head bobbing up and down in the combers. He yelled a few words of encouragement, but no one knows whether Inagaki heard. His drowned body later washed up on the beach.

As Sakamaki struggled through the surf, he realized that the charge had not gone off in the sub. Five . . . ten minutes passed. The hideous truth dawned—on this too he had failed. He wanted to swim back but just couldn't make it. He had lost all his strength. He no longer swam at all. He just swirled about—coughing, swallowing, spitting up salt water. He was utterly helpless. Everything went blank.

When he came to, he was lying on the beach near Bellows Field, apparently cast up on the sand by a breaker. He glanced up into the curious eyes of an American soldier standing beside him. Sergeant David M. Akui was on guard, packing a pistol at his hip. The war that was just beginning for so many men had just ended for Prisoner of War Kazuo Sakamaki.

At this moment it was 12:20 P.M. in Washington, D.C., and ten highly polished black limousines were just entering the Capitol grounds. The first was convoyed by three huge touring cars, nicknamed *Leviathan*, *Queen Mary*, and *Nor-*

mandie. These were filled with Secret Service men guarding President Franklin D. Roosevelt, who was on his way to ask Congress to declare war on the Japanese Empire.

The cars stopped at the south entrance of the Capitol, and the President got out, assisted by his son Jimmy. Roosevelt wore his familiar Navy cape, Jimmy the uniform of a Marine captain. Applause rippled from a crowd that stood behind sawhorse barricades in the pale noonday sun. The President paused, smiled, and waved back. It was not his campaign wave—this was no time for that—but it wasn't funereal either. He seemed trying to strike a balance between gravity and optimism.

The Presidential party moved into the Capitol, and the crowd lapsed back into silence. Here and there little knots clustered about the portable radios which the more enterprising remembered to bring. All were facing the Capitol, although they couldn't possibly see what was going on inside. They seemed to feel that by studying the building itself, a little history might somehow rub off onto them.

Like the President, the people were neither boisterous nor depressed. They had seen movies of the cheering multitudes that are supposed to gather outside chancelleries whenever war is declared, but they didn't feel that way at all. Occasionally someone made an awkward, halfhearted attempt to follow the script. "Gee," said a teen-age girl, clinging to a bespectacled, rather unbelligerent-looking sailor, "ain't there some way a woman can get into this thing?"

It was almost painful, yet it was typical. Like the men at Pearl, who kept linking their experiences to football and the movies, the people had nothing better to go by. A nation brought up on peace was going to war and didn't know how.

Ever since the news broke early Sunday afternoon, they had groped none too successfully for the right note to strike. "Happy Landings!" cried a man who phoned a Detroit paper for confirmation—and the editor detected the tone of false gaiety. "Gotta whip those Japs!" a Kansas City newsboy chanted self-consciously as he passed out extras. And at Herbert's Drive-Inn Bar in the San Fernando Valley, a customer pulled one of a thousand forced, flat jokes: "You guys with Japanese gardeners—how do you feel now?"

Along with the awkwardness went a naïveté which must have seemed strange to the more sophisticated warring nations of the world. The Vassar faculty passed a resolution formally offering its "special training" to the service of the country. A Washington cab driver phoned the White House, offering to carry any government worker to his job free—a proposal likely to astonish any official who did time in Washington during the ensuing years. Members of the Pilgrim Congregational Church in St. Louis debated whether to bomb Tokyo, decided not to—"we're a people of higher ideals." A man in Atlanta wired Secretary of Navy Frank Knox to hold Japanese envoy Kurusu until all Navy officers on Wake were released, and ex-Ambassador Joseph Davies to Russia seriously discussed the possibilities of using Vladivostok as a base.

But most people didn't worry about bases; they were sure the United States could defeat Japan with absurd ease. The country at large still regarded the Japanese as ineffectual little brown men who were good at imitating Occidentals but couldn't do much on their own. "I didn't think the Japs had the nerve," said Sergeant Robert McCallum when interviewed on a Louisville street corner. As reports spread of disquietingly heavy damage at Pearl Harbor, many agreed with Professor Roland G. Usher, a German authority and head of the History Department at Washington University in St. Louis —Hitler's *Luftwaffe* may have helped the Japanese out.

But rising above the awkwardness, the naïveté, and the overconfidence ran one surging emotion—fury. The day might come when formal declarations of war would seem old-fashioned, when the surprise move would become a stock weapon in any country's arsenal, but not yet. In December, 1941, Americans expected an enemy to announce its intentions before it fought, and Japan's move—coming while her envoys were still negotiating in Washington—outraged the people far beyond the concept of any worldly-wise policymaker in Tokyo.

Later, Americans would argue bitterly about Pearl Harbor —they would even hurl dark charges of incompetence and conspiracy at one another—but on this day there was no argument whatsoever.

Young Senator Cabot Lodge of Massachusetts had been an ardent "neutralist" (just a month earlier he had voted against allowing U. S. merchant ships to enter Allied ports), but right after he learned of Pearl Harbor from a filling-station attendant, he was on the air . . . urging all Americans, no matter how isolationist they might have been, to unite against the attack. Senator Arthur Vandenberg of Michigan, leader of the isolationist bloc, had heard the news in his bedroom, where he was pasting up clippings about his long, hard fight against U. S. involvement in the war. He immediately phoned the White House, assuring President Roosevelt that whatever their differences, he would support the President in his answer to Japan.

It was the same with the press. The isolationist, rabidly anti-Roosevelt Los Angeles *Times* bannered its lead editorial, "Death Sentence of a Mad Dog." Some papers tried to prod isolationist leaders into controversial statements, but none were coming. Senator Burton Wheeler of Montana, for instance, snapped back, "The only thing now is to do our best to lick hell out of them."

And the sooner the better. There was an overwhelming urge to get going, even though no one knew where the road might lead. At Fort Sam Houston, Texas, Brigadier General Dwight D. Eisenhower got the word as he tried to catch up on his sleep after weeks of long, tough field maneuvers. He was dead tired, had left orders not to be disturbed, but the phone rang and his wife heard him say, "Yes? . . . When? . . . I'll be right down." As he rushed off to duty, he told Mrs. Eisenhower the news, said he was going to headquarters, and added that he had no idea when he would be back.

The Capitol swelled with the same spirit of angry unity and urgency as the Senators filed into the House Chamber to hear the President's war message. Democratic leader Alben Barkley arrived arm in arm with GOP leader Charles McNary; Democrat Elmer Thomas of Oklahoma linked arms with the old isolationist Senator Hiram Johnson of California.

Next the Supreme Court marched in, wearing their black robes, and then the members of the Cabinet. Down front sat the top military leaders, General Marshall and Admiral Stark. Further back, five Congressmen held children in their laps, lending the curious touch of a family gathering. In the gallery Mrs. Roosevelt, wearing black with a silver fox fur, peeked from behind a girder—she had one of the worst seats in the House. Not far away sat an important link with the past—Mrs. Woodrow Wilson.

At 12:29 P.M. President Roosevelt entered, still on Jimmy's arm. There was applause . . . a brief introduction by Speaker Sam Rayburn . . . and the President, dressed in formal morning attire, stood alone at the rostrum. He opened a black looseleaf notebook—the sort a child uses at school— and the Chamber gave him a resounding ovation. For the first time in nine years Republicans joined in, and Roosevelt seemed to sense the electric anger that swept the country, as he grasped the rostrum and began:

> Yesterday, December 7, 1941—a date which will live in infamy—the United States of America was suddenly and deliberately attacked. . . .

The speech was over in six minutes and war voted in less than an hour, but the real job was done in the first ten seconds. "Infamy" was the note that struck home, the word that welded the country together until the war was won.

Facts About the Attack

Most Americans caught in the Japanese attack on Oahu went through successive stages of shock, fear, and anger—a poor climate indeed for pinning down exactly what happened. And even about the basic statistics it's dangerous to be dogmatic. There are different ways of counting things: should, for instance, an obsolete airplane that is out of commission anyhow be counted as "destroyed by the enemy"? Keeping these cautions in mind, here are the answers to some basic questions that are bound to arise:

How many ships were in Pearl Harbor? Best answer seems to be 96. Most maps show 90 ships, but omit the *Ontario, Condor, Crossbill, Cockatoo, Pyro,* and the old *Baltimore.*

What was U.S. air strength? Some 394 planes, according to Congressional investigation, but many were obsolete or being repaired. Available aircraft: Army—93 fighters, 35 bombers, 11 observation; Navy—15 fighters, 61 patrol planes, 36 scout planes, 45 miscellaneous.

How big was the Japanese Striking Force? There were 31 ships—six carriers, two battleships, two heavy cruisers, one light cruiser, nine destroyers, three submarines, eight tankers. Air strength—432 planes used as follows: 39 for combat air patrol, 40 for reserve, 353 for the raid.

What was the strength of the Japanese Advance Expeditionary Force? Probably 28 submarines—11 with small planes, five with the famous midget subs. (The Congressional investigation set the figure at 20, but this is too low, according to the Japanese.)

When did various events occur? Most reliable sources agree the raid began about 7:55 A.M., ended shortly before 10 o'clock. At Pearl and Hickam few noticed the five neat phases spelled out in the CINCPAC Official Report. To the men it was a continuing battle, flaring up and down in intensity, with a 15-minute lull around eight-thirty. The most stunning single moment—the *Arizona* blowing up—seems to have taken place about 8:10. Some eyewitnesses feel that the explosion came at the very start of the attack, yet this couldn't be so, judging from the experiences of the five *Arizona* survivors who were located.

In fixing the time for various events, this book depends on both official records and the memory of eyewitnesses. Neither source is infallible. Logs and reports were sometimes worked up long after the event, and in the excitement of battle a fighting man could lose all track of time.

The time range at the top of each left-hand page is intended only as a rough guide. Some incidents necessarily start before or continue beyond the period indicated.

What were the American casualties? Navy—2008 killed, 710 wounded, according to the Navy Bureau of Medicine. Marines—109 killed, 69 wounded, according to Corps Headquarters. Army —218 killed, 364 wounded, according to Adjutant General's figures. Civilian—68 killed, 35 wounded, according to the University of Hawaii War Records Depository. Of the 2403 killed, nearly half were lost when the *Arizona* blew up.

What was the damage? At Pearl Harbor 18 ships were sunk or seriously damaged. Lost: battleships *Arizona* and *Oklahoma*, target ship *Utah*, destroyers *Cassin* and *Downes*. Sunk or beached but later salvaged: battleships *West Virginia, California*, and *Nevada;* mine layer *Oglala*. Damaged: battleships *Tennessee, Maryland,* and *Pennsylvania;* cruisers *Helena, Honolulu,* and *Raleigh;* destroyer *Shaw;* seaplane tender *Curtiss;* repair ship *Vestal.*

At the airfields 188 planes were destroyed—96 Army and 92 Navy. An additional 128 Army and 31 Navy planes were damaged. Hardest-hit airfields were Kaneohe and Ewa. Of the 82 planes caught at these two fields, only one was in shape to fly at the end of the raid.

During the attack there were about 40 explosions in the city of Honolulu—all, except one, the result of U. S. antiaircraft fire. These explosions did about 500,000 dollars' worth of damage.

What were the Japanese losses? Tokyo sources agree that the Striking Force lost only 29 planes—nine fighters, 15 dive bombers, and five torpedo planes. In addition, the Advance Expeditionary Force lost one large submarine and all five midgets. Personnel lost: 55 airmen, nine crewmen on the midget subs, plus an unknown number on the large submarine.

Acknowledgments

"Uniforms meant nothing," recalls Chief Albert Molter, reflecting on Pearl Harbor. Others agree that it was a day when rank was forgotten, when all that counted was the good idea, when people wanted only to pitch in together.

They have shown the same spirit in contributing to this book. Admirals, sailors, generals, privates, ordinary civilians—some 577 participants—have unselfishly joined forces to help me piece together this picture of that famous Sunday.

Some of these people are still in Oahu, and sitting down with them on that balmy, tranquil island conveys best of all what a shock the attack must have been. You feel it when Brigadier General Kendall Fielder painstakingly reviews that last peacetime evening with General Short . . . when James B. Mann describes seeing the first planes in the early sunlight above Haleiwa . . . when Webley Edwards explains how he desperately tried to make his radio audience believe the news . . . when Tadao Fuchikami tells of his motorcycle ride with the famous message from General Marshall to General Short.

As they tell their stories, nothing seems to be too much trouble. Vivid impressions still linger—Richard Kimball delving into old registration books at the Halekulani Hotel; George Walters rooting through his papers on Drydock No. 1; Dr. Robert Faus wading through dusty files on the emergency ambulance service. And there was the evening Master Sergeant Robert McMurtrie dug out the letter which explained better than a dozen investigations how little grasp anyone had of radar at the time. Six weeks before Pearl Harbor, McMurtrie (then a private) had been shifted from

221

radar work to KP, and he joyfully wrote home, "In the kitchen you can take pride in what you're doing."

Sometimes nothing short of a personally conducted tour would explain a point, and I want to thank Master Sergeant Francis Clossen for showing me around Wheeler; Technical Sergeant Billy Kerslake for guiding me through Kaneohe; Mrs. Anne Powlison for a tour of the Kailua area; Colonel Robert G. Fergusson for going over the old Coast Artillery setup; and Mrs. Paul Young for re-enacting her harrowing morning in the family laundry at Wahiawa. The Army, Navy, and Air Force public information offices, of course, paved the way at Pearl, Hickam, Schofield, and Fort Shafter; and though I must have stretched their patience to the breaking point, I never found any limit to their help.

Many of the participants are now far from Hawaii, but they were no less willing to take time out and talk about Pearl Harbor —sometimes under circumstances that must have been trying, to say the least. Lieutenant General Truman Landon was on the verge of leaving for Latin America, but he seemed to have all the time in the world as he recalled the B-17 flight from California. Rear Admiral William Burford was cornered on the golf course near San Diego, but was as amiable as if he had just broken par, while he described how the *Monaghan* rammed the midget sub. And I'll never know what lunch plans Admiral Halsey sacrificed to sit with me instead, relating the story of the *Enterprise* planes.

Some of these people gradually evolved into my "experts" on certain localities . . . and found themselves more ruthlessly imposed upon than ever. These unsung heroes included Commander Victor Delano on Battleship Row . . . Edmond Jacoby on Ford Island . . . Master Sergeant John Sherwood on Hickam . . . Master Sergeant Francis Clossen on Wheeler . . . Chief Walter Simmons on Kaneohe . . . Chief Charles Leahey on Pearl Harbor.

Others I depended on greatly for their specialized knowledge on certain points: Vice Admiral Walter Anderson for background on fleet organization; Dr. John Moorhead for the medical side of the story; Admiral Charles M. Cooke for incidents on the flooding of Drydock No. 1; Admiral Claude Bloch for information on the midget submarine penetration of the harbor. I especially appreciate the time Joseph Lockard and Joseph McDonald spent, helping on the riddle of the Opana radar contact.

Often eyewitnesses not only gave me their time but lent me personal papers to fill out the story. Among them: Lieutenant Colonel George Bicknell, Brigadier General Kendall Fielder, Rear Admiral William Furlong, Rear Admiral Peyton Harrison, Rear Admiral S. S. Isquith, and Captain William Outerbridge. Invaluable diaries were contributed by Commander J. G. Daniels, Thomas Lombardi, and Henry Sachs. Mrs. Hubert K. Reese also made available the diary of her gallant son Lieutenant Hubert K. Reese, Jr., who was lost on convoy duty in 1943.

Most of the Japanese participants were later killed in the war, but fifteen were located and contributed firsthand accounts. Their task was not easy, but they tackled it with vigor and frankness, and the result is a vital part of the story. I am extremely grateful to Takahisa Amagai, Dr. Sukao Ebina, Dr. Tadataka Endo, Shigeru Fujii, Mochitsura Hashimoto, Toshio Hashimoto, Lieutenant Colonel Masanobu Ibusuki, Kazuyoshi Kochi, Vice Admiral Ryunosuke Kusaka, Kazuo Sakamaki, Yoshio Shiga, Shin-Ichi Shimizu, Suguru Suzuki, Yoshibumi Tanbo, and Hoichiro Tsukamoto.

Where eyewitnesses were not available, and in some cases to supplement their accounts, I have relied on a mountain of written material. The 40 volumes of the U. S. Congressional investigation are full of nuggets. The War Records Depository of the University of Hawaii has much data, including a priceless collection of school children's themes. The Honolulu Harbor Master's records have essential facts on wind, weather, and shipping. The Honolulu Board of Water Supply has the best information on damage to the city.

The Honolulu papers had lively coverage, and I'm indebted to Editors Ray Coll of the *Advertiser* and Riley Allen of the *Star-Bulletin* for letting me rummage through their files. Special thanks go to Managing Editor Thurston Twigg-Smith of the *Advertiser* for digging out material on Niihau.

Numerous books contain valuable information on the attack. *The Rising Sun in the Pacific* by Samuel E. Morison (Little, Brown, 1948) and *Battle Report: Pearl Harbor to Coral Sea* by Walter Karig and Welbourne Kelley (Farrar & Rinehart, 1944) have detailed over-all accounts. Blake Clark's *Remember Pearl Harbor* (Harper, 1942) preserves many colorful incidents. The civilian side is thoroughly covered by Gwenfread Allen's *Hawaii's War Years* (University of Hawaii Press, 1945). On the question of responsibility, *Admiral Kimmel's Story* by the Admiral himself (Henry Regnery, 1955), *The Final Secret of Pearl Harbor* by Rear Admiral Robert A. Theobald (Devin-Adair, 1954), and Walter Millis' fascinating *This Is Pearl* (William Morrow, 1947) should all be read by anyone trying to understand this knotty problem. Lieutenant Clarence Dickinson's *Flying Guns* (Scribner's, 1942) and Eugene Burns' *Then There Was One* (Harcourt, Brace, 1944) both touch on the story of the *Enterprise* planes.

Various aspects of the Japanese side are covered in *Midway* by Mitsuo Fuchida (U. S. Naval Institute, 1955); *Sunk* by Mochitsura Hashimoto (Cassell & Company, 1954); *I Attacked Pearl Harbor* by Kazuo Sakamaki (Association Press, 1949); *Zero!* by Masatake Okumiya and Jira Horikoshi with Martin Caidin (Dutton, 1956).

Additional information can be found in many magazine articles that have been written on the subject. To name a few of the best: Robert Ward's account of Japanese planning in the December, 1951, issue of the *United States Naval Institute Proceedings;* Captain Fuchida's own story of leading the air attack in the September, 1952, issue of the same magazine; Barry Fox's touching reminiscences of a housewife's feelings in the January, 1943, issue of *Harper's.*

A more personal kind of help has come from every side. Vice Admiral John F. Shafroth graciously arranged off-the-record interviews with various key figures. Richard MacMillan and Adney Smith gave indispensable guidance in Honolulu. Captain Ralph Parker generously shared his deep understanding of Navy life. Eugene Burns, Russell Starr, and Captain Joe Taussig offered invaluable leads. Lieutenant (j.g.) Herbert E. Hetu and Chief William J. Miller proved that they could locate anybody who had ever been in the Navy. Lieutenant Commander Herb Gimpel worked miracles in getting pictures on a moment's notice. Rear Admiral and Mrs. Hall Mayfield helped in more ways than I could ever list.

In pulling the story together, *Life* magazine supplied wonderful research assistance, and in this connection I am especially indebted to Charles Osborne of the *Life* staff. Roger Pineau, Malcolm Boyd, and Harold Daw contributed other valuable research. Miss Florence Cassedy joined that brave band of typists who have faced my handwriting, and my mother performed as valiantly as ever on the index.

But all these contributions, great as they are, would not be enough without the 464 eyewitness accounts written especially for my use by the people listed on the following pages. These are the heart of the matter, for while no one person is necessarily infallible, the consensus of several hundred is very likely to approach the truth. Like the Armed Services and the individuals mentioned in this Acknowledgment section, these people share no responsibility for my thoughts and conclusions, no blame for my errors or inadequacies, but all the credit for whatever new understanding may emerge from this story of December 7, 1941.

List of Contributors

Each name is followed by the vantage point from which the account was written. Where supplied, the present rank of those still on active duty is also included.

Charles H. Abrams, Pearl Harbor
Edwin W. Adams, Wheeler Field
Carp. Harry R. Adams, *Vestal*
FPC Wayne Lax Adams, *Vestal*
Donald B. Addington, *Phoenix*
CPO Enrique S. M. Aflague, *Minneapolis*
E. H. Akins, Wheeler
Donald B. Alexander, Kaneohe NAS
Bruce G. Allen, B-17 flight
Frank Allo, Hickam Field
Walter C. Anderson, *Nevada*
V. Adm. Walter S. Anderson, USN (Ret.), *Maryland*
Carroll T. Andrews, Wheeler
John V. Armstrong, *Oklahoma*
Terrance J. Armstrong, *Oklahoma*
Thomas E. Armstrong, *Oklahoma*
Kenneth Atwell, Hickam
Marlin G. Ayotte, Pearl Harbor

Charles O. Backstrom, Hickam
M/Sgt. John W. Baker, Tripler General Hospital
Woodrow Baily, *Tennessee*
Robert W. Ballou, Kaneohe NAS
QMC Willard A. Beal, *Oklahoma*
Cdr. John R. Beardall, *Raleigh*

Earnest T. Bedell, *Shaw*
Mrs. Monica Conter Benning, Michigan hosp.
Robert S. Benton, *West Virginia*
Charles E. Bergdoll, B-17 flight
Joseph Berry, *Helena*
S 1/c Ben Bill, Navy housing
HMC V. G. Biskup, Naval Hosp.
H. E. Blagg, *Maryland*
Maj. Gen. Gordon A. Blake, USAF, Hickam
QMC John D. Blanken, *San Francisco*
Stanley J. Blazenski, Naval Mobile Hosp. No. 2
Alec C. Boatman, *Tennessee*
Erwin J. Bohenstiel, Ford Island
Charles M. Bohnstadt, *Sacramento*
Nicholas T. Bongo, Hickam
P. E. Bos, Ford Island
C. E. Boudreau, Navy Receiving Station
S. F. Bowen, *Tennessee*
Maj. Samuel Bradlyn, USAF, Hickam
Clarence Bruhl, Submarine Base
Albert E. Brawley, B-17 flight
Samuel Lester Brayfield, *New Orleans*

225

Brainard J. Brewer, construction
work near Schofield
Chester L. Brighton, *Helena*
Donald W. Brown, *West Virginia*
E. F. Brown, Pearl Harbor
K. R. Brown, *Tucker*
W. M. Brown, PT boats
Norman C. Brunelle, Pearl Harbor
Wilfred J Brunet, *Honolulu*
Lester T. Buckley, Schofield
Mrs. Mary Buethe, Navy housing
R. Adm. J. W. Bunkley, USN
(Ret.), *California*
R. Adm. William P. Burford, USN
(Ret.), *Monaghan*
Joseph John Burke, *Patterson*
J. P. Burkholder, *Tennessee*
Martin T. Burns, *Phoenix*
J. W. Burton, Ford Island
Max E. Butterfield, Hickam

PNC Edward P. Campbell, *Tennessee*
Mrs. Lorraine Campbell, Navy
housing
CWO W. M. Canavan, *St. Louis*
Chief Gunner Ralph A. Carl, Jr.,
Tennessee
Kenneth D. Carlson, *Selfridge*
Brig. Gen. Richard H. Carmichael,
USAF, B-17 flight
Richard M. Carse, Schofield
Peter A. Chang, Submarine Base
S. B. Chatfield, *Wright*
Donald C. Christensen, *Phoenix*
George A. Cichon, *California*
Erwin F. Cihak, B-17 flight
Fred R. Claesson, Ft. Kamehameha
Henry B. Clark, Jr., *Cockatoo*
Peter M. Clause, Schofield
M/Sgt. William M. Cleveland,
Hickam
E. J. Clifton, *Sumner*
Chandler Cobb, Pearl Harbor
Leslie Coe, *Nevada*

Charles Coleman, *St. Louis*
TEC Durrell E. Conner, *California*
Charles R. Cunningham, *Jarvis*
Carl E. Currey, *Maryland*
A. J. Corizzo, *Bagley*
Mrs. Aletha Cote, Hickam housing
Felder Crawford, *Maryland*
Edward G. Creighton, *Monaghan*
Capt. Mark Creighton, USAF,
Hickam
John Crockett, Navy Yard
George V. Cruise, *Helena*
Carlos J. Cunningham, Ford Island
PNC L. L. Curry, Jr., *Oklahoma*

Mrs. Iva Daniels, Navy housing
Cdr. J. G. Daniels, *Enterprise*
flight
Henry R. Danner, Drydock No. 1
Sydney A. Davis, Hickam
William H. Deas, *Castor*
Cdr. Victor Delano, *West Virginia*
W. E. Dellegar, *Oglala*
George E. Denning, Schofield
Thomas A. Denton, 1010 dock
Fred L. Dickey, Wheeler
Cdr. Cleo J. Dobson, *Enterprise*
flight
James W. Dollar, *Phoenix*
Ambrose A. Domagall, *Ward*
Thomas J. Donahue, *Monaghan*
George A. Dorfmeister, *Detroit*
Raeburn D. Drenner, Wheeler
Ivan C. DuBois, Hickam
James Duncan, civilian plane
Y. Dupre, *Dobbin*
Mrs. Rhea Dupre, Navy housing
M/Sgt. J. H. Dykema, Hickam
Albert A. Dysert, *Helena*

Douglas A. Eaker, Submarine Base
Mrs. F. M. Earle, Navy First Aid
Sta.
R. Adm. A. R. Early, USN (Ret.),
Pearl Harbor

Mrs. E. M. Eaton, Navy housing
Charles P. Eckhert, Hickam
AD1 George W. Edmondson, Ford Island
Leonard T. Egan, Wheeler
Wilfred Eller, Naval Mobile Hosp. Unit
Fred R. Elliott, *West Virginia*
BTC H. E. Emory, *California*
Walter F. England, Oiler *Y.O.44*
EN1 Charles W. Etter, *Blue*
G. Taylor Evans, Jr., *California*

Mrs. Florence E. Fahrner, Hickam housing
Maurice Featherman, *West Virginia*
MMC William R. Felsing, *Pennsylvania*
Ernest L. Finney, *Nevada*
Mrs. Joseph G. Fischer, Navy housing
John P. Fisher, Ft. Shafter
Joseph W. Fleck, *New Orleans*
Don Flickinger, Wheeler
Charles A. Flood, *Helena*
Brig. Gen. William J. Flood, USAF (Ret.), Wheeler
Charles L. Flynn, *Pruitt*
Jack F. Foeppel, *Raleigh*
Mrs. Claire Fonderhide, Hickam housing
James L. Forbis, *Arizona*
Frank G. Forgione, *Oglala*
Cdr. Howell M. Forgy, USN (Ret.), *New Orleans*
Roy Foster, Schofield
Cdr. Vance Fowler, *West Virginia*
W. R. Frazee, *Argonne*
Dr. Arthur F. Fritchen, Naval Hosp.
Arthur W. Fusco, Wheeler

John M. Gallagher, *Solace*
Capt. Wilmer E. Gallaher, *Enterprise* flight

Mrs. Joseph Gallaway, Navy housing
RMC R. L. Gamble, *Tennessee*
LeRoy V. Gammon, Ft. Shafter
Mrs. Jeanne D. Gardiner, Makalapa housing
Carey L. Garnett, *Nevada*
BM1 Thomas Garzione, *Vestal*
L. George Geiger, Hickam
Antonio Gentile, Jr., Hickam
M/Sgt. J. D. Gentry, *Pennsylvania*
Alvin Gerth, *Pennsylvania*
Fiore Gigliotti, *St. Louis*
Roy W. Gillette, Ft. Shafter
Mrs. Alice N. Gillis, Honolulu
David Wynne Gilmartin, *Utah*
ATC Frederick W. Glaeser, Ford Island
John M. Gobidas, *Rigel*, *Oklahoma* rescue
Daucy B. Goza, Ford Island
John D. Grabanski, *California*
Cdr. Leon Grabowski, Naval Hosp.
C. A. Grana, *California*
Capt. Lawrence C. Grannis, USN (Ret.), *Antares*
Tony J. Gregory, Schofield
MUC C. S. Griffin, *Nevada*
Edward J. Gronkowski, Hickam
A. M. Gustchen, *Honolulu*

Glenn W. Haag, *Argonne*
Robert Paul Hagen, PT boats
Ralph B. Haines, motor launch
George H. Haitle, *Maryland*
Francis L. Haley, *Nevada*
Joe Hallet, *Tautog*
Maj. Robert W. Halliday, Hickam
George W. Halterman, Hickam
LCDR Frank S. Handler, *Helm*
Joseph Patrick Hanley, *Rigel*
G. S. Hardon, *Monaghan*
Verdet Windford Harpin, *New Orleans*
Joseph C. Harsch, Waikiki

C. J. Harrold, Honolulu, Ft. Shafter
Fred C. Hart, Submarine Base
Alfred B. Hauft, Ft. Shafter
CMC Gilbert J. Hawkins, *Sacramento*
Harry Haws, *Montgomery*
Dr. Will Hayes, Waikiki, Hickam, Pearl Harbor
Mrs. Maurine K. Hayter, Alewa Heights
Maj. Gen. Leonard D. Heaton, Schofield hosp.
BMC K. V. Hendon, *Nevada*
John E. Henry, Hickam
Roy Henry, *Honolulu*
Thomas A. Henry, *Bagley*
Maurice J. Herman, Schofield
John E. Hewitt, *Widgeon*
Robert L. Hey, Hickam
Robert F. Hilbish, Schofield
Ralph F. Hinkle, Navy Yard
Carl Hoffman, Hickam
William Hole, *Medusa*
M/Sgt. John K. Hollwedel, Honolulu, Hickam
Mrs. John K. Hollwedel, Honolulu
Henry H. Homitz, Hickam
Otto Honegger, *Honolulu*
LCDR R. L. Hooton, *West Virginia*
James C. Hornberger, Jr., Ft. Shafter
Alfred D. Horne, Jr., *Pelias*
Wilbur K. Hunt, Hickam
Joseph S. Hydrusko, *Solace*, *Oklahoma* rescue

William T. Ingram, *Oklahoma*
R. Adm. S. S. Isquith, USN (Ret.), *Utah*

C. H. Jackson, Submarine Base
LCDR Gerald M. Jacobs, Pearl City, Ford Island
Edmond M. Jacoby, *West Virginia*

1st Lt. Haile H. Jaekel, USAF, *Salt Lake City*
John Jaskowski, Hickam
BM/1 James H. Jensen, USCG, *West Virginia*
Glenn A. Jewell, *Ontario*
CWO R. E. Johnsen, *Rigel*
Doir C. Johnson, *West Virginia*
H. G. Johnson, Schofield
James Albert Jones, motor launch
Mrs. Imogen Jones, Wahiawa
BMC R. E. Jones, *Pennsylvania*

M/Sgt. Nicholas H. Kahlefent, USAF, B-17 flight
Capt. J. B. Karstein, USAF, Hickam
Warren G. Kearns, Kaneohe NAS
Lt. Col. Bernard T. Kelly, USMC, *Helena*
Maj. William T. Keogh, Ft. Shafter
Francis X. Kiefer, *Helena*
Richard L. Kile, *Avocet*
Cdr. David L. G. King, *Helena*
Howard E. King, Hickam
Lewis A. Kirk, *Honolulu*
Oliver A. Kirkeby, *Tennessee*
Charles W. Knapp, *Raleigh*
Joseph F. Kneeland, *Helena*
Richard P. Knights, *Oklahoma*
Wilbur F. Kohnle, *St. Louis*
EMC Jan Kolodziej, *Oklahoma*
James Korthe, Navy housing
Mrs. James Korthe, Navy housing
George C. Kovak, Maui, Hickam
Arnold E. Krause, *New Orleans*
Kenneth Krepps, Wheeler

Peter A. La Fata, *Swan*
James C. Lagerman, Ford Island
Mrs. Bess Lalumendier, Wheeler
William D. Land, *Tangier*
Lt. Gen. Truman H. Landon, USAF, B-17 flight

John Landreth, *Nevada*
Col. Frank H. Lane, USAF, Hickam hosp.
Glenn Harvey Lane, *Arizona*
Ansell C. LaPage, *Blue*
Lt. Gen. Claude C. Larkin, USMC (Ret.), Ewa Field
C. J. Lawrence, *Phoenix*
Howard L. Lawson, Schofield
ATC James S. Layman, Ford Island
EMC W. R. Leckemby, *Shaw*
Vance B. Leneave, *Medusa*
Charles A. Leonard, Schofield
Frank A. Lewis, *Dobbin*
Cdr. Julien E. Lindstrom, *St. Louis*
GMC Robert E. Linnartz, *Nevada*
William C. Long, *Honolulu*
Russell A. Lott, *Arizona*
Charles Lowe, *Maryland*
Jack C. Lower, Navy Yard
Jack J. Luscher, *Detroit*
William A. L. Lynch, *California*

James W. McAdams, Wheeler
William E. McCarthy, Jr., Ft. Shafter
TMC Eugene N. McClarty, *Downes*
Malcolm J. McCleary, *Oklahoma*
J. E. McColgan, Ford Island
Dr. H. P. McCrimmon, Kaneohe NAS
Mrs. A. C. McCullaugh, Navy housing
W. Payton McDaniel, *Nevada*
James H. McDonough, Honolulu
R. Adm. John M. McIsaac, USN (Ret.), *MacDonough*
Lt. Oden L. McMillan, USN, *Nevada*
Robert L. McMurray, *St. Louis*

Kenneth Magee, Hickam
Fleet Chaplain William A. Maguire, Pearl Harbor

Cdr. Everett A. Malcolm, *Arizona*
TDC Cecil S. Malmin, Kaneohe NAS
TDC Thomas S. Malmin, Ford Island
LeRoy G. Maltby, Kaneohe NAS
Guido J. Mambretti, Hickam
Charles Mandell, *Maryland*
Aloysius J. Manuszewski, Schofield
Vern L. Marcum, Schofield
Donald J. Marman, *Honolulu*
Orion C. May, *San Francisco*
Mrs. Hall Mayfield, Makalapa housing
ALC Harry R. Mead, Ford Island
Stanley Meldrum, Schofield
Cdr. Charles J. Merdinger, *Nevada*
Kenneth M. Merrill, Hickam
Mrs. Annette E. Merritt, Honolulu
Joseph C. Messier, *Helena*
Charles J. Michaels, Jr., *Swan*
Harvey H. Milhorn, *Arizona*
Edward Miller, Submarine Base
Russell F. Miller, *Maryland*
Walter Miller, Jr., tug in Pearl Harbor
JOC William J. Miller, *Castor*
Albert J. Miskuf, *Helena*
Albert H. Molter, Ford Island
M. G. Montessoro, *Castor*
Joseph T. Moore, Hickam
Rev. F. E. Morgan, Pearl Harbor
L. A. Morley, *Honolulu*
Shirl P. Morrill, *Pennsylvania*
ADC Russell C. Morse, Ford Island
Lt. (j.g.) Don Morton, Pearl City
George Murphy, Jr., *Oklahoma*
John A. Murphy, *Vestal*
Howard E. Myers, *St. Louis*

Charlie Ross Naylor, *Breese*
George L. Newton, Jr., B-17 flight
Joseph F. Nickson, *San Francisco*
R. N. Nilssen, Kaneohe NAS
Raymond B. Nolde, *Ward*

Quentin P. Norcutt, *St. Louis*
J. Harold North, *Maryland*
John R. Nugent, Schofield

Burdette E. Odekirk, *Maryland*
Robert A. Oborne, Jr., Ford Island
Edward F. J. O'Brion, *Arizona*
Carroll J. Oliver, *Pennsylvania*
Persifor S. Oliver, *Bagley*
Edward M. Ovecka, Hickam
BMC Allen S. Owens, *Nevada*

John E. Parrott, *San Francisco*
Gilbert R. Patten, *Nevada*
Maj. Earl S. Patton, USAF, deep-sea fishing
GMC L. R. Peacock, *Enterprise* patrol boat
Capt. Carl A. Peterson, USN, *California*
Robert J. Peth, Ford Island
Emmett Pethoud, Jr., Hickam
R. Adm. John S. Phillips, USN (Ret.), *Neosho*
John F. Plassio, Wheeler
ADC Henry Popko, Kaneohe NAS
James H. Power, Jr., *Pennsylvania*
William Power, *West Virginia*
ADC William N. Powers, *Neosho*
Louis A. Puckett, Navy Yard
Charles T. Putnam, Navy tug

CPO Harand N. Quisdorf, Ford Island

Stanley H. Rabe, harbor craft
James G. Raines, *Curtiss*
M/Sgt. Walter T. Raisner, USAF, Schofield
Lt. Col. R. L. Ramsay, USAF, B-17 flight
R. Adm. Logan C. Ramsey, USN (Ret.), Ford Island
Weldon V. Rash, *St. Louis*
Waldo H. Rathman, *Whitney*
Lt. Col. Ernest L. Reid, USAF, B-17 flight

Glenn Homer Robinson, *Oklahoma*
Joseph H. Robinson, *MacDonough*
Robert J. Robinson, Ft. Shafter
E. H. Robison, Pearl Harbor Marine Barracks
Don E. Rodenberger, *Oglala*
Jack Rogo, Ford Island
F. A. Rogue, *San Francisco*
John J. Romanczyk, *Vestal*
Mrs. Alexander Rowell, Pearl City, Red Hill
Raymond G. Roy, *Selfridge*
Vernon C. Rubenking, Wheeler
Millard J. Rucoi, *Pennsylvania*

George J. Sallet, *Bagley*
W. V. Samples, Honolulu, Navy Yard
Brig. Gen. LaVerne G. Saunders, USAF, Hickam
HMC T. A. Sawyer, *Solace*
Albert F. Sandall, *Oklahoma*
George Santella, *Allen*
Cdr. D. S. Schroeder, Pearl Harbor
Walter H. Schuh, *Maryland*
Raymond Senecal, Schofield
Marion T. Shepherd, Hickam
M/Sgt. John P. Sherwood, Hickam
Bert F. Shipley, Hickam
Thomas F. Shook, Jr., *Phoenix*
Carl W. Shrader, Wheeler
Capt. W. B. Sieglaff, USN, *Tautog*
R. Adm. R. B. Simons, USN (Ret.), *Raleigh*
CPO Walter Simmons, Kaneohe NAS
Eldon E. Smart, Pearl Harbor
Capt. Billie J. Smith, USAF, Hickam
YNC George B. Smith, *Oklahoma*
Gordon F. Smith, Wheeler
CWO Hugh W. Smith, Jr., Navy Receiving Sta.
Joseph W. Smith, *Dale*

Ray C. Smith, *Vestal*
Robert W. Snyder, *Detroit*
Frederick Sommer, Schofield
James A. Spagnola, Navy Yard
Capt. Paul E. Spangler, USN, Naval Hosp.
Mrs. Paul E. Spangler, Alewa Heights
Mrs. Jackie Bennett Sprague, Hickam housing
Leonard M. Stagich, *Montgomery*
Arnold J. Stengtein, *Nevada*
Mrs. Barry Fox Stevens, Kaneohe Bay
Virgil A. Stewart, Hickam
John G. Stirnemann, *Solace*
Frank P. Stock, *Vestal*
Capt. Herald F. Stout, USN, *Montgomery*
Anthony Sudano, Pearl Harbor
Douglas Sugate, *Medusa*
Charles A. Super, *MacDonough*
John Swanson, Submarine Base
Capt. H. E. Swinney, USAF, Hickam

Cdr. William P. Tanner, PBY patrol
Homer R. Taylor, B-17 flight
Hoyle A. Taylor, *San Francisco*
William E. Taylor, *Phelps*
Gordon E. Tengwall, *Oklahoma*
R. Adm. William R. Terrell, USN (Ret.), *Tucker*
R. Adm. Francis J. Thomas, USNR (Ret.), *Nevada*
J. H. Thompson, Hickam
Luther Thompson, Hickam
Mrs. Margrett S. Timmons, Waikiki
E. A. Titsworth, Hickam

A. M. Townsend, *St. Louis*
Mrs. A. M. Townsend, Honolulu

CTC Earle K. Van Buskirk, Ford Island
BMGC Elmer A. Vandenberg, *Solace*
JOC H. C. Varner, *Rigel*
LCDR Valera C. Vaubel, Naval Hosp.
QMC Edward M. Vecera, *West Virginia*
Mrs. Robert B. Vokac, Schofield housing

R. A. Wadsworth, *Vestal*
Mrs. Ellison Wallace, Tripler
Cdr. W. G. Wallace, *St. Louis*
Mrs. W. G. Wallace, Honolulu
Maj. Leo G. Wears, USMC, *Oklahoma*
Harold R. Webb, *Nevada*
Paul J. Weisenberger, *Helena*
Mrs. Elizabeth S. White, Honolulu
EN1 Robert W. White, *Ontario*
QMC Robert J. Whited, *Antares*
Ralph E. Wiley, Hickam hosp.
Frank B. Wilkes, *Tangier*
Warren S. Wilkinson, Hickam
Donald R. Williams, *Argonne*
Robert D. Williams, Wheeler
John W. Wilson, Hickam
V. Adm. L. J. Wiltse, USN (Ret.), Detroit
Blaine K. Wolff, *Narwhal*
Henry T. Wray, *Argonne*

Charles A. Yokom, PT boats
Stephen B. Young, *Oklahoma*

Adolph J. Zlabis, *Vestal*

Index

233